VANISHED CITIES

VANISHED CITIES

Hermann and Georg Schreiber

TRANSLATED FROM THE GERMAN BY
RICHARD AND CLARA WINSTON

NEW YORK   ALFRED A. KNOPF   1957

L. C. catalog card number: 57-7550

© *Alfred A. Knopf, Inc., 1957*

THIS IS A BORZOI BOOK,
PUBLISHED BY ALFRED A. KNOPF, INC.

FIRST AMERICAN EDITION

The quotations on pages 39 and 42–4 are from THE ROYAL WAY *by André Malraux, copyright 1935 by Random House, Inc. Reprinted by permission of Random House, Inc.*

Originally published in German as VERSUNKENE STÄDTE. *Copyright 1955 by Paul Neff Verlag.*

TO THE MEMORY OF OUR PARENTS

HERMANN SCHREIBER

BOOKSELLER IN VIENNA

IONE SCHREIBER

NÉE ELSINGER

Alas, poor man, you do not tread upon the ground of this, your earth, but upon the roof of your own house, which many deluges have shaped into its present form for you.

—HERDER

PREFACE

Returning from Asia Minor, a Roman politician, whose only claim to fame is his friendship with Cicero, was once sailing along the Greek coast. In a letter of condolence to Cicero on the death of his daughter, he recalled his impressions of that voyage. "Behind me lay Ægina, before me Megara, on the right the Piræus, on the left Corinth— cities which had once flourished marvelously, but which now lie before us cast down and shattered. And this thought came to me: we human beings take it very hard when one of us is ruined or killed, although in one single place the dead shells of so many cities lie. . . ."

What Cicero's friend felt two thousand years ago affects us even more strongly today. Some law we cannot wholly fathom ordains that everything human beings have created must undergo the same great transformation. A house, a citadel, a palace can survive for many generations; but the cities, those stone shells of human life, are in a fascinating way subject to the vicissitudes of human destiny. It would even seem as if they in their turn affect the people dwelling within them, as if the essence of a city, the significance of its situation, the fate of its walls shape a particular breed of men; as if many and perhaps all cities develop into monstrous organisms which are linked in a mysterious way to the mollusk life of the human creatures swarming in their stone channels and chambers.

Because they are thus animated, thus alive, cities the world over have become not only objects of historical study, but also cores of stories and myths, and, like so many heroes or kings, cities after their deaths have become entangled with legends which grow as rankly as the vines and creepers that choke the gray stones.

It was in the form of some such image that the mystery of vanished glory touched our hearts in the lecture halls and libraries of Vienna University, when the breath of the past first swept over us. We sat over books and inscriptions written thousands of years ago, and from the records of peoples long since vanished we seemed to hear the noisy bustle of the markets in lost commercial cities, the clatter of arms in the hands of guards at the gates of thriving metropolises whose walls were fated to be razed perhaps only a hundred, perhaps a thousand years afterward. And when we ourselves came to stand on the reefs where cities now buried beneath the waves had once flourished, when we walked over sod beneath which they lay, only a few yards deep and yet sleeping forever—the houses, streets, and palaces of ancient civilized peoples—we knew that the lost cities would never again release us from their spell.

Scattered over the globe are the sites of hundreds of cities which were founded, which flourished, and which met their end through war, fire, or flood. Precisely because there are so many, we can be lavish with our materials and discard everything doubtful, dispense with the fables of those who do not find reality wonderful enough in itself. Why move heaven and earth, why delve into astrology for proof of the existence of Atlantis, when ancient Thamugadi lies glittering in its riches before our eyes? Why make moons draw up oceans and set giants tramping across the Peruvian plateau, when our hearts can be stirred to a sense of reverence by the Sun Gate of the pre-Inca god Kon-Tiki? In such works we sense, across oceans and the high peaks of the Andes, that we are the brothers of those builders.

In order to make more vivid glory and doom, growth and decay, we have chosen only cities that no longer exist or, if they still remain, live on in a form which has nothing in common with their past importance. We also have omitted the well-known ones which have been treated individually in recent books, such as Ur, the cities of Crete, Egypt, the Hittite Empire, and the Mayan civilization. For Babylon we have concentrated on the somewhat less familiar era after the end of its existence as an independent state. The detailed discussion of Pompeii was advisable because of its connection with hitherto wholly neglected cities like Stabiæ. By restricting our subject in this way we have been able to give more space to a number of cities, and to introduce others (e.g., Spina, Ezion-Geber, Thamugadi, Tara and Cendro, Karakorum and Khambalu) to the non-specialist public for the first time.

HERMANN SCHREIBER

Vienna, July 1955   GEORG SCHREIBER

C O N T E N T S

I FORCES OF NATURE

1 *Unholy Cities*   5

Dead Sea and Hot Springs. Gomorrah, the Land under the
Lake. The Exiles' Curse. Sodom's Wealth. Why Lot's Wife
Looked Back. The Princess with the Golden Key. Ys, the End
of the Earth. A Roman Road into the Sea. Vineta's Sunken Bells.
Arab Coins in the Baltic Region. Twelve Gates and a Beacon.
Farmer Busch and His Discovery. Rungholt and Haithabu. Rev-
els and Sin. The Great Flood of 1362.

2 *Holy Cities*   28

Pastor Spanuth Seeks Atlantis. Primordial Disasters and the At-
lantic Island Bridge. Cyclopean Cities of the Early Seafarers.
Plato's Fable of Atlantis. The City of Cities. Angkor: Astronomy
in the Jungle. A Lagoon City in the South Seas. Across the
Pacific, but in Which Direction? Saurat's Giants. Tiahuanaco:
Kon-Tiki's City.

3 *Cities of the Storied South*   68

Pozzuoli, the City beneath the Mineral Spring. Where the Amber Route Ended. Spina, an Older Venice. Atria, Name-
giver to a Sea. Pæstum, City of Temples and Roses. The Land
of Cattle. The Original Home of the *Commedia dell'arte*. The
cows of Stabiæ. Theaters with More Seats than the City Had
Inhabitants. The Warning Earthquake. Nero in a New Light.
The Victims of Vesuvius.

II GOLD

4 *Coined Gold*   119

A Deserter. The Tower of Babel and the Hanging Gardens. The
Ass from the Mountains and the Ass from the Sea. Murashu &
Sons. Darics and Shekels. Hit Songs, Boxing Matches, and Bar-
becues. What Happened to Doctors Who Made Mistakes.
Alexander and Babylon. The Metropolis Becomes a Hunting

Preserve. Palmyra, the City of Great Bel. The Black-eyed Queen. City of Bishops and Exiles. The Bedouins Have the Last Word.

5 *Gold and Garrison*   149

Rome and the Alps. Celtic Mining. Pilgrimage to the War God. Carrus Navalis and Carnival. The Sacred Remains Sacred. Æneas Lands at Ostia. A Meteorite from Asia Minor. The Goddess Hears Claudia Quinta. Skyscrapers in Ancient Ostia. Early Christianity in the Baths. The Dead Rest in the Theater. Saracens and Popes. Lovely Baiæ. Luxury and Loose Morals. Science of Wine. The Curse of a Jealous Poet.

6 *Silver from Atlantis and Gold from Ophir*   180

Biblical Tarshish. Flounced Skirts and Castanets. Barbarians Drink Water. The Prehistoric Seafarers, Invention of the Blockade. The Golden City of the Sun-Worshippers. Where Was Ophir? King Solomon and the Queen of Sheba. Ruins "From the Abysses of Time." Ancient African Ruins. The Murder of the Sacred King. Slave Trade for Humanitarian Reasons. The Bead Game in the Jungle. Cosmic Order in the Kingdom of Drums. The Thudding Heart of Black Africa.

III WAR

7 *Heroes and Sibyls*   230

Homer and Guesses. Toll Passage of the Dardanelles. Mycenæ and Tiryns. Life in Troy. The Ten-Year War. The Oldest Greek Settlement in Italy. Æneas Goes to the Sibyl's Grotto for Advice. Dido Founds Carthage. A Naval Power. Riches. Recovery. Trade Rivals Know No Mercy.

8 *Cities and Legionaries*   261

A Pipeline for Wine. The Sybaritic Way of Life. Anti-Noise Campaign in Antiquity. Competition for the Olympic Games. Musical Counteroffensive. Rich Campania and the Queen of Roads. Hannibal as Liberator. The Soldiers Who Wintered in Capua. The Ranks of Cities. The Restive Mountains. The City Built in a Year. Arab Market in Timgad. Refuge for Hermits and Doorless Monastery.

9   *Dim Scripts and Dark Oracles*   292

   White Stone Age Men in the Fifteenth Century. Cave Cities and
   Dual Kingship. Strange Justice. The Etruscans in the Alps.
   Rome's First Kings. The Science of the Liver. Stagnation on the
   Indus. The Priest City with the Sacred Baths. The Aryan In-
   vaders. The Chariot Conquers Culture. The Great City of
   Shang. Cosmopolitan Karakorum. The Residence of the Tartar
   Khans. The Revolt of the Beardless. 5,000 Astrologers. The
   Province of Beautiful Girls.

EPILOGUE   338

CHRONOLOGICAL TABLE   340

INDEX   *follows page*   344

L I N E D R A W I N G S

Leaping hinds, from Tell Beit Mirsim   11

Chariot horse of Rameses III   35

Phæthon   70

Greek freighter   78

Young shepherd with flute   82

A chariot overthrown at the circus   92

Oxcart, from an ancient allegory   94

Market scene   99

Silenus astride a wine-bag   103

A painter's studio   113

Building a brick wall in Egypt   122

Assyrian musicians   127

A Roman military camp   136

Egyptian war chariot   147

Sale of wine   155

The war god Latobius   160

Coin of Emperor Claudius   164

Constantine the Great and Fausta   169

Bath scene   173

A cymbalistria   178

Greek fifty-oared ship   182

Horse kneeling   187

Negroes fleeing Pharaoh's soldiers   206

A potter   235

The body of Patroclus   241

Ancient Greek basket-chaise   264

Building a camp   283

Roman foot-coverings   287

Figure of a ship carved on rock   297

Mural in Clusium: wrestling match   308

Greek funeral   313

Seal from Mohenjo-daro   320

Statuette of a dancing girl   321

Miniature from Harappa   324

Kublai Khan   328

MAPS

BY GUY FLEMING

Ancient Cities of Italy   73

The Mediterranean World   152

Africa: Gold from Ophir   193

LIST OF PLATES

FOLLOWING PAGE 72

PLATE I Guardian lions of Angkor
By Life *photographer Eliot Elisofon;* © *Time, Inc.*

II Angkor-Vat: air view
Eliot Elisofon.

III Buddha images
Eliot Elisofon.

IV Floral designs and an apsaras
Eliot Elisofon.

V The Mucalinda Buddha
Eliot Elisofon.

VIA Giant ancestors in stone, Tiahuanaco
Ewing Galloway.

VIB Man with cat's head
Courtesy Skrifola Ltd., Copenhagen.

VII Relics of Toltec gods
Paul Popper Ltd.

VIII On Easter Island
Courtesy Skrifola Ltd., Copenhagen.

IX Temple of Serapis
Photo by Giulio Parisio; © *Federico Arborio Mella, Milan.*

XA Pigeonhouse at Puteoli
Courtesy Italian State Tourist Office.

XB Vestibule in the amphitheater
Courtesy Italian State Tourist Office.

XI Pæstum: Temple of Poseidon
Courtesy Italian State Tourist Office.

PLATE XII   Where Apollo was worshipped
Courtesy Italian State Tourist Office.

XIIIA   Out of the rubble and ashes
Archæological Collection, Vienna University.

XIIIB   The great amphitheater, Pompeii
Photo by Vasari; © Federico Arborio Mella, Milan.

XIVA   Victim of Vesuvius
Publifoto-Black Star.

XIVB   The house of Cornelius Rufus
Photo by Vasari; © Federico Arborio Mella, Milan.

XVA   Forum at Pompeii
Courtesy Italian State Tourist Office.

XVB   Street of Abundance
Courtesy Italian State Tourist Office.

XVIA   A house in Herculaneum
Courtesy Italian State Tourist Office.

XVIB   Wine tavern
Courtesy Italian State Tourist Office.

FOLLOWING PAGE 168

XVII   Towers of the Ishtar Gate
From The Excavations at Babylon, *by Robert Kaldeway* (*Macmillan & Co. Ltd., London*).

XVIIIA   Darius's palace at Persepolis
Photo by Ella Maillart, from Paul Popper Ltd.

XVIIIB   Giant sculpture at Nineveh
Courtesy Skrifola Ltd., Copenhagen.

XIX   Agora at Palmyra
© Institut français d'archéologie de Beyrouth.

XX   Head of a Palmyrene woman
Photo by André Vigneau; © Editions TEL, Paris.

XXI   Colonnade and the temple of Baal
© Institut français d'archéologie de Beyrouth.

XXII   Bathtub in a Celtic town
© Verlag des Geschichtsvereines für Kärnten, Klagenfurt.

PLATE XXIII A home in Ostia
Photo by GFN; © Federico Arborio Mella, Milan.

XXIVA House of the Round Temple
Photo by GFN; © Federico Arborio Mella, Milan.

XXIVB Ostia: the public latrine
Photo by Anderson, Rome.

XXVA Ostia: theater square
Courtesy Italian State Tourist Office.

XXVB Ships on a mosaic floor
Photo from the authors' collection.

XXVIA Terraces at Baiæ
Wide World.

XXVIB A section of the baths
Wide World.

XXVII The Lady of Elche
Photo by André Vigneau; © Editions TEL, Paris.

XXVIIIA Before excavations at Tell-el Kheleifeh
Courtesy Nelson Glueck.

XXVIIIB Walls of King Solomon's city
Courtesy Nelson Glueck.

XXIXA Brickyard at Ezion-Geber
Courtesy Nelson Glueck.

XXIXB Grave of a bricklayer
Courtesy Nelson Glueck.

XXX Conical tower of Zimbabwe
Photo by Ronald D. K. Hadden; © Federal Information Department, Southern Rhodesia.

XXXI Temple and the Valley of Ruins, Zimbabwe
Photo by Ronald D. K. Hadden; © Federal Information Department, Southern Rhodesia.

XXXIIA In the Elliptical Temple
Photo by Ronald D. K. Hadden; © Federal Information Department, Southern Rhodesia.

XXXIIB The temple of a royal city
Photo by Ronald D. K. Hadden; © Federal Information Department, Southern Rhodesia.

FOLLOWING PAGE 264

PLATE XXXIII   Citadel at Mycenæ
Courtesy Dr. Stiglitz, Vienna.

XXXIV   Cave of the Cumæan sibyl
Photo by Giulio Parisio; © *Federico Arborio Mella, Milan.*

XXXVA   Tunnel to Lake Averno
Photo by Alinari, Florence.

XXXVB   Entrance to the underworld
Photo by Alinari, Florence.

XXXVI   Temple at Delphi
Photo by A. Reeber; courtesy Skrifola Ltd., Copenhagen.

XXXVIIA   Governor's box at the amphitheater
Photo from the authors' collection.

XXXVIIB   Floor-heating in Carnuntum
Photo from the authors' collection.

XXXVIII   Negro boy in bronze
© *Museum Carnuntinum, Bad Deutsch-Altenburg, Austria.*

XXXIX   Carnuntum: a young boy
© *Museum Carnuntinum, Bad Deutsch-Altenburg, Austria.*

XL   Ruins at Timgad
Paul Popper Ltd.

XLIA   Main street in Thamugadi
Courtesy French Embassy Press and Information Division.

XLIB   Temple of Venus
Paul Popper Ltd.

XLII   Triumphal arch of Diocletian
Paul Popper Ltd.

XLIII   Armchair in a burial chamber
Courtesy Skrifola Ltd., Copenhagen.

XLIV   An Etruscan warrior
Photo by Alinari, Florence.

PLATE XLVA   Etruscan buck goat
Photo by Alinari, Florence.

XLVB   Bronze chimera from Arezzo
Photo by Alinari, Florence.

XLVIA   Terra-cotta head of a warrior
Courtesy Metropolitan Museum of Art, New York.

XLVIB   Chariot from the sixth century B.C.
Courtesy Metropolitan Museum of Art, New York.

XLVIIA   Etruscan warrior in bronze
Courtesy Metropolitan Museum of Art, New York.

XLVIIB   Mural in a tomb at Tarquinii
Photo by Alinari, Florence.

XLVIIIA   Great Bath at Mohenjo-daro
Courtesy Press Information Bureau, Government of India.

XLVIIIB   Humped bull on a stamp seal
Courtesy Press Information Bureau, Government of India.

PART ONE

FORCES OF NATURE

▣ THE EARTH BEARS US UNWILLINGLY UPON her back. We carve into her in order to sink the foundations for our houses, and now and again she shakes herself and with a brief shudder tumbles these houses about as if they were children's blocks.

For hundreds of thousands of years men lived as pitifully at the mercy of wind and weather as animals, and every natural force was to them a god with power over their lives. When their presumptions increased they created houses for themselves. As they put these houses together into citadels and settlements upon which the rain pounded vainly and the wind lashed harmlessly, they were measuring their strength against the powers of nature, against the elements.

They measured it, and grew immoderate, and once, no doubt, they reared a building up toward the clouds, a building to which men had to raise their eyes as ordinarily they did only in prayer. And when this building did not go on growing, when instead it fell to ruin, they felt that the wrath of God must be the cause.

But the cities themselves spread out in all those places favored by men: on the shores of pleasant bays, by lakes and rivers, on capes extending far out into the sea, on plateaus, and in the heart of jungles. Over the seas and across the lakes came ships bringing wealth; from the capes the people put out their seines for fish; and on the sunlit plateaus livestock throve. Who, in the midst of life and livelihood, gave a thought to the slender pillar of smoke which rose into the sky from the strange, cone-shaped mountain behind the city? Who imagined that the friendly sea would roar up over the land, that the little lake would pour into a volcanic fissure? The people were men, not gods. They built houses that withstood wind, rain, and cold. But these houses could not withstand the glowing torrent of lava which the mountain's wrath spewed forth. The walls collapsed, the courtyards became filled with hot ash, and the houses buried the people.

If nature and the earth, those kindliest of mother-goddesses, were so aroused as to annihilate cities, men could only conclude that the fault was theirs. They communed with themselves and sought to find the sin, until thousands of years and innumerable acts of destruction showed them how blindly nature rampages: temples are shattered and dens of vice remain standing; the just are drowned and the unjust escape. Time rules by his own laws.

I

UNHOLY CITIES

DEAD SEA AND HOT SPRINGS. GOMORRAH, THE LAND
UNDER THE LAKE. THE EXILES' CURSE. SODOM'S
WEALTH. WHY LOT'S WIFE LOOKED BACK. THE PRIN-
CESS WITH THE GOLDEN KEY. YS, THE END OF
THE EARTH. A ROMAN ROAD INTO THE SEA. VI-
NETA'S SUNKEN BELLS. ARAB COINS IN THE BALTIC
REGION. TWELVE GATES AND A BEACON. FARMER
BUSCH AND HIS DISCOVERY. RUNGHOLT AND HAI-
THABU. REVELS AND SIN. THE GREAT FLOOD OF
1362.

I F WE would speak of the downfall and disappearance
of human habitations, we must speak first of all of the
ancient elements: fire, water, earth, and air. For these,
by sudden onslaught or by the slow, inexorable, gnawing
attrition of centuries, have ever gained ascendancy over
the frail constructions of men.

The Book of Genesis gives us the first accounts of disasters in which great cities were swallowed up. After the
tale of the catastrophic Deluge the Book describes a second retribution visited upon cities which are specifically
named and more or less located, so that archæology has
been able to look into the truth of the tradition.

The Bible says: "And the waters prevailed exceedingly

upon the earth." But the whereabouts of the disaster is extremely vague, and science has not decided to this day whether the story is based upon a local flood in the valley of the Tigris and Euphrates, upon the sinking of a continent, upon a deluge affecting the whole surface of the earth—perhaps the emptying of a central Asiatic sea to the east, south, and southwest—or perhaps even a tremendous precipitation of the dense atmosphere of water vapor which, according to Johannes Riem, once surrounded the entire earth and which to this day veils the planet Venus in eternal cloud.

In describing the destruction of Sodom, however, Genesis gives better data, which are, moreover, confirmed by other sources. Claudius Ptolemy, the Egyptian astronomer and geographer who lived in Alexandria in the second century A.D., speaks of the Dead Sea as the "Sea of Sodom." And even earlier Strabo, the Greek geographer, wrote of the annihilation of Sodom: "We may credit the traditions of the natives that in ancient days thirteen cities flourished in this region. The walls of the capital city of Sodom are, it is said, still preserved. They say that a great earthquake shook the cities, fire rose out of the sea, and sulfurous water poured forth, so that the very rocks caught fire. The cities either sank into the ground or were abandoned by the inhabitants, who fled in terror." Philo, a contemporary of Strabo, also speaks of the destruction of Sodom, as does Josephus in his *Antiquities of the Jews.* Everything, then, points to the fact that the event is historical. The question remains, what natural catastrophe could correspond to Strabo's rather fantastic-sounding description?

Geologists have pointed out that the relative heights and the geological structure of the West Jordanian and East Jordanian plateaus are exactly alike; the River Jordan must have broken through them and formed its valley as

late as the Tertiary, about 60,000,000 to 600,000 years ago.
The frequent earthquakes to which this region is subject
and the numerous hot springs are evidence for the hypothesis. The villages of Hamam near Tiberias, Amatha (near
present-day Mkes), and the valley of the Wadi Zerka
Ma'in are still faintly overcast by a sulfurous mist from the
thermal springs which suggests the explanation of the
Biblical "rain of brimstone."

It has been proved, however, that no volcanic eruption
has taken place in this vicinity for more than ten thousand
years. The period when an extinct volcano was last active
can be deduced with fair certainty from the layers of lava
and the composition of the volcanic stone. It is evident,
therefore, that Sodom and Gomorrah did not undergo the
same sort of destruction that later overwhelmed Pompeii
and Herculaneum.

The meaning of *gomorrah* is "land covered by water."
From the location of the two cities it is evident that only
the waters of the Dead Sea could have flooded Sodom
and Gomorrah. According to Max Blanckenhorn, who
spent many years in the region, the Dead Sea had its origin in a deep subsidence of the land, but assumed its present form only as the result of a second, smaller subsidence. "It was a sudden downward movement of the
earth's crust forming the floor of the valley to the south
of the Dead Sea, accompanied by an earthquake, of
course. The earth sank along one or several faults, de-
stroying the cities of Sodom and Gomorrah and literally
overturning them so that the salt sea could sweep over
them," Blanckenhorn writes. We can assume that in the
process great sections of the earth's crust tipped up and
turned over—so that the passage in the Bible was describing an event by no means legendary. "And He overthrew those cities, and all the plain, and all the inhabit-

ants of the cities, and that which grew upon the ground."

As a matter of fact, the Biblical text apparently adheres so closely to historical truth that doubt is cast upon the asserted reason for the catastrophe. For up to this point the story speaks only of the *cities,* which the Lord threatens with destruction because of their sinfulness. However, in the description of the disaster itself, not only the sinful cities are destroyed but "all the plain . . . and that which grew upon the ground." When the land sank and the Dead Sea overflowed, no distinction was made between the righteous and the sinners, between the innocent countryside and the corrupt cities.

But could any cluster of huts by the shore of the Dead Sea in those remote times actually be dignified by the name of city? Had the nomadic people of Israel, accustomed to wander from pasturage to pasturage, already developed into an urban folk? Geologists assign the probable date for this catastrophe at the southern tip of the Dead Sea to the first half of the second millennium B.C. —that is, to the centuries during which, archæologists assume, the Israelites first migrated from Ur across Palestine to Egypt. Sodom, therefore, was not an Israelite city. The Bible relates that the "men of the city . . . of Sodom" came to Lot's house and surrounded it, "both old and young, all the people from every quarter." And they said to him: "Go away. You are the only stranger here and would be a judge."

Lot, the Jew, was a stranger, the only foreigner, and the people of Sodom expelled him. He was neither the first nor the last exile to wish dire destruction upon those who drove him away. Nor was he the first, when a natural calamity ensued, to connect this with his own expulsion or the expulsion of his forefathers. An early Jewish historian may have known of the doom of Sodom and looked upon it, or chosen to look upon it, as punishment for the expulsion of a Jewish family. To make religious capital of this connection would require that the situation be reversed: the Almighty decides upon the annihilation of the city and warns the single representative of the chosen people to flee.

The first half of the second millennium B.C. is one of the most obscure phases in the history of Palestine. In the seventeenth century B.C., Palestine was the heart of a Semitic kingdom which the Hyksos controlled from Avaris; in fact, it is a fair assumption that they located this capital of theirs in the northeastern corner of the Nile Delta with the aim of keeping their grip on Palestine. In spite of local unrest that forced the cities to build massive encircling walls, trading and raiding brought such prosperity to this kingdom that the Jews, an impoverished nomad people passing through Palestine, were prompted to speak of the sinful gluttony and luxury of the cities. Sodom was, in all probability, a Canaanite city.[1] We must imagine it as protected by a strong, thick wall of rammed earth. Palestine became the principal trade artery between Asia and Africa, or, to be more precise, between the Land of the Two Rivers and the Egyptian culture on the Nile. This is proved by the innumerable scarabs found by archæologists, and also by weapons, ornaments, and those charmingly naïve clay vessels on which the name of a political enemy was written before the vessel was smashed—the idea being that the power or health of the enemy would thereby be shattered. The rammed-earth walls, reinforced with stones, were so solid that

---

[1] An argument in favor of this assumption is the close connection between Canaanite and Israelite tradition, especially in the stories of Genesis, as the papyrus finds at Ugarit have shown. A good many scholars go so far as to consider the Canaanite and Israelite texts merely deviant editions of a common original text.

they survived for many centuries and were constantly being reinforced and improved. But the enemy to which
Sodom succumbed was mightier than any human army.

The city that vanished amid clouds of noxious sulfur
fumes under the churned-up waves of the Dead Sea
never came to light again. Strabo reports that it was possible to pace off some sixty stadia around the outer fortifications. That is, the perimeter of the city was some six
to seven miles long—a sizable settlement indeed for those
days. The gates probably resembled those solid triple
gates that have been excavated at Sichem. The clever
towers and passages that have been excavated in Palestine indicate that the times were extremely insecure, in
spite of the prevailing economic prosperity. Archæologists
have detected in the ruins of Tell Beit Mirsim no less than
four complete and four partial destructions during the
two and a half centuries from 1800 to 1550 B.C. In Megiddo, farther to the north, five complete and an as yet unknown number of partial destructions took place during
the same period. As in our own twentieth century A.D.,
every generation participated in several wars and saw
buildings, property, fields, and families ruined. In no
phase of the history of Palestine do we find cities more
strongly fortified. These cities were essentially castles to
which the inhabitants of the surrounding countryside fled
in time of stress, and the hectic urban life to which the
Bible refers may, perhaps, have been only a kind of brief
celebration after battle, a hasty seizing of pleasure before the next aggressor struck.

Between the homes of the wealthy and the huts of the
poor and the semi-servile populace there existed an extraordinary gulf. The largest homes of this period covered
an area of some twenty thousand square feet. Exterior
walls six feet thick were usually raised on a stone base,

so that the houses were small forts within the big fortress. The servants lived in rooms on the ground floor, the master and his family in the upper story. Only in death were these class differences erased; the poor are often found buried in tombs like the rich, and there is scarcely any difference in the size of the tombs, though the burial gifts were naturally more valuable in the case of the rich. The rich man was buried with his expensive weapons, and

LEAPING HINDS IN INLAY WORK FROM TELL BEIT MIRSIM, CIRCA 1600 B.C.

(from W. F. Albright: The Archaeology of Palestine; *Pelican Books)*

the women of his family took their jewels and other ornaments with them to the grave. In all graves we find numerous clay vessels painted with Egyptian motifs of leaping gazelles, plants, etc., in monochrome.

The most resplendent building of Sodom was undoubtedly the temple. Although the Canaanites produced no architecture of signal artistic merit, they lavished labor and material upon their temples. The priests enjoyed great prestige and performed many sacrifices—not only of animals, but of human beings also, especially prisoners, which may be one reason for the horror the Israelites expressed in their Biblical narrative.

The fertility goddesses were highly important; they were usually represented naked, with the sexual characteristics strongly emphasized. Sacred prostitution was a feature of the Canaanite temples. This rite probably persisted at the time of the Israelite migration, and it is easy to imagine that the practice which was a form of divine service to the Sodomites must have struck the Jews as sinful abomination.

Possibly the Jewish womenfolk were more strongly drawn to these foreign cults (as Roman women were to the Mysteries) than their men. Lot's wife disobeyed the prohibition, looked back upon Sodom, and turned to a pillar of salt, and Lot's daughters, who fled with him, soon afterward sinned with their father. The prosperous commercial cities may well have been a temptation to which various clans among the Hebrews yielded until the disaster that befell Sodom and Gomorrah stirred their consciences, for it must have appeared as a warning from heaven.

The landscape is one that makes it easy to believe in divine wrath. "With its desolation and the long line of high, dreary chalk walls, barren, stony slopes and ragged gorges," comments the mid-nineteenth-century Orientalist Jakob Philipp Fallmerayer, "it fills the spirit of the wandering stranger with gloomiest melancholy." If we add the facts that birds avoid the Dead Sea on account of the poisonous vapors rising from the crevasses of the mountains, that the sea is too salty for fish, and that for most of the year a merciless sun blazes down upon the shimmering salt plains along the shore, we can easily understand that in such a landscape belief in supernatural forces must have been impressed upon the minds of

the people with unusual force. When, moreover, a geo-
logic upheaval causes the collapse of a land strip many
miles in extent, so that the waters of the silent, deadly,
fishless sea pour over cultivated soil, the rising sulfurous
vapors can easily be interpreted as portents of evil, and
the event itself as an act of divine punishment.

Men have always been prone to attribute to events in
nature meanings that suit their own doctrines. That is
why the most impressive legends of such "heavenly judgments" have arisen at times and in places where a new
religion was fighting its way against a native cult. The
interpretation of elemental catastrophes is one of the
strongest weapons in such a struggle.

Two thousand years later we meet with another
"Sodom." The story of its doom provided many a cleric in
medieval France with material for rousing sermons
against licentiousness and gluttony.

This is the way the legend is told. In the shelter of
perilous Pointe du Raz—the terror of sailors, where even
on windless days the swells of the Atlantic dash wildly
against the Breton coast—lay the rich and flourishing
city of Ys. The city was located on an inlet, and the inhabitants had erected a dike across the entrance to the
inlet to hold back the sea. A great lock in this dike
permitted shipping to enter. King Gradlon ruled wisely
over this city, but his beautiful daughter Dahut (or Ahès,
according to other sources) was led astray by luxurious
living and indulged in many excesses. One day she stole
from her father the golden key to the lock, the key that
permitted the heavy gates to be raised and lowered, and
went to visit her lover. In her lover's arms she forgot the
passage of time; the tide came in, the water rushed
through the open gates and destroyed the city.

The most obvious flaw in this story is its failure to attribute any motive to the princess's theft of the key; it does not seem likely that Dahut needed it in order to keep a rendezvous with her lover. Such lacunæ almost always indicate a break in the tradition. The Christian preachers who took over the old legend did not know what to make of the magical symbol of the key. In the later forms of the Celtic religion the key had a special role in connection with ideas of mastery and possession, but it also frequently stood for the realm of the dead. The underlying tale may well represent a Celtic version of the Greek Orpheus myth. The Isles of the Blessed, the realm of the dead in the Celtic religion, were assumed to be in the farthest west, where the sun sinks into the tempestuous, unexplored, and seemingly boundless sea. Princess Dahut wanted the key in order to fetch someone she loved back from the realm of the dead, or else in order to wed the king of the dead. In this same countryside we find, along with the legend of Ys, the age-old fairy tale of the bride of Death (or of the god of the dead). The Byzantine historian Procopius also speaks in his *Gothic War* of the Land of Shades beyond the Western Sea.

In connection with the city of Sodom we have seen some indications of a mode of life which might appear sinful to a foreigner. But the allegations of vice and divine judgment cannot, in the case of Ys, refer to anything but a conception dear to the earlier religions: the port of embarkation for the realm of the dead, the Isles of the Blessed. Historically there is no evidence for the existence of any especially rich and luxurious commercial city at this spot on the Breton coast. The great block of granite upon which green Brittany now rests presumably rose out of the primordial ocean as early as the Primary, about

540,000,000 to 200,000,000 years ago. For millions of years it has defied the onslaught of the waves. A glance at the map shows us how deep are the incursions the ocean has been able to make here. The bays of Carnac and Concarneau, of Saint-Anne and Brest, represent victories of the sea over the land, though the peculiarly wild and gashed aspect of this coast is not entirely due to such erosion; rather, according to many geologists, it came about because the sea level rose several yards during the Quaternary.

Nevertheless, we possess reliable evidence of great flood tides in early historical time. All around Britanny larger and smaller settlements have been drowned by the waves. But only Ys became famous; Ys alone captured men's imaginations, for Ys lay on that westernmost tongue of land which represented the end of the human world, the outermost extreme, the arm of this world that extends out into the Void. By relating the doom of Ys the Christian priests were striking at the religion of the druids.

Fishermen of Cancale on the northern coast of Brittany will to this day show strangers extensive remains of walls on the bottom of the sea. Visible only when the water is calm and clear, these walls suggest that a city once stood here. It must have been swallowed up when the sea broke through between the Chausey Islands and Mont Saint-Michel during the famous storm tide in the days of Charlemagne. It was that flood which gave the Channel coasts approximately their present shape.

But the fishermen of Cancale are mistaken in thinking that these are the walls of the sunken city of Ys. For annals of the Carolingian period refer portentously to the fate of the citadel of Gardoine, which resisted Charlemagne's army during a lengthy siege and in punishment was swept under by a flood. Ys itself was no longer in

existence during the Carolingian period. It was, therefore, not overwhelmed by the great eighth-century storm
tide, nor did it succumb to the steady attrition of the
sea waves. As so often in these dark periods of history,
the question is settled for us by the Romans.

For the Romans had included Ys in their network of
roads, and around A.D. 400 a map of these roads was
prepared. Consequently, we know the exact course of the
Roman road that ultimately ran straight into the sea at
the Bay of Dounarnenez.

If, in clear weather, we sail a short distance out into
this bay, we will see the stone edges of the road, and at
ebb tide the walls of a settlement are visible. These remains may have been much more plainly visible in the
past. A sixteenth-century chronicler records that the people of Douarnenez *"osoient bien assurer qu'aux basses
marées estant à la pesche, avoir souvent veus des vielles
maseures de murailles"*—that is, they insist that when
fishing at ebb tide they have seen the ruins of ancient
walls.

These walls and the map of the Roman road permit
us to date approximately the destruction of the city of
Ys. We know that in Brittany the Romans began building
extensive fortifications only toward the end of the third
century. Until then they had relied on the inhospitable
character of the region, which in fact had proved difficult
to conquer for this reason. Ys must therefore have been
drowned at the earliest by the flood of the year 395;
might equally well have succumbed to the nocturnal
floods of 441, which were so dreadful that they long remained in memory.

Ys, however, was certainly not a great and rich city,
since simple walls were considered sufficient for it; it
was not provided, like Condevincum (Nantes) or Con-

date (Rennes), with elaborate fortifications. Nor is it possible to see where wealth could have come from; the
period when the Breton ports flourished fell much earlier.
The Celts who migrated into Brittany from the fifth century B.C. on encountered a population that had already
acquired from Spain, by the sea route, a knowledge of
bronze tools. Since Brittany was well supplied with tin,
the inhabitants of the southern coast in particular developed a flourishing manufacture and trade. Deep into
the Roman period Brittany continued to supply wide
areas of Gaul with tools and weapons. Iron came slowly
and many centuries later than in other regions.

With the triumph of iron, however, the Breton towns
slumbered contentedly in the quiet life of the Pax Romana. The land grew poor. Ys, supposedly so wanton, did
not even have a theater; stone theaters in this vicinity
were found only in the far more important cities of
Locmariaquer and Nantes. The town subsisted, as do so
many Breton towns today, on fishing. The fishermen went
out to sea after salmon, and hunted mussels in the muck
at ebb tide. The Greek poet Oppianus, who lived in Asia
Minor during the second century A.D., was familiar with
the methods of Celtic fishermen and described them in
his didactic poem on the piscatorial art, the *Halieutica*.
The Celts painted their boats, which were equipped with
structures resembling fish heads and fins at prow and
stern. When they ran across a school of fish, they speared
the biggest fish with tridents. Even if we assume that the
French coast in those days was far richer in fish than at
present, it is hard to see how any people could become
rich and haughty by such a mode of earning their livelihood. It is true that the people of Ys were skilled craftsmen; they made pretty ornaments and highly esteemed
textiles. (The Celts were probably the only folk who pos-

sessed a "god of inventions," but they were unfamiliar
with so simple a tool as the mortar and pestle, and did
not know the art of creating large buildings in stone.)

The houses of Ys were frequently nothing but roofed
cellars. Sometimes they were round, with walls and roofs
supported on wooden poles. The women sometimes held
exceptional rank in Celtic society; women with balances
and other insignia are depicted on vases. They often
served as priestesses, especially during the Gallo-Roman
period—that is, the final two or three centuries in the
life of Ys. Earlier they may have functioned as female
druids; so the generally well-informed geographer and
seafarer Pomponius Mela asserts. The men wore trousers,
which the Romans soon discovered were highly practical
in the raw climate of Brittany, leather belts, and in war
a shirt of chain mail. Agriculture, which was scarcely
profitable on their rocky slopes, was held in low esteem;
there was not even a special god of the soil.

When the flood tide came, dike and lock gate could
not withstand it. For how could the men of Ys have
built large and solid dikes when they had always been
small craftsmen, not builders of great cities? In citing
them as examples of sinful luxury, the medieval bishops
were being most unjust.

About a thousand years after the Atlantic storm tides
overwhelmed the Celtic settlement of Ys, there were
catastrophic floods in northern Germany. The exact dates
of these have come down to us. The All Saints' Day flood
of the year 1304 devastated extensive portions of the
coastline along the mouth of the Oder River, tore loose
from the island of Rügen the strip of land known as the
Ruden, and swallowed the northwest tip of the island of

Usedom, at the mouth of the Peene. The so-called Marcellus (January 16) flood of 1362 remained for centuries
the worst of the North Sea floods; it cut such deep gashes
into the North Frisian coastline that a later, equally severe
flood on October 11, 1634, was able to split the island
of Nordstrand into four parts.

Each of these disasters devoured fishing villages and
ports of varying sizes. If, however, we examine closely
the documents and eyewitness accounts of those days,
we come to appreciate the classical clarity of Strabo,
Philo of Alexandria, or Pomponius Mela, who provide us
with incomparably more information about far remoter
times than do the medieval chronicles. The confusion of
these medieval documents begins with the very names of
the places destroyed by the sea.

There was, for example, a Slavic city on the Baltic Sea
named Yumne. An early chronicler Latinized this as
Jumneta and wrote it as IVMNETA. Someone else read
these letters as VIMNETA, from which it was ultimately
made into storied Vineta.

In the popular imagination of the Germans in the High
Middle Ages, the north was an icy wilderness of mists,
the east a mysterious and endless expanse. Splinter groups
of Slavic tribes extended long wedges into the area of
solid German settlement. Their fairy tales and their
strange religion with its many-limbed gods perplexed the
minds of the German peasants on the frontiers.

In this still pagan eastern land a city was destroyed.
Exaggerated rumors of its onetime wealth and brilliant
life circulated among the Germans, for the link between
wealth and destruction, paganism and ruin, seemed obvious to all. Tales were told of strange ships that had
come from distant places, with dark-skinned men on

board: Saracens. It was obvious and inevitable that God must send a great flood, causing the sea to swallow up all this sinful pomp.

Legends are folk tales, and the people work away at them industriously. Within a few centuries pagan "Vineta" had been blessed with churches and church towers. The weird tale went that on certain days the entire city rose so far from the bottom of the sea that the steeples of the church towers protruded out of the water like dangerous reefs. If a ship was wrecked upon them, neither survivors nor corpses would be found, for the inhabitants of the sunken city drew the ship's crew down to join them. Only the faint tolling of the sunken bells gave a hint of their fate.[2]

For centuries the exact location of Yumne or Vineta remained uncertain. Richard Hennig has shown, however, through ingenious studies and prolonged discussions with various regional historians, that Vineta must have been situated on the northwestern corner of the island of Usedom, near Rügen Island. His strongest point is geographical: a flourishing trading city must have had a good port and been located at the terminus of a heavily traveled inland trade route. Moreover, Usedom is marked as the site of Vineta on a map by Jansonius dated 1649. Jansonius comments: *"Vineta emporium olim celeber aquar. æstu absorptum"*—"Vineta, formerly a famous mart, which was swallowed up by the waves of the sea."

Legend was embroidering when it attributed to Ys a rocky Breton village, great wealth and even a king. But legend was right about Vineta. Scholars have come to the conclusion that it was indeed a rich commercial town,

---

[2] The theme of the "sunken bell" became a favorite motif in German literature, and was most notably employed by Gerhart Hauptmann in the famous play of that name.

probably the metropolis of Baltic trade before the rise
of the Hansa. This still half-pagan city of the Wends, as
the Germans called the neighboring Slavs, did really trade
with the infidel, as hundreds of thousands of Arabic coins
found in the southern and central Baltic regions prove.
Here was more than enough reason for "divine punishment," especially since the German Baltic cities of Kiel
and Lübeck and the German merchants in Swedish Wisby
would have liked the lion's share of Vineta's business.

The chief enemies of East-West trade were the Danes.
These Vikings did not wait for divine punishment to visit
Vineta. In 1098, or possibly twenty years later, the rich
city so well situated for commerce but poorly located
for defense was conquered and plundered by the Danes.
It was nearly destroyed and was not rebuilt. The Hol-
steinian historian Helmold, who in his *Chronica Slavorum*
described the Christianization of the Slavs, mentions in
1168 the ruins of the city. These ruins and the surrounding land were swallowed up by the sea in the great flood
of 1304.

As it turned out, the Danes had only injured themselves by inflicting premature destruction upon the
doomed city. With Vineta out of the way as a competitor,
Lübeck waxed rapidly in power, welded the Slavic cities
into a league, and led the Hansa blockade that in 1361
smashed the power of Denmark.

Thus, the city of Vineta, by the time it sank into the
sea, was probably inhabited only by rats. But we possess
a good many references to its way of life before its destruction. In the Jomsviking Saga, for example, we may
read: "Thereafter Palnatoki hastily caused a great fortress
to be erected, and this was later called Yomsburg. Fur-
thermore he had so large a harbor built for this fortress
that a good two hundred and fifty long ships could find

room there, and all of them would be enclosed within the fortress." The city of Yomsburg-Yumne-IVMNETA-Vineta was thus originally a kind of port of refuge for merchant ships—highly essential in days when piracy was rampant in the vast reaches of the Baltic Sea. To enclose the port within the fortress was the only solution to the problem of protecting so fortunate a city; yet it thereby became all the more tempting to the sea robbers.

The saga continues its description of Vineta's efforts to protect its trading port: "Everything inside the harbor was arranged with great artfulness, and there was also a kind of gate barring the entrance. Above the narrow waterway a huge stone arch was erected. Set in the gates were strong iron bolts which could be locked from within by iron pins. Above the stone arch was a large outwork in which many catapults were kept. Part of the fortress extended out into the sea . . . so that the harbor was entirely within Yomsburg."

This was around the year 980. About this same time Ibrahim Ibn Jakub, a much-traveled Arab merchant, wrote of a Slavic tribe that lived on the seacoast to the west of the Poles: "They have an important city on the encircling sea. It has twelve gates and a port, and the arrangements in this port are excellent."

At first glance this seems like the kind of nonsense so common in the narratives of medieval travelers—the tales of giants, duck-headed men, sea serpents, and so on. After all, a city would have twelve gates only if twelve highroads led out of the city. And if the city were situated by the sea, the twelve roads would have to run close together, providing a communications network of absurd density for medieval conditions. The gates referred to must therefore be harbor gates permitting ships to enter, and it is understandable that a harbor of that sort would have made an impression even upon so traveled an Arab.

Vineta was distinguished by another feature. Evidence seems to indicate that the city had the first beacon light in the Baltic area. Adam of Bremen, the eleventh-century chronicler of missionary work among the Scandinavians, writes in his *Descriptio insularis Aquilonis* that in Vineta there was an *olla vulcani,* a "fire-spewing pot" "which the inhabitants call Byzantine fire." Beacon fires, which had been common in ancient Rome, were forgotten by the eleventh century; only Alexandria and a few ports of the Byzantine Empire used them to guide sailors. The inhabitants of Vineta, therefore, must have learned the custom from Byzantium, for trade between Greek, Sicilian, and Arab ports and the Baltic cities was much closer than is generally assumed. That is why we must turn again to an Arab writer to find out whether so rich a city as Vineta was actually completely abandoned after being plundered and burned. The Arab geographer Abu Abdallah Mohammed ash Sherif al Edrisi also traveled widely. For King Roger II of Sicily (1093–1154) he constructed a celestial globe and a silver disk on which a map of the world was etched. For Roger's son William he also composed a detailed geography, unfortunately now lost. In a shorter "Roger's Book," however, Edrisi mentions that there were three abandoned cities on the Baltic whose inhabitants had moved "deeper inland."

It appears to be true, then, that the citizens of wealthy Vineta fled when the Danes ravaged their beautiful city; they did not have the tenacity to rebuild upon the blackened ruins. Thus, the greedy sea that rolled forward upon Rügen and the mouth of the Oder on the night of All Saints' Day in the year 1304 drowned only untilled land and empty houses, raged against encircling walls where sentinels no longer stood, and completed the work of de-

struction begun by Danish arms with such thoroughness
that to this day no more of Vineta has been found than
eight gold rings that a German fisherman dug out of the
sand at the mouth of the Peene.

Rungholt, the "Vineta of the North Sea," which was
swept by the flood of 1362, is far more historical and
less legendary than Yumne-Vineta. Myths and ghost stories have sprung up around Rungholt also, of course. But
undeniable traces of sunken Rungholt have been discovered—which is not the case with Vineta, in spite of all
efforts.

The most important discovery was made by a farmer
of Nordstrand named Andreas Busch, who was well acquainted with local history and interested enough to pursue investigations. In an article he published in 1923 he
wrote:

"Not far from the present shoreline of the island, where
the silted ground was recently once more washed clean
by the waves, the ancient sea-level of the place could be
determined accurately. . . . After wading through an
old ditch we entered the easternmost and largest of the
seven wharfs. In 1921 this was still some 150 by 200
feet wide and rose between two and three feet above
the surrounding terrain. On the southwest and especially
on the northwest sides decayed stumps of piles protruded
here and there. On the wharf itself traces of six wells
were found, each with an inner diameter of about four
feet." Busch then goes on to speak of a harbor sluice and
of weapons and tools washed out of the muck by the tide.
Some of these are now to be found in the Town Museum
of Husum. There are swords with heavy bronze heads,
several in leather sheaths; the point of a lance; a number
of axes; a mace; and a good many household utensils.

So many wells and boundary lines have been found that ancient Rungholt is estimated to have had at least a thousand inhabitants—far more than any simple fishing village could boast in the thirteenth or fourteenth centuries. A town on that inhospitable coast could, however, hardly have been graced by much splendor and wealth. Richard Hennig has demonstrated that Rungholt's situation was far less favorable than Vineta's. It is true, of course, that in those times the North Frisian Islands formed sizable bodies of land, even though much of the land was marshy, so that at least until 1240 Rungholt could have been considered a mainland port. Considerable trade passed through Schleswig because the captains of the frail vessels of the High Middle Ages justifiably dreaded stormy Cape Skagan. But Rungholt was not situated directly on the mouth of the Eider, stopping-place for virtually all ships laden with cargo for the Baltic; between the Eider and the Schlei there was only a relatively narrow strip of land to be crossed by expensive land transportation. On the Schlei was the great transshipment port of Haithabu, a populous harbor town located approximately where the seaport of Schleswig now lies.

Because of the remote and virtually unexplored fur and amber regions to the east, this part of the Baltic was a desirable trading area for the ports of the vicinity. But it was far from the only one, and the citizens of Rungholt appear to have possessed considerable enterprise. They traded not only with their neighbors in Hamburg, but also sent their vessels as far as Flanders, as recently discovered documents from Ghent demonstrate. Such vigorous commercial activity bespeaks considerable prosperity. Could the hardheaded moorland farmers and sailors have been so seduced by the profits from Flanders cloth that they wallowed in vice and blasphemy? So we are told by a chronicler writing in 1635. "Returning home laden with gold from a successful voyage to Flanders, a group of young men of Rungholt capped their long revels by stealing a pig, placing it in a bed, and calling a priest to give it extreme unction. When the priest arrived, he saw through the joke and refused to play his part. Thereupon the youths snatched the holy chalice from him, filled it with beer, and drank from it. It is said that the outraged pastor invoked the wrath of God, and the very next night the tide rose; it poured over the undiked islands, turned the canals into roaring torrents, and in the end swept away the city and harbor of Rungholt."

Like Vineta, Rungholt is reputed to rise above the waves now and again—according to some tales, every seventh year on Midsummer Night. Undoubtedly a mirage akin to the fata morgana has actually been seen, for these reports are very common. This particular natural phenomenon is said to have been unusually distinct on September 17, 19, and 20, 1939.

Rungholt did not go under all by itself; some thirty villages, settlements, and island farms fell prey to the waves on that January day in 1362, and it is highly probable that not all thirty had sinned in the same tasteless fashion. The elements are not concerned with guilt or blamelessness; they strike as the phase of the moon and the pressure of the atmosphere direct them. They leave it to the men crowding in terror on the roofs of their houses while the waves lash round to seek for guilt and ask for reasons. That seeking and asking has taken place again and again, in the salt deserts around Sodom, upon the Atlantic reefs, and among the foggy shoals of the Frisian Islands—wherever death lurks.

Sometimes the elements yield up again the prize they

have concealed for centuries. For a few years the land rose around the island of Südfall, the waves washed away the loose silt, and the plow furrows of the Rungholter farmers could be seen, the men who did not sail to Flanders but got their bread by honest tilling of the soil. Andreas Busch, who first found these recovered fields, takes occasion in his account to comment on the skill or clumsiness of the farmers who had driven their crude plows through this marshland.

II

HOLY CITIES

PASTOR SPANUTH SEEKS ATLANTIS. PRIMORDIAL DIS-
ASTERS AND THE ATLANTIC ISLAND BRIDGE. CYCLO-
PEAN CITIES OF THE EARLY SEAFARERS. PLATO'S
FABLE OF ATLANTIS. THE CITY OF CITIES. ANGKOR:
ASTRONOMY IN THE JUNGLE. A LAGOON CITY IN THE
SOUTH SEAS. ACROSS THE PACIFIC, BUT IN WHICH DI-
RECTION? SAURAT'S GIANTS. TIAHUANACO: KON-
TIKI'S CITY.

ON JULY 30, 1952, an Egyptologist, a North German
regional historian, and a Swiss archæologist rode out in
a motorboat to Helgoland. About six miles from the island a diver descended into the water and found, twenty-
five feet below the surface, a stone wall protruding some
two feet from the sand. Then came a ditch, and beyond
it a second stone wall.

A find of this sort is interesting but not particularly
sensational. The North Sea coast is known to be sinking
steadily. Many now flooded areas were once settled—
the Zuider Zee, for example, Jade Bay, and the entire
vicinity of the Frisian Islands. Even the English Channel
began gradually to open up only in the fifth millennium
B.C., thus separating the British Isles from the mainland.
If that stone wall in the sea were not just a glacial moraine

but really the work of human hands, it simply proved that
the region was habitable and inhabited in prehistoric
times.

But Pastor Jürgen Spanuth, the leader of this expedition, gave a far weightier interpretation to the find. The
stone wall he took as tangible proof for his thesis that
the legendary island of Atlantis had been situated near
Helgoland.

In making this assertion Spanuth was saying nothing
fundamentally new; he was only reviving a hypothesis
put forward in the 1930's. At that time some German
had written a book entitled *Atlantis-Helgoland, Motherland of Aryan-Germanic Racial Thoroughbreeding and
Colonization.*

In the seventeenth century a Swede named Olof Rudbeck had claimed his native land as the true site of Atlantis and as the homeland of every imaginable people:
the Scythians, Giants, Amazons, Goths, Trojans, Moors,
Gauls, and Teutons. Ever since, Atlantis has been "discovered" in many places in the world: in Palestine, in
South, West, and North Africa, in the Azores, the Canary
Islands, St. Helena, North and Central America, the Caucasus, Ceylon, Spitzbergen, and Crete. In 1912, Paul
Schliemann, grandson of the discoverer of Troy, drew
highly dubious comparisons between the finds in Troy
and other finds in Egypt and Central America. His con-
tention was that a sunken continent of Atlantis had been
the common original home of these various cultures. Finally, he claimed to possess coins that had been the currency of Atlantis forty thousand years ago.

There would be no point in examining this and much
similar humbug that has been written about Atlantis,
were it not partly based upon facts that are in themselves correct and quite interesting. The tendency to

search for Atlantis in the vicinity of the Azores is based
upon the existence of numerous undersea volcanoes in
that area. These may once have annihilated a large island; the "Azores plateau" extends a great distance several hundred yards below the surface. Moreover, the Atlas
Mountains march toward the Atlantic Ocean and there
break off quite abruptly. The legend of the doom of the
island of Atlantis might, therefore, be based upon the
natural catastrophe in which the end of this mountain
chain was swallowed up.

Bones of the ancestor of our present-day horse, the
protohippus, have so far been found only in the Americas,
while the horse itself was unknown in America at the
time the New World was discovered. It had evolved only
in Europe, Asia, and Africa, but must have reached the
Old World from the New. Similar reasoning applies to
the distribution of the banana and other fruits. A prehistoric land bridge between South America and Africa
has therefore been deduced—and this hypothetical land
bridge has also been named as the site of sunken Atlantis.

It can be objected, of course, that great changes in
the surface of the earth (among which could be included
the sinking of a land bridge between South America and
Africa) took place several million years ago. No record
could have come down to us of such primordial natural
catastrophes, so there is no reason to connect them with
the Atlantis myth.

Legends of floods are to be found over the entire world,
but they all refer either to the Sumerian flood legend
(which influenced the Biblical and Greek stories), which
is based upon a historically demonstrable flood, or to
floods of the Amazon or Rio Grande rivers; or else they
were basic cosmological myths of the origin of things from
primal waters.

The simplest—and for the layman the most convincing —method of proving theories about Atlantis is that of adducing supposed parallels between American and European cultures, thereby proving what the author of the theory set out to prove: that the sunken continent or the land bridge of Atlantis once existed.

The best known of these "proofs" was put forth in 1882 by an American, Ignatius Donnelly. But many of the cultural aspects that Donnelly lists as common to Europe and America are common to all human cultures that have gone beyond extreme primitivism. Moreover, many of Donnelly's detailed data are simply inaccurate—as, for example, the assertion that the Peruvians knew the plow before Pizarro, or that they mined iron. The fact that they brewed intoxicating beverages can be explained as a universal human activity, without reference to cultural communication!

Even more rash, in view of the limited number of sounds the human vocal cords can produce, are conclusions drawn from chance similarity or identity of words. If a Mexican city is named Panuco, there is no reason to connect it with the Greek god Pan. We have similar accidental identities within the same cultural sphere: the city of Paris has no connection whatsoever with the beautiful Homeric shepherd of the same name. But Donnelly is not alone in such false reasoning. Even modern writers like Braghine can print fantastic statements, such as that a Basque missionary preached to the natives of Guatemala in the language of his region and was understood. Comprehensive comparisons of the Guatemalan Indian dialects with Basque have shown that there is not the slightest relationship between the languages.

As a matter of fact, to the chance relationships between

European and American cultures there are opposed a number of fundamental differences in key cultural elements, such as the numerical system.

Serious scholars are often compelled to deal with the problem of a wonderful sunken city or land of Atlantis because of the enormous and constantly swelling literature on the subject. But most of them come to the impatient conclusion: "As for Atlantis as a supposed island bridge over the ocean, geologists are generally agreed that if any such island or direct land connection between the continents ever existed, it was at a time when no human beings walked this earth on either side of the ocean." [1]

Occasional contact across the ocean remains a possibility. For that neither sunken cities nor sunken islands, much less continents, need be hypothesized. Modern scholars have shown that the achievements of prehistoric seafarers have been generally underestimated. The oceans of the world were traversed a good while before the Phœnicians, Carthaginians, and Etruscans sailed out upon them. We still do not know very much about these earlier voyages. But they have left their traces: gigantic stone buildings, tombs, stone memorials, and fortress walls. "Cyclopean walls" these were called in antiquity, for it was thought that only the Cyclops, one-eyed giants like Homer's famous Polyphemus, could have erected such walls. H. G. Wells speaks of a "heliolithic" cultural sphere because the builders of these walls seem to have practiced a solar cult. Among other symbols, they used the sun's disk and the swastika. Most scholars refer to their cultural sphere as the megalithic (big stone). Since these Cyclops left monuments almost exclusively in coastal regions,

[1] Quoted from Hans Dietrich Disselhoff: *Geschichte der altamerikanischen Kulturen* (Munich, 1953), pp. 12 f.

it is evident that they were familiar with the sea and seafaring. The tombs of these people were found first in Scandinavia and northern Germany; consequently, they were first thought to be Germanic and their swastika was taken to be a "Nordic" or at least an "Aryan" symbol. It has since been learned that they had no connection with the peoples of the Indo-European linguistic family. These "Cyclops"—if they may be considered a unified people, which is questionable—sailed the coasts of Europe from Scandinavia to Ireland and Spain, as far as the Canary Islands, into the Mediterranean, up rivers deep into the heart of Europe, and even to Armenia, Palestine, India, and Japan. They may well have occasionally reached America. But they have nothing to do with Atlantis!

Many Atlantis "scholars," of course, are fond of referring to these seafarers. Pastor Spanuth, however, claims other sea peoples for his particular Atlantis. His theory is that the Danauna, Zakkara, Pursta, Shardana, and Washasha, who are mentioned in documents of Pharaoh Ramses III, came from Helgoland-Atlantis when the greater part of their homeland was swallowed up by the sea. Since the Egyptians have left pictorial representations of their victories over these foreign invaders, Spanuth has been able to reproduce pictures of his "Atlanteans." What part of the Mediterranean these sea peoples actually came from need not be discussed here; it is enough to note that they certainly did not come from the North Sea coast. Moreover, Ramses III reigned at the beginning of the twelfth century B.C., while Atlantis is supposed to have been submerged eight thousand years earlier, according to Plato.

Plato is, as a matter of fact, the only real "authority" for the Atlantis myth. In his dialogue *Timæus* an Egyptian

priest is supposed to have told the Athenian lawgiver
Solon the following tale:

"Our histories tell of a mighty power which was ag-
gressing wantonly against the whole of Europe and Asia,
and to which your city put an end. This power came
forth out of the Atlantic Ocean, for in those days the
Atlantic was navigable; and there was an island situated
in front of the straits which you call the Pillars of Heracles.
The island was larger than Libya and Asia put together.
. . . Now in this island of Atlantis there was a great and
wonderful empire which had rule over the whole island,
and several others, as well as over parts of the continent,
and besides these they subjected the parts of Libya
within the Pillars of Heracles as far as Egypt, and of
Europe as far as Tyrrhenia [Italy]. . . . In later times
there occurred violent earthquakes and floods; and in a
single day and night of rain all the warlike men in a
body sank into the earth, and the island of Atlantis in
like manner disappeared, and was sunk beneath the sea.
And that is the reason why the sea in those parts is im-
passable and impenetrable, because there is such a quantity of shallow mud in the way; this was caused by the
subsidence of the island."

This description of Plato's certainly contains little to
serve the purpose of Pastor Spanuth. There is, however,
a second and much more detailed story of Atlantis in
Plato's dialogue *Critias,* also known as the "Atlantean"
dialogue. Since it occupies almost twenty pages in Bur-
net's edition of Plato (Oxford, 1902), it is almost always
quoted in extracts, each Atlantis scholar choosing the particular sections that suit his theory. (We, too, cannot
quote the entire text here, but will endeavor to cover
the essential points.)

The island of Atlantis was the property of Poseidon,

god of the sea. There lived his descendants and "the earth-born primeval men." Poseidon fell in love with a girl named Kleito. In order to be with her undisturbed, the god placed three circular zones of sea and two of land around the hill on which she lived, and provided springs of cold and warm water and many fruit trees.

CHARIOT HORSE OF RAMESES III.

Later this became the site of the king's castle, and the god's ten sons ruled as kings over Atlantis, the neighboring islands, and parts of the mainland. The island was rich in metals, wood, spices, fruit, vegetables, and animals wild and domestic. There were even elephants. Temples, palaces, harbors, docks, bridges, and canals were built. The royal palace was magnificent beyond belief. A temple for Kleito and Poseidon was sheathed in silver, with spires of gold, a ceiling of ivory, gold, silver, and copper alloy. In it stood statues of gold and a huge altar. The port was crowded with ships and merchants who came from all parts of the world and who swarmed in such numbers that they created a tremendous din by day and by night.

The island towered steeply out of the sea. It was mountainous; only the region around the city itself was flat. A great irrigation system watered the plain so well that crops could be harvested twice a year. The plain contained sixty thousand farms of the same size. The number and kind of warriors, chariots, and sailors to be supplied by each farm was fixed in advance, so that in case of war all the archers, armored men, and the crews for twelve hundred ships would be in readiness.

Ten kings ruled over this land, each an absolute despot in his territory. These rulers obeyed the injunctions of their ancestor Poseidon; Poseidon's laws were engraved upon a pillar that stood in his sanctuary in the middle of the island. There the kings met every five or six years to confer with one another and hold court. To initiate the tribunal, there was a curious ceremony: the kings alone, armed only with clubs and cords, must hunt down one of the sacred bulls that pastured freely around the temple. They sacrificed the bull, promised to obey the law and judge justly, and then dined together. When darkness fell and the sacrificial fire died down, they donned resplendent blue garments, extinguished all the fires in the sanctuary, sat down on the bare ground, and discussed all night long any disputes that had arisen among them. They were not allowed to make war against one another.

These kings were true models of wisdom, gentleness, and unselfishness; they cared not at all for wealth, but only for friendship and unity. Thus, everything went well for a long time. But in the course of generations the portion of divine blood they had inherited from Poseidon was increasingly diluted; human weaknesses won the upper hand; the rulers degenerated.

"Zeus, the god of gods, who rules with law, and is able to see into such things, perceiving that an honorable race was in a most wretched state, and wanting to inflict punishment on them, that they might be chastened and improve, collected all the gods into his most holy habitation, which being placed in the center of the world sees all things that partake of generation. And when he had called them together, he spoke as follows. . . ."

With this, Plato's tale of Atlantis breaks off. We know the fate of the island from the preceding dialogue, the *Timæus;* earthquakes and floods caused it to be swallowed by the waves as punishment for unrighteousness—the familiar story.

If we take the trouble to examine the Atlantis story in conjunction with Plato's complete works, we will not be inclined to take the legend literally. No poet and no mythographer before Plato ever mentioned any such legend, or so much as hinted at it; it is strictly the intellectual property of the great poet-philosopher and is directly related to his treatise on the ideal republic. No one goes hunting for the cave of Plato's famous parable. Similarly, neither Plato nor his great disciple Aristotle, nor any other contemporary, believed in the reality of Atlantis. It was reserved for a Byzantine geographer to include this island in his *Christian Topography*. But such is the mania for wonders in this age of ours that people have looked for the imaginary island upon this earth. In consequence, none of the real lost cities has ever become so famous as the city and country of Atlantis, which never existed. Mythical Atlantis has become a symbol both of

the ideal state and of the vanished glories of earlier phases
of human history.

   As such a wish-dream, Atlantis is by no means restricted
to European culture. The "city of cities" also figures in
the imaginations of other peoples, though of course under
other names. Some two centuries after Plato introduced
this most stubborn of delusions, a subject of the Han Emperors, a Chinese named Jang Kien, set out on a voyage
of discovery lasting twelve years. From the stories he
brought back his countrymen formed their conception
of their own land as the "Middle Kingdom." Hitherto
they had conceived the whole earth as a square with
sides no more than ten thousand Chinese miles in length,
giving an area of 6,200,000 square miles—about two and
a half times the area of present-day China. Mythical and
geographical conceptions are intimately interwoven in
all Asiatic cultures. Thus, the seas were seen as mythical
waters bounding the ends of the world; high mountain
chains or vast deserts were likewise taken for boundaries
of the earth. The dimensions arrived at in this way were
projected not only to the courses of the stars, but were
also observed in the building of temples and even in the
building of many cities, which were thus intended as
microcosmic images of the whole of creation. Certain
cities were accounted sacred, especially those laid out in
later stages of the development of the religions; in their
physical plan they expressed cosmological and religious
ideas. They remained places of pilgrimage for centuries
after the significance of their original layout ceased to
be understood by the pilgrims.

   The youngest city of this sort is Mandalay in Upper
Burma. It was founded only in 1857. Its walls form a
square slightly less than a mile on the sides, laid out in

the directions of the compass. The most imposing cosmo-magical city plan, however, is that of Angkor, the temple city of the god-kings of Khmer, now buried in the jungle of Indochina. It was arranged on the square, and in its earliest stages had moats and encircling ponds around artificial temple mounds, symbolizing the oceans encir-cling the center of the world, Mount Mandara or Meru.

The clarity of this cosmological scheme gave way to utter chaos when the primeval jungle burst in and over-whelmed the works of man.

"For four days past they had seen nothing but the forest. Even the villages near which they camped seemed bred of the forest like their wooden Buddhas and palm-thatched huts asquat like monstrous insects on the spongy soil. In the glaucous sunlight, dense as the sheen of an aquarium, every thought grew turbid, decomposed. . . . Some unknown power assimilated the trees with the fungoid growths upon them, and quickened the restless movements of all the rudimentary creatures darting to and fro upon a soil like marsh-scum amid the steaming vegetation of a planet in the making. Here what act of man had any meaning, what human will but spent its staying power?" (André Malraux)

In the border area between Cambodia and eastern Siam lies the *tonle-sap,* the Great Lake, which is more than sixty miles long. To the north of it is the lush Indo-chinese jungle, so impenetrable that from an airplane only the brownish-green waves of the treetops can be seen, concealing everything beneath them. This jungle has engulfed the most magnificent temple city we have knowledge of, and it is unlikely that in the unknown in-teriors of South America, Borneo, or Tibet anything even nearly comparable will be discovered in the future. The temple ruins of Angkor mark the site of the noblest, mightiest, and probably most inaccessible of all the mysterious lost cities on the face of the earth.

And yet the interval between the time the glorious sacred city of the Khmers was abandoned by its inhabitants and the time the first European settlements were established in Indochina amounted to only a hundred years. When around 1280 the Venetian Marco Polo, on his journey from China into Burma, set foot in Cambodia, the civilization of the Khmers and the power of their kings were at their height. In 1292, Niccolò Polo traveled with his brother Maffeo and his son Marco across Indochina, Sumatra, and Ceylon back to Europe, and around 1320 the Franciscan father Odoric of Portenone mentions a stay in this region. European penetration of the country began with the Portuguese discoverers. Like Pizarro in Peru, they were able to profit by the internal dissension of the country. The various pretenders to the throne who fought one another in Cambodia looked for allies wherever they could find them. Toward the end of the sixteenth century Diego Belloso, a Portuguese, and the Spaniard Blas Ruiz de Hernan Gonzalez promised hard-pressed King Sotha I of Cambodia the aid of the Iberian kingdoms, which had been united since 1580. By the time this aid finally arrived, King Sotha had already fled—wisely, since the greater part of the fleet sent from the Spanish Philippines had been shattered by a typhoon. Perhaps a victory of King Sotha would have been the saving of the ancient temple of Angkor; but, as it was, the King went to Laos. With the head of state gone and political chaos persisting, the inhabitants of those vast, weird edifices ceased to fight the advance of the jungle. Slowly, like a monstrous octopus, it gathered pillars and gates, walls and cupolas, into the lustful green arms of its lianas.

Since nothing came of the promised military aid, Indo-chinese relations with Europe remained for a long time purely economic in nature. But "Indochina derived great advantages from trade with the Portuguese, and Divine Providence," as a Jesuit chronicler of the seventeenth century put it, "chose this way to smuggle a *patre* into the country along with every shipment of goods."

With persecution of the Christians the bloodiest phase in the history of Indochina began; the country became more inhospitable to Westerners than any other colonial territory. Scholars therefore kept away, though the land had long been recognized as the site of ancient, highly developed cultures. It was 1908 before the territory in which Angkor is situated came under French domination. To this day any expedition into the realm of the ancient rulers of Khmer is a perilous adventure. Under Paul Doumer, who did more for Indochina than any other European, a law was promulgated for the protection of ancient sanctuaries and monuments. The difficulty of transporting huge blocks of stone on two-wheeled ox-carts and down narrow jungle paths did the rest to preserve the inviolability of the holy places and the ancient royal residences. But the conditions hindered scholars also. To carry on research in the tropical jungle demanded more than mere scientific pertinacity. A man who wished success in this field had to have retained, through all his years of scholarly study, a spirit of youthful adventure and daring. We can scarcely speak of the temples of the Khmers without mentioning André Malraux, who has done so much to make the architecture and sculpture of the lost city in the jungle meaningful to the civilized world.

In his novel *The Royal Way*, Malraux describes the battle with the jungle that has made it almost impossible

for archæologists to obtain an over-all view of the Khmer
culture. Again and again, after exhausting journeys
through the primeval forest, they have encountered dis-
appointments.

"Night fell, the dawn came, another night, another
dawn, and at last they reached a remote village dithering
with malaria, a village lost amid the universal disintegra-
tion of all things under an unseen sun. Now and then they
caught sight of the mountains, and each time they loomed
nearer. Low-growing branches swished noisily against the
hoods of the carts, but even their intermittent rustle
seemed muted by the heat. The warm miasma steaming
up from the earth half suffocated them, but they had
a consolation—the last guide's positive assurance that
there was sculpture on the temple towards which they
were proceeding.

"But they had grown used to such affirmations. For
all his doubts regarding this temple—and indeed any
specific temple they might go in quest of—Claude was
held to his general idea of them by a half-skeptical belief, a complex of logical assurances and doubts so deep
as to have become almost physiological. It was as if his
eyes and nerves protested against his hope, against the
unkept promises of this phantasmal road.

"At last they reached a wall.

"Claude's eyes were growing familiar with the forest.
When near enough to discern the centipedes scurrying
across the stonework, he realized that their guide had
shown more intelligence than his predecessors, and had
led them to a fault which obviously marked the site of the
former entrance. Like all the other temples this one was
ringed by a tangled palisade of cane-brake. Perken, who
was beginning to know the habits of the vegetation round
such sites, pointed to a spot where the green barrier was

less thick. 'Pavement,' he said. There, doubtless, was the pathway leading to the sanctuary. The cartmen set to work. With a noise like crumpled paper, the canes fell slowly right and left, leaving behind them tiny specks of white, shining like stars across the gloom—the pithy stumps slashed diagonally by the wood-knives. . . ."

Today we know of some hundred large and small sanctuaries that were erected in the so-called Khmer era and still exist, though the data on the individual temples differ sharply, their separate identities are by no means clear, and some are discovered by chance only to be lost in the jungle once more. André Malraux tells us what it felt like to make such a discovery:

"Before him lay a chaos of fallen stones, some of them lying flat, but most of them upended. It looked like a mason's yard invaded by the jungle. Here were lengths of wall in slabs of purple sandstone, some carved and others plain, all plumed with pendent ferns. Some bore a red patina, the aftermath of fire. Facing him he saw some bas-reliefs of the best period, marked by Indian influences—he was now close up to them—but very beautiful work; they were grouped round an old shrine, half hidden now behind a breastwork of fallen stones. It cost him an effort to take his eyes off them. Beyond the bas-reliefs were the remains of three towers razed to within six feet of the ground. Their mutilated stumps stuck out of such an overwhelming mass of rubble that all the vegetation round them was stunted; they seemed socketed in the débris like candles in their sticks. The shadows had shortened; an unseen sun was climbing up the sky. An imperceptible tremor, a perpetual vibration, began to stir within the leafy depths, though there was not the faintest breeze. The great heat was beginning.

"A loose stone fell and sounded twice in falling, first

with a muffled thud, then clearly; and Claude, in his
mind's ear, caught an echo of the word: eer-ie. But it
was not only the dead stones which the clumsy frogs
quickened to fugitive life on this their first encounter
with mankind; it was not only the utter desolation of
this forsaken temple, nor was it but the veiled yet active
malevolence of this vegetation that made the place seem
so uncanny. Something inhuman brooded over all these
ruins and the voracious plants which now seemed petri-
fied with apprehension; a presence of numinous awe
guarded with its dead hand these ancient figures holding
their lonely court amongst the centipedes and vermin of
the forest."

A Chinese traveler who visited Angkor toward the end
of the thirteenth century has left a highly fantastic description of the city. Some of his statements, however,
have been confirmed by modern scholarship.

Angkor—the word means capital city—was not only a
seat of government but a religious center, a much-fre-
quented place of pilgrimage. Many roads led from this
metropolis, which was once ringed by a belt of fertile
ricelands. The jungle now surrounding the ruins is therefore relatively young. In the center of the city were some
twenty temples, the most important, the Bayon Temple,
being a kind of national sanctuary which our Chinese
traveler described as "golden." This may mean that its
towers or roof were covered with gold leaf, though no
traces of gold are to be found on the ruins. The towers
display characteristic giant faces on all four sides, faces
whose brows merge into the cornices. The eyes are half
or fully closed, and the mouths under the broad noses
are smiling with blissful, transfigured contentment. René
Grousset, the late specialist in Asiatic art and history,
relates the expression of these faces to the influx of Indian

religious feeling. The huge faces on the temple towers, he says, showed all believers the "happiness without desires of the soul that has at last entered nirvana." We may well imagine that the enormous, smiling, stylized faces looking down from countless towers and gates gave to the swarms of pilgrims a foretaste of the peace they hoped to find within the temple itself.

To the north of the Bayon Temple was the Royal Palace; its splendid terrace with the life-size sculptures of elephants still stands.

The entire central temple area with the square pond in front of it makes an overwhelming impression upon the traveler who emerges from the wilderness of the jungle. There is a complete and amazing harmony about the whole plan, as if it were the product of a single creative will; brilliant architectural ideas have here become convincing stone realities. Hundreds of faces look down upon the observer; hundreds of scenes of dancing, play, and battle are depicted on pillars and façades, some in earnest, some in mocking distortion.

Hans Nevermann, who collected the legends, fairy tales, and mythology of this land, describes the people as endowed with a keen sense of humor and a rather considerable delight in mockery, satire, and caricature. To this day they call themselves Kao-Mon, which means literally "high portal" but which is probably only a derivative from the word *Khmer*. For, remote as is the glory of the ancient kings of Khmer, the Cambodians still like to apply the name to themselves. The heroes of their stories and of the episodes depicted on the façades and pillars are usually kings who wish to marry off their numerous daughters, or princes who clamber in disguise over fences at night in order to pick some especially tasty squashes. The reliefs deal most frequently with stories of court life, and there are whole courtly romances in pictures; parallels to the ancient Sanskrit heroic epics are common.

What the Chinese traveler has to tell us about the life and luxury of the court indicates that extreme of luxury which is rarely found among a healthy, rising nation but which is so frequently present in an empire that has reached its peak and is stagnating while awaiting destruction.

It is true that the buildings, constructed of brick and sandstone crudely hewn into large blocks and laid without mortar, could probably have been put up quite rapidly. But the sandstone, for example, had to be brought from quarries fifteen miles away—a distance requiring enormous labor power in view of the massiveness of the blocks and the primitive transportation of the twelfth and thirteenth centuries.

If in addition we consider the lavishness of the court appurtenances, the thousands of concubines, the bodyguard of women our Chinese traveler reports, we can picture the king himself as very much like one of those fat, smiling, satiated statues—the kind of king sword-waving barbarians have easily overcome in all ages. And in fact the glory of the Khmers, whose grandiose architecture has been preserved for us, lasted a comparatively short time. The Khmer region lies in the western part of Indochina, which is exposed to Indian influences (the north and east is influenced by China); the people themselves are related to the inhabitants of old Pegu (southern Burma). The kings, however, traced their ancestry back to the fearsome Hindu god Siva, and Sanskrit (in the variant known as Pali) became the language of inscriptions and of the church.

The golden age of Khmer began with King Djayavarman II. For his "ancestor" Siva the King built a splendid temple on Mount Koulen, to the north of Angkor, and one of his successors named Yacovarman I (889–910) founded the capital city of Angkor. However, the Bayon Temple in the heart of Angkor seems, according to the latest research, not to have been built until the reign of King Djayavarman VII (1181 to about 1218). Upon this temple appear for the first time the faces with that characteristic inward smile and closed or almost closed eyes. The peak of the temple, which is visible from a great distance, displays the four faces of the Bodhisatva Avalokitesvara. He is the most popular of the innumerable Bodisatvas and is considered to be the quintessence of mercy; in Tibet he is embodied in the Grand Lama of Lhasa.

It is curious to reflect that this temple was built contemporaneously with the cathedrals of Notre Dame and Chartres. But probably the temple of Khmer was not open to the faithful; priests alone scurried through the narrow corridors between the richly carved walls; priests and dignitaries alone moved upon the wide terraces between the towers. The populace gathered below in great throngs and looked up at the splendid works of art. These temples were for gods; they were at the same time funeral monuments for god-kings, of whom the greatest were identified after their deaths with Vishnu.

Thus the temple of Angkor-Vat was the tomb of Souryavarman II, and the Bayon Temple was a gigantic mausoleum for Djayavarman VII; most of the reliefs adorning this temple refer to incidents from his life.

From the west the vigorous Thai tribes pressed into this kingdom. From the east came a new variety of Buddhism whose adherents sought salvation in complete renunciation, in modest living and contemplation; they had

no use for pompous liturgy or resplendent temple buildings. And from the moist lowlands the jungle, which had
once been thrust back by man, advanced once more
against the exhausted peoples of Khmer. In the fifteenth
century a king named Pona Yat decided to abandon the
too splendid capital that was so close to the warlike
Siamese tribes. A large part of his people followed him
to the new capital south of the Great Lake, where today
the city of Pnompenh lies. Those who remained behind
were slaughtered or dragged away into slavery by the
Thai.

The city and temple of Angkor remained abandoned
to the jungle, which, while slower to wreak destruction
than the young Siamese warriors and their raging war
elephants, was more thorough. The jungle swallowed
small buildings entirely, hiding them completely under
branches and vines. And it transformed even the mightiest edifices by the grip of its roots and the thrust of its
shoots into loosened, then swaying, and soon collapsing
heaps of hewn stone.

Among the people, however, the strangest legends of
the great kings were preserved. These tales show them in
quite a different light from that given by the perhaps
colored narrative of the Chinese traveler and diplomat—
who had, after all, come to demand tribute. According to
the folk tales, King Djayavarman VII erected more than
one hundred hospitals throughout the land, and Khmer
was a kingdom of righteousness in which no one had to
go hungry. Thus these grandiose buildings acquired a
life of their own after they had been abandoned by men.
Out of the concealing green embrace and darkness of the
jungle they began to shine forth anew as they had in the
days when hundreds of thousands of the faithful sought
them out.

In modern times these remarkable edifices suggested to the Austrian archæologist Robert Heine-Geldern the possibility of a fecundation of Central American culture from Southeast Asia. About halfway between India and America, and almost on the same latitude as the temple city of Angkor, lies the Caroline island of Ponape, also called Bonepe or Puinipet. For a long time this island was the heart of the Spanish colony in Micronesia. It is surrounded by a coral reef broken by a number of passages, so that the island possesses several excellent harbors. And yet it is a dying land, a dying paradise where only a few people now live—far less than dwelt there fifty or a hundred years ago, and only a fraction of the happy population that built a remarkable culture about A.D. 1650.

The island was discovered by the Portuguese navigator Pedro Fernandez de Quiros. He gave the mountains of basalt rock which rise to a height of almost six thousand feet the name of Monte Santo, but otherwise observed little about Ponape. It remained for two German scholars, W. S. Kubary and Paul Hambruch, to investigate the ninety-odd mysterious buildings of crude basalt blocks which are scattered over an area of nearly a square mile. Hambruch attempted to discover the former use of these structures, which his colleague thought to be the royal tombs of a people who had once inhabited the island.

In the island's lagoon, now filled with silt, the unknown subjects of the kings of Ponape built their sacred city out of great blocks of dark basalt, a city that, as soon as the last artisan had left the holy precincts, the people were forbidden on pain of death to enter. The buildings of gray basalt and coral rock are overgrown by moss and partly hidden by trees and underbrush. But it is evident that the builders possessed a knowledge of architecture not found elsewhere among the peoples of the oceanic islands, who live in flimsy huts. Some have speculated that the buildings stemmed from a settlement of ship-wrecked sailors, perhaps an early colony of Japanese whose vessel had been driven to the island by a storm, or of Spanish mutineers who had been deliberately left there. But the structures show not the remotest traces of Japanese or Spanish character, and both Kubary and Hambruch agree in considering them the products of a native culture.

For a long time it was taken for granted that the Polynesians could not have developed a high civilization independently. This theory was, however, largely due to the prejudices of the early travelers, the first of whom were rough sailors, followed by traders, and finally by narrow-minded Puritan missionaries who had no under-standing whatsoever for the traditional ways and the charming nature of the islanders. Naturalness was for them savagery, and simple candor the equivalent of im-morality. Adelbert von Chamisso, the German poet and naturalist who took part in Count Nikolai Romanzov's voyage around the world in 1815–18, has left the first account of the Polynesians which did some justice to this people. Kubary, coming after Chamisso, began writing down old legends from the island of Palau, but until the beginning of the twentieth century knowledge of this fascinating insular culture increased only very slowly. Paul Hambruch collected tales and old legends in the Carolines, especially on Ponape, and found that they repeatedly mentioned the old kings and their city in the land known as Matolenim. One story would tell of an old wizard of the basalt mountains who kidnapped a beauti-ful princess from the city, or there would be references to the preparation of food for the royal court. Names were uncertain. The intelligent and story-loving Polynesians are fond of puns and symbolic appellations, so that it is difficult to determine what the original names may have been. Hambruch, on the basis of his many records of old traditions, believes that all the kings of the lagoon city were called Shautelur, and that the palace was known as Pankatra or Pan-Katara.

The city, partly built on artificial islands with channels among them, was divided into three parts: walls used as tombs, the priest's city on the heights, and the lower city, which contained the royal palace. The king's residence was at the same time the temple of the supreme god, so that we may assume the existence of a god-kingship like that among the Khmer kings. Bathing pools, hearths, and oyster ponds can still be recognized; but the people themselves, except for bones found in the wall graves, and a few ancient legends, have completely vanished from the island.

Hans Nevermann doubts that these kings were Polynesians at all. "In ancient Polynesia the small islands were ruled by chiefs to whom the entire population was subject. On larger islands and island groups, however, there were always several independent political units side by side, each of which had its chieftain. . . . Whenever there is talk of the king of a larger island in the ancient tales, the person in question is always merely the chief of the district. The chieftain Tu of Tahiti, who came from a family of upstarts, was mistaken by the white discoverers for the king of Tahiti. As a result he acquired great prestige and with the aid of the foreigners actually climbed to that estate and became the founder of the royal dynasty of Tahiti. Every royal dynasty in Polynesia was established with the aid of whites, through their weapons and their moral support."

Such obscurities, and the unique architecture of the royal lagoon city on Ponape—for nothing resembling it is to be found on any of the other islands—make for a double mystery. Perhaps shipwrecked Europeans did actually have some part in the creation of the strange kingdom of Ponape. If that were the case, white men created something that they themselves destroyed—by the diseases they imported with them. In the nineteenth century the population of Ponape was steadily diminishing. An epidemic of smallpox swept away thousands of natives, and the remaining population was decimated by tuberculosis, which accompanied the acquisition of clothing. The clothes the missionaries forced upon these children of nature dried slowly after the frequent tropical rains; the result in a people with no immunity, who had long been spoiled by the mildness of the climate, was frequent colds that weakened the lungs. In addition, the forced adoption of alien views destroyed the natural relationship of these people to the rain, the wind, and their island soil. Thus, the green islands of the Pacific Ocean, which seem to us paradises on earth, were visited by diseases that had their origin in our sooty factory belts. The low point seems now to have been passed; doctors have joined the missionaries, and the natives have learned to recognize what is bad for them. They are no longer innocent, but their numbers are slowly increasing. Yet the moss-covered basalt palaces on the coral reef of Matolenim will continue to stand empty, for the tropical jungle has meanwhile conquered them and rendered them uninhabitable. King Shautelur the Last will remain the last of his race, a race we know nothing of.

· · ·

Along with his account of the stories and legends of the Carolines, Paul Hambruch has published pictures of two slyly smiling, good-humored natives to whom he was indebted for most of the old tales he collected on Ponape. There were certain narrator families in which the stories were transmitted from father to son along with the inherited art of recitation. When one of these storytellers finished his tale, the whole audience would break into the mellifluous, untranslatable refrain "*o uay.*"

Like the preservers of the legend of the sunken Breton city of Ys, the storytellers of Ponape stocked their lagoon city with kings and beautiful princesses; the darker the present, the more gloriously does the splendor of remote times glitter.

Certainly storytelling is a primal human impulse, like singing and dancing. Moreover, particular basic motifs reappear in the most primitive tales of all peoples: mythical explanations of natural phenomena, nature symbols, hero tales, tales of knaves, of trickery of the gods, tall tales, and so on. And yet we feel a shudder of awe every time we come across similarities between the old tales of some remote insular folk and the sagas of more familiar peoples, or the myths of classical antiquity. The more the listener knows about the magical realm of folk tales, the more strongly his own imagination collaborates. The stranger and more primitive the language of the story-teller, the stronger is the listener's impression of teetering upon the verge of mythic revelation.

For a whole year Thor Heyerdahl, the young Norwegian ethnologist, lived with a group of white companions on the small Marquesas island of Fatu Hiva, in the middle of the Pacific Ocean. He describes the suggestive atmosphere of the folk tales in these words:

" 'Tiki,' the old man said quietly, 'he was both god and

chief. It was Tiki who brought my ancestors to these islands where we live now. Before that we lived in a big country beyond the sea.'

"He poked the coals with a stick to keep them from going out. The old man sat thinking. He lived for ancient times and was firmly fettered to them. He worshiped his forefathers and their deeds in an unbroken line back to the time of the gods. And he looked forward to being reunited with them. Old Tei Tetua was the sole survivor of all the extinct tribes on the east coast of Fatu Hiva. How old he was he did not know, but his wrinkled, bark-brown, leathery skin looked as if it had been dried in sun and wind for a hundred years. He was one of the few on these islands that still remembered and believed in his father's and his grandfather's legendary stories of the great Polynesian chief-god Tiki, son of the sun.

"When we crept to bed that night in our little pile hut, old Tei Tetua's stories of Tiki and the islanders' old home beyond the sea continued to haunt my brain, accompanied by the muffled roar of the surf in the distance. It sounded like a voice from far-off times, which, it seemed, had something it wanted to tell, out there in the night. I could not sleep. It was as though time no longer existed, and Tiki and his seafarers were just landing in the surf on the beach below. A thought suddenly struck me, and I said to my wife: 'Have you noticed that the huge stone figures of Tiki in the jungle are remarkably like the monoliths left by extinct civilizations in South America?' "

The story of what happened next is a familiar one: how a young botanist and zoologist turned his attention to ethnology and finally set out on a balsawood raft to follow the route that the ancient god-king or chieftain-god Tiki may have taken when he emigrated with his people from South America to Polynesia. A chain of mysterious remains of ancient civilizations stretches between southern Asia across various Polynesian islands and Easter Island all the way to Meso-America, the name given to the ancient American cultural region that extended from Chichén Itzá in northern Yucatán to the southernmost outposts of the Inca civilization in what is now Chile. The most impressive specimens are to be found in southern Asia and South America; the islands between contain sparser remains, like a bridge between rich shores. But, despite Thor Heyerdahl's madcap voyage on a raft from the Peruvian coast to Polynesia, we have to this day no certain knowledge of whether cultural fertilization followed the trade winds from east to west, or whether the ancient cradle of peoples, Asia, sent emissaries of its culture with the seafaring Polynesians as far as Easter Island and still farther eastward.

Angkor, with its distinctly Indian-influenced temple reliefs, would probably have been the first station of the eastward journey. The lagoon city on Ponape probably still lies within the sphere of influence of Asia. On barren Easter Island with its mysterious gigantic sculptures there was in all probability no city to disappear. But at the eastern end of the supposed ancient cultural bridge a tall broken gate rises toward the sun: the Sun Gate of the holy city of Tiahuanaco on the southern shore of Lake Titicaca.

The more barren a landscape is, the more imposing is the impression made by stone monuments. In the vast wasteland of this thirteen-thousand-foot plateau the traveler suddenly comes upon fantastically hewn pillars, stone colossi so curiously arranged that they could scarcely have been the columns of a building. Then there is a huge gate of rough stone blocks bearing strange and artistic drawings. Such sights inspire even the least fanciful observer to weird guesses, wild assumptions, putative explanations that will not stand the light of cold logic. The earliest white men to see them, the soldiers of the conquistadors, paused in awed amazement before these mysterious structures and asked the Indians who had built them. But the Indians maintained a terrified silence; there was no information to be had from them.

The Spanish monks were ready enough with an explanation. Only devils, they averred, could have moved and piled such monstrous stones; all these ruins must have been devils' work. A historian of half-Inca, half-Spanish origins, Garcilaso de la Vega, whose *Commentarios Reales* (1609) is a principal source of early Peruvian history, seems to have held the same opinion, and a good many later Spanish studies seriously take up this "theory." However, it was at any rate clear from the narratives of the conquistadors that the culture of Tihuanaco was older than that of the Inca kingdom and represented another people entirely. That fact was certainly calculated to stimulate the imaginations of travelers and scholars. If these people were not the Incas, who were they? A Mr. Nanking suggested in a book published in London in 1827 that very probably "the first Inca of Peru was a son of Kublai Khan." Fritz Rock, former director of the Ethnological Museum in Vienna, in describing one of the giant masks from Tiahuanaco pointed out its "lucid, tranquil features which vividly remind one of certain types to be found in the Buddhist cultural sphere of Asia. Large slant eyes with distinctly marked lower lid, the bridge of the nose high and broad, the flattened tip spreading out to either side and more than twice the width of the bridge, nostrils open to the front, broad septum and only slightly distended sides. Lips are broad, the lower half of the face wider than the upper. Brow, temples and cheeks are marked off by the brim of a special headcovering which displays large volutes in the front and on both sides." Paul Ehrenreich has shown astonishing parallels between one solar myth (concerning K'oni-tikki's predecessor K'oniraya) and certain Siamese tales. And Walter Krickeberg concludes that certain elements in the folk tales of the Inca kingdom must have found their way south via the Isthmus of Panama.

The last and most fantastic link in this chain of hypotheses which scholars have forged by laborious investigation and bold guesswork is offered in a book by a French cosmologist named Denis Saurat, published in the latter part of 1954. He holds that the founding of Tiahuanaco took place 250,000 years before Christ—a dating we assuredly cannot take seriously. In concerning ourselves with his book we do so not because we admit even the glimmer of probability for his theory, but because it deals with the numerous South American legends of a onetime population of giants. From the coast of Colombia as far as southern Peru such tales about the huge stone monuments of Tiahuanaco repeatedly crop up.

Saurat proceeds from two facts.

1. Along the main ridge of the Andes, running in approximately a north-south direction in a line about 450 miles long, marine deposits are found at an altitude of thirteen thousand feet.

2. Lake Titicaca is extremely salty, which can be explained only on the assumption that it remained behind when the primal ocean retreated to its present level.

The extremely high level of the ocean at a period presumably three hundred thousand years ago is explained by Saurat on the basis of Hans Hörbiger's unscientific theory that the earth had three moons before the present moon. The third moon supposedly created, by the strength of its gravitational attraction, a bulge of water around the equator. Out of this water only five islands protruded: the Andes at Tiahuanaco, the Mexican plateau, New Guinea, Tibet, and the Abyssinian plateau. "We can imagine," Saurat writes, "that the men of the port of Tiahuanaco possessed ships with which they could sail the whole of their vaulted sea, and that a common culture prevailed over all five of the islands." Drawing upon the theories of the British writer H. S. Bellamy, Saurat concludes that the people who created this culture were giants between thirteen and sixteen feet tall. Giant plants, giant lizards, and giant insects also arose, he maintained, because the moon counteracted the gravitational attraction of the earth and diminished gravity favored the development of large forms of life. Saurat also supports his idea of giantism by a number of other hypotheses (mutation caused by cosmic rays, etc.) that need not concern us here.

There is likewise no need for us to disprove Saurat's theories in detail. In regard to Tiahuanaco, however, it must be said that even the great Sun Gate would have been too small for men sixteen feet tall.

According to Saurat, the culture of Tiahuanaco was developed during the second interglacial period, an era during which men produced hand axes and shaped flints but, so far as we know, not the slightest trace of even the most primitive art. Art begins with the Aurignacian period (60,000–40,000 B.C.). Thus, if we are to credit Saurat, Tiahuanaco knew a period of artistic creation which was followed by some two hundred thousand years of human evolution in which no art was created. Moreover, human skeletal remains from this second warm age (the Steinheim skull and the finds at Swanscombe,

England) show no signs of giantism. Such tools of the era as have been found point to a purely appropriatory way of life for these early men—that is to say, they lived by hunting and gathering whatever foodstuffs nature provided. Such a mode of life naturally excludes the possibility of communal life for any sizable aggregation of human beings. Men in those days lived in packs of from five to twenty families. But twenty families do not constitute a city and certainly could not have undertaken such monumental transportation and raising of materials as was involved in the building of Tiahuanaco.

Science has, it is true, given a name to the hypothetical giant. As *Meganthropus* (big man) he became a subject of discussion after G. H. R. von Königswald discovered near Sangiran in eastern Java two fragments of lower jaw whose size suggested bodies of astonishing dimensions. Moreover, various scientists between 1900 and 1940 procured in various Chinese pharmacies enormous molars of a human type. Interesting as it might be to consider that these finds confirmed the innumerable legends of giants, it turned out that these "big men" were in reality simply big-headed men. The rest of their bodies were not proportionately so large as the jawbones and teeth, and did not, in fact, exceed the normal standard of humanity. They represented a type of early man exceptionally well equipped for biting and chewing.

Consequently, the legends of giants, which were widely disseminated in ancient America, remain for the present unconfirmed and unexplained. Such tales form part of the Aztec creation myth; parallels to them are found in various parts of South America and even share the strange detail that these giants were homosexual cannibals who treated women merely as food, for which crime they were ultimately destroyed by heaven.

Tiahuanaco itself is not linked with the giants in these

legends. It is, however, related to the creation of the
world, which, according to the beliefs of the plateau Indians of the Quechua and Aymara tribes, took place in
highly peculiar alternations of creation and destruction.
The names for the creating god vary. In some places he
is called Pachaiachachic, which means something like "the
teacher (the tamer) of the world." But usually the name
for him is K'oni-tikki, "the source of the sun's warmth."
He created the earth and men, but men disregarded him
and worshipped mountains, rivers, springs, and rocks instead of the god himself. In punishment he poured un-
ending rain down upon mankind, and only a few guilt-
less ones whom he permitted to flee to the highest mountains escaped the great flood. After the rain ceased, the
god allowed the few survivors to come out of the caves
and mountains, and ordered them to repopulate the
earth. Out of gratitude men held the caves, mountains,
trees, and other such refuges in high esteem, and their
children began to worship these places by making each
one of them a *huaca*, a holy place. Thereupon the god,
who wished to be reverenced alone, once more became
wrathful and transformed all those who had founded
this new religion into stones. (This was the explanation
of the upright stone sculptures found especially in Tiahuanaco.) Then the god, laboring in Tiahuanaco, created
the sun, the moon, and the stars.

The substance of the above tale was written down by
Antonio de la Calancha before A.D. 1638. Pedro Sarmiento
de Gamboa in his *History of the Inca Kingdom* has told
another version with many illuminating details.

K'oni-tikki created the world dark at first, without sun,
moon, or stars. After the creation he formed a race of
giants of huge size out of some plastic material, in order
to see whether it would be well to create men of that

size. But since they seemed to him far too huge compared to his own size, he made men in his own image, as they are today. And they lived their lives in darkness. K'oni-tikki commanded them to live in harmony and gave them other injunctions, the content of which is not reported in the tradition. When arrogance and selfishness awoke among men and they violated his laws, the god cursed men and sent upon them a deluge during which it rained for sixty days and sixty nights. With only three servants, whom he had retained, the god then set about re-creating the world after the flood. For this purpose he went with his servants to the great lake in the Collao region (Lake Titicaca). His first efforts resulted in a moon brighter than the sun. Thereupon the sun became envious and hurled a handful of ashes into the moon's face; that is why the moon now displays dark spots. Then the god crossed to the southern shore of the lake. On huge stones in Tiahuanaco he made drawings of all the things and peoples he intended still to create. When he had breathed life into the men he had made, they moved down into various valleys and to the coast, all still speaking the same language, and became the tribes of Peru. Before they left, however, they erected a magnificent residence for their creator in Tiahuanaco.

Both versions of the myth end similarly. The god K'oni-tikki, after having traveled for a long time through all the districts of Peru, departs by striding off across the sea to unknown lands in the west. From this exploit he received the attributive name Uiracocha, which means something like "The Swimmer upon the Sea" but which was a word originally referring only to inland waters, presumably to Lake Titicaca.

These ancient legends contain all the various elements upon which both Saurat's and Thor Heyerdahl's Kon-

Tiki thesis are based. Saurat proceeds from the mention of the giants and the flood—though, of course, even sixty days of rain could not have raised the level of the ocean by thirteen thousand feet, so that a cosmic cause had to be dragged in to explain this. Heyerdahl, for his part, was struck by the tradition that a god with a name so similar to that given him by the old native on Fatu Hiva should be said to have departed westward across the sea. Moreover, the legend spoke of a balsawood raft—though the K'oni-tikki of the Peruvian story used this raft not for sailing the ocean, but only for traveling the distance between the island and the shore of Lake Titicaca.

For our own purposes—namely, for some light on the ruins of Tiahuanaco—these myths contain, in addition to later and probably Christian elements, three fundamental features. They represent:

1. An attempt by the Indians to explain to themselves the existence of the tremendous ruins and stone sculptures;

2. Vague memories that Tiahuanaco once played an important part in the religious life of the people many centuries before;

3. Reverberations of a conflict between two religions or forms of one religion. The first and older religion seems to have been characterized by nature myths, in which trees, rocks, and mountains were held sacred; whereas the second proclaimed a personal god-creator and a central sanctuary.

The ancient legends were unknown to Alexander von Humboldt when he reached Tiahuanaco in the year 1802. With an intuitive grasp of the meaning of the ruins, however, the great scholar offered the suggestion "that some informed traveler ought to investigate the shore of Lake Titicaca, the district of Callao and the plateaus of Tiahu-

anaco, these sites of an earlier American culture." The
archæologists who undertook this assignment in the following decades indeed found much to ponder. They saw
ruins and stone fragments, caryatids, lines of walls firmly
embedded in the earth, distributed over an area of some
125 acres. Foundations for buildings and a water reservoir can still be seen. But more impressive than these
are the remains of the Calasasaya. This is a large square
bordered by standing stone figures, and was perhaps a
temple to the sun. The mighty encircling wall was
made of stone bonded with earth; unlike the Incas, the
builders of Tiahuanaco apparently did not know the use
of mortar. Although here and there the stones were held
together with copper clamps, the seventeenth-century
Spaniards, when they were building La Paz, the present
capital of Bolivia, had no trouble prying free innumerable
huge stone blocks from the ancient buildings at Tiahuanaco and carting these off to serve as building material
for churches and dwellings, barracks and government
buildings.

The tallest of the ruins is a pyramid more than 165
feet high, with an irregular trapezoidal base. A natural
hill some sixty feet high was incorporated into its building. This pyramid seems at one time to have been the
center of a larger group of similar pyramids. It is about
thirteen hundred feet from the Calasasaya and was perhaps the place of sacrifice, for a stone-lined channel running down from the flattened peak has been discovered;
this perhaps served as a duct for the blood from the
sacrifice. Here, as at the temple of Khmer, the people
assembled outside the temple and the sacrificial altars.

The most famous part of these ruins is, of course, the
great monolithic Sun Gate. It is carved out of a single
block of gray volcanic stone some sixteen inches in thick-

ness, and faces the east—that is, the rising sun. The
broad crossbeam, containing a magnificent relief, is split
diagonally, which seems to indicate that Tiahuanaco was
at some time visited by a severe earthquake. This may
well have happened during the city's most flourishing
period, for numerous stone blocks have been found which
were left lying half-finished, as though the workmen had
dropped their chisels and fled in superstitious fear. The
bas-relief above the opening of the gateway, extending
the whole width of the gate, has given the name "Tiahuanaco culture" to a style that dominated the arts and
crafts of South America for almost a millennium. This is
the era which began about the first century A.D., and
during which the theocratic cultures of Mexico reached
their peak. In Peru a branch of Tiahuanaco culture won
predominance over the other regional cultures in the
southern mountain lands. We find reflections of the Tiahuanaco style in pottery decoration and weaving patterns far to the south of the borders of Peru. The style
continued to dominate until the rise of smaller kingdoms
and of the Inca city of Cuzco around A.D. 1200. Early
students of the question attempted to explain the sway
of the style by political expansion; they assumed a great
empire of the Aymaras several centuries before the Incas
embraced the entire area. But in local names and in the
more technical aspects of a civilization there are few
supports for such a thesis. The cultural dissemination
seems to have been purely spiritual in nature; that is, the
gods of Tiahuanaco, and especially the sun god K'oni-
tikki, proved to be superior to the regional divinities, and
the sacred motifs and symbols belonging to the Tiahuanaco gods were therefore adopted in the textiles and
other crafts of remote tribes.

Hans Dietrich Disselhoff has described and interpreted

the bas-relief on the great Sun Gate. "The central and chief figure, a god standing upon a graduated pedestal, carries in both hands staffs or scepters which terminate in the heads of condors. From his rigid countenance rays shoot out in all directions, ending in the heads of animals. This central figure has been interpreted as the sun god or creator. Probably it represents the sun. Winged angels approach from both sides in three friezes one atop the other. Some have human faces, some are masked as birds. On the fourth and lowest frieze appear faces surrounded by rays, smaller replicas of the head of the god. Attempts have been made to interpret the entire relief as some form of calendar, but none of these interpretations is convincing. However, it is evident that some cosmic processes have been given symbolic expression here. It is probable that a precise understanding of this ancient, strange religious world will never be vouchsafed us."

Archæologists know of no other people of the ancient Andean world who were as competent in working stone as the unknown builders of Tiahuanaco. Nevertheless, we find strikingly few sculptures; bas-reliefs and geometrical patterns scratched in the stone predominate to such an extent that it seems evident that the builders were copying textile ornamentation. As we know from burial gifts and other finds, ancient Peruvian weaving was developed to a high art. Hundreds and even thousands of labor hours were spent on making textiles for religious purposes.

To all appearances Tiahuanaco—today a Bolivian village inhabited by impoverished highland Indians—was not heavily populated during any phase of its history; the barren plateau would scarcely have prompted the establishment of a sizable city. Tiahuanaco was a sanctuary, a holy city like Mecca or Jerusalem, a city linked with mythic conceptions of the creation of the stars—

perhaps because from valleys and from the coast the sun could be seen rising over the highlands. For centuries the fishermen of the coast and the farmers of the valleys made pilgrimages to this holy place, just as the Brazilians on the other side of the Andes continued into the nineteenth century to brave rides of ten or twelve days in order to participate in the annual pilgrimage to Monte Santo in northern Brazil.

Thousands of people were needed to transport the heavy stone blocks from the quarries more than three miles distant, more thousands to work these great monoliths and, finally, to set them up. All of this was probably done by the pilgrims, who often come from afar, for among the reliefs are representations of the fauna of warmer regions, such as the jaguar and the rattlesnake.[2] Otherwise, however, the classical Tiahuanaco style is without individual features, and seems so strictly religious in character that we cannot help thinking the work must have been directed by powerful priests. While Tiahuanaco motifs appear in the ceramics and textiles of many other regions, no comparable or similarly ornamented architecture is found anywhere else in South America. This fact further supports the assumption that Tiahuanaco was a most holy sanctuary that was intended to be unique. The sun god had only one home—there on the high plateau, close to the sun.

From all that has been said, it seems evident that the mysterious city of the Andes, with its megalithic stairs and giant gateway, is not nearly so old as romantic theorizers wish to believe, and certainly has not survived the

---

[2] From the occurrence of such reliefs Disselhoff concludes that the creators of the Tiahuanaco culture were immigrants from the lowlands on the other side of the Andes. But a little later in his book he himself adopts Wendell C. Bennett's pilgrim theory, which seems a sufficient explanation.

quarter of a million years Saurat assigns to it. The plateau with its salt-water lake may have aroused superstitious wonder ever since the people of these regions began reflecting upon their world; but the first stones for a sanctuary were probably cut out of the sandstone and Andean rock around the time that Jesus was born in Nazareth, many thousands of miles to the east and not far from another salt lake.

Thor Heyerdahl places the ancient Peruvian migrations that supposedly reached as far as the Polynesian islands between A.D. 500 and 1100. This was also the era when the religiously dominated Tiahuanaco civilization burgeoned and spread widely in the Andean regions. Is it likely that the Tiahuanaco people were driven by so powerful an impulse toward expansion that they set out on rafts to cross the unknown ocean, rafts of the same sort that K'oni-tikki employed to cross from one shore of Lake Titicaca to the other? There are numerous Indian legends of men coming ashore from ships that had sailed the Pacific, or that had come from the north. But while such stories of immigration are frequent, there is only one tale of an emigration: the impressive story of K'oni-tikki, the god of the sun's heat, who departed from the land by floating over the waves of the ocean like sea foam and went toward the west, where the sun sets. Stirred though we may be by the magnificent achievement of Heyerdahl and his companions in braving the ocean aboard a raft, we still do not know whether the ancient legend records an actual migration, or whether it is merely a reverent account of the death of an old god who succumbed to the growing power of the Inca kingdom, with its god-kings, and went down to the seacoast, where for centuries the Peruvians have placed their tombs facing the setting sun.

III

CITIES OF THE STORIED SOUTH

POZZUOLI, THE CITY BENEATH THE MINERAL SPRING. WHERE THE AMBER ROUTE ENDED. SPINA, AN OLDER VENICE. ATRIA, NAME-GIVER TO A SEA. PÆSTUM, CITY OF TEMPLES AND ROSES. THE LAND OF CATTLE. THE ORIGINAL HOME OF THE COMMEDIA DELL'ARTE. THE COWS OF STABIÆ. THEATERS WITH MORE SEATS THAN THE CITY HAD INHABITANTS. THE WARNING EARTHQUAKE. NERO IN A NEW LIGHT. THE VICTIMS OF VESUVIUS.

THE PENINSULA of Italy preserves so much of the grandeur of the past in the midst of contemporary reality that all seems confusion. Past and present are inextricably intermingled. We may step out of the railroad station at Rome and amid the city traffic come upon a long fragment of ancient city wall, or see contemporary apartment buildings rising beside rows of classical columns. The process of growth and decay is still in full flux in this country.

We do not find in Italy the abrupt gaps that on other continents have been brought about by contact with European civilization. Neither time nor the Renaissance builders who used ancient monuments for quarries wrought such destruction as did the Pizarros in the golden temples of the Inca kingdom.

Geologically, too, this peninsula on the central axis of Europe's vital inland sea has not yet come to rest.[1] Vesuvius, Etna, and Stromboli continue to belch forth smoke; fragments of volcanic stone whirl through the air; and earthquakes shake the ground trodden by so many soldiers, from Hannibal's Carthaginians with their elephants to Americans with their tanks.

Around 530 B.C. a small band of Greeks fled from the tyrant-ruled island of Samos. They reached the bay west of the Gulf of Naples and in this promising region founded a settlement that they called Dicæarchia, meaning "the rule of justice." In Roman times this settlement became the town of Puteoli, for decades the most important port on the west coast of Italy.

Our reason for beginning with this town is, however, not its former importance but the fact that Pozzuoli, as it is now called, displays so graphically the slow burial of a city, the literal subsidence of a city into the earth.

Puteoli possessed the third-largest amphitheater in Italy; its extensive subterranean passages are still excellently preserved. But even more interesting is the market building of the town. This is situated in the heart of modern Pozzuoli. It must have been a splendid structure, with a fountain in the middle, surrounded by columns of African marble; the domed roof was covered with

---

[1] The contemporary traveler in Italy can see for himself that the small town of Civita Castellana in the district of Viterbo, near the remains of the Etruscan city of Falerii, is plainly falling to pieces. The cliff on which it was built rests insecurely on a base of watery clay; since about 1560 large and small pieces of rock have been breaking off, causing houses, vineyards, or barns to collapse. For this reason the peasants take their entire families with them when they go out in the mornings to work in the fields.

bronze tiles, the upper story adorned with loggias. An arcade surrounded the central court; then came individual peddlers' booths, reminiscent of an Oriental bazaar. The visitor can see such booths to this day, but he cannot get to the center of the building to admire the mosaics of the floor. For the remains of the market building have sunk, along with the rest of the town.

PHÆTHON, FROM A GREEK CAMEO.

The reason for this subsidence is well understood by geologists. The coast in this region, full of hot springs and volcanoes, has for centuries been sharing the slow movements of the earth's crust. Three thirty-foot upright pillars of the gray limestone known as cipolin serve as a measure of the sinking. The holes of marine borers extend as high as nineteen feet, which indicates that the sea must at one time have flooded the entire surface of ancient Puteoli. Up to the beginning of the last century the ground level was rising again; it was possible to make close studies of the Roman market building, which at the time was taken for a temple of Serapis because a statue of this Greco-Egyptian god who had also been worshipped in Italy had been found on the premises. Since then a new phase of subsidence has begun. The water from the mineral springs in the immediate neighborhood can no longer flow off into the sea. The water level above the precious marble floor is rising an inch annually. Yet perhaps the floor will sometime rise again, five or ten or even fifteen feet. Whether or not this shall be is determined somewhere deep within the earth, far deeper than men have ever penetrated with their petroleum probes or drills.

Where the ground was known to be unsteady, buildings were set upon piles, thus protecting them as much as possible from the perils of the unpredictable soil. Two thousand years before the flowering of the lagoon city of Venice we find a comparable miracle of the ancient world, whose center was at that time Greece.

The Greeks believed the end of the world lay to the west, where the sun set. There they placed the entrance to the underworld; there in the west was to be found everything fabulous; there lay the limits of the realm of humanity. There, too, the River Eridanos was supposed to flow into the northern sea. Eridanos, like his brothers Nil, Istros (the Danube), and many other rivers, was a son of Oceanus, the great world-encircling sea. There in the west Phæthon lay buried, that luckless son of Helius who drove the chariot of the sun for one day and proved too weak to control it. Amber, Greek legend had it, arose from the tears his sisters wept for him.

The farther the Greek seafarers penetrated into the world, the more the fabulous lands receded, or became definite and known places. Legendary Eridanos was none other than the River Po, and people of the region around it did have amber, for northern Italy was the terminus of the Amber Route by which this precious ma-

terial for ornament was brought from the Baltic Sea. Thus
there arose in the wide delta of the Po many settlements
of seafaring traders—Greeks and Etruscans especially,
for the dominion of the Etruscans at that time extended
deep into northern Italy.

One such mercantile town, Spina, became rich and
powerful around the middle of the first century B.C. Probably it was built on piles; in any case, as a city-state that
commanded the sea and also dominated by trade a considerable portion of the hinterland, it played a part similar to that later taken by Venice.

The outward aspect of the city cannot as yet be re-
constructed. Perhaps there was enough firm ground so
that single- or two-story houses in the Greek, or sometimes the Etruscan, fashion could be built. But it seems
probable that the swampy land in the delta of the great
river made drainage canals necessary, and wherever these
crossed the city some of the houses would have had to
be built on piles. (Drainage canals dug around the city
would also serve as protection against the barbarians of
the surrounding regions.) Piles also supported bridges
and footwalks, while goods were transported along the
canals. It appears likely that, at least in part, Spina was
a prototype of the Venice of a thousand years later.

There were temples, and Spina had the wealth to ornament these lavishly. On the agora, the market place and
chief center of the city, where all of public life took
place, there stood statues of the gods and columns of
marble or bronze in honor of distinguished citizens; in
the morning, hawkers met there, and money-changers,
officials, householders buying food for their families, and
idlers. The agora was the place for popular assemblies,
parades, and public feasts. Wares were cried: amber
from the north, oil and wine, vases and honey from

The guardian lions of Angkor-Vat, buried deep in the jungles of Cambodia.

PLATE I

Air view of Angkor-Vat, the ancient residence of the Khmer kings.

PLATE II

Angkor: a group of Buddha images stored in the temple court.

PLATE III

A doorway at Angkor is decorated with floral designs and
an apsaras—one of the celestial dancers of Hindu mythology.

PLATE IV

The Mucalinda Buddha, a Cambodian sculpture of the late twelfth century.

PLATE V

Huge stone sculpture stands am
the ruins of the mysterious holy
of Tiahuanaco on the shore of L
Titicaca in the Bolivian Andes.
Indians consider these the spirits
gigantic ancestors turned to st

Statue of a man with a
cat's head at Tiahuanaco.

PLATE VI

Toltec stone images of the gods, found at Tula in Mexico.

PLATE VII

Giant stone sculpture of unknown origin
found on Easter Island in the South Pacific.

PLATE VIII

The water of thermal springs continues to rise around the pillars of the Temple of Serapis in the center of modern Pozzuoli. Actually this was the covered market place of the Roman city of Puteoli.

PLATE IX

A Roman pigeonhouse i
coastal town of Puteoli,
stroyed by a gradual su
ence of the earth's crust

Vestibule in Puteoli's amphitheater, which was the third
largest in Italy.

PLATE X

Pæstum: the so-called Temple of Poseidon; in reality it was dedicated to the Greek fertility goddess Hera.

PLATE XI

The Temple of Apollo at Pompeii, where Greeks, Etruscans, and Romans worshipped Apollo until the ashes from Vesuvius buried the city, A.D. 79.

PLATE XII

the rubble and ashes at
...i splendid works of art
...een dug, such as this
...of a youth.

The great amphitheater at Pompeii, one of the city's major
attractions. People came from all the neighboring towns
and villages to watch the gladiatorial combats in the arena.

PLATE XIII

Archæologist Amadeo Maiuri examines the plaster-of-Paris cast of a victim who was caught and suffocated by the ashes and lapilli of Vesuvius as he tried to flee Pompeii. His body formed a cavity in the ashes, and the plaster cast gives a minutely detailed reproduction of his features.

Interior of the house of Cornelius Rufus at Pompeii, showing the atrium and, in the background, the peristyle.

PLATE XIV

The forum at Pompeii: the city's meeting-place and trade center.

A typical street in Pompeii: the Via dell'Abbondanza or Street of Abundance.

PLATE XV

Entrance to a house in Herculaneum, buried in the avalanche of mud that poured forth from Vesuvius, A.D. 79.

A wine tavern in Herculaneum.

PLATE XVI

ANCIENT CITIES OF ITALY

Greece, metal tools from Etruria. Slaves were traded, artisans hired. Besides the wealthy merchants there were innumerable itinerant peddlers who traveled on muleback to the many small villages lying between the sea and the mountains. They visited the remotest valleys of the Apennines and even reached the Alps. The safety of these peddlers depended entirely on the laws of hospitality; their risks were great, their profit margins equally great. For that reason many of the rural folk came to the commercial metropolis. Sturdy peasants from Umbria and proud, red-mustached Celts mingled with wily Greeks and fat, property-conscious Etruscans. The wealth of the city grew steadily, and in sacred Delphi, where Kings and cities sent a tenth part of their profits in gratitude to the gods, stood, beside the treasuries of great kings like Gyges and Crœsus and famous cities like Sybaris and Athens, the treasury of the citizens of Spina.

This treasury was still being shown as a sight of Delphi when Strabo wrote his book on geography, around the time of the birth of Christ. His comment on Spina itself, however, is a reminder of the transitoriness of all worldly goods. "Spina is now a village but was once a famous Greek city. In Delphi, for example, a treasury built by the Spinetans is shown, and it is said that they once ruled the sea. The city is reputed to have been situated by the sea, but now it is some ninety stadia [about nine miles] inland." As the coast silted over, the city became separated from the sea that was its life blood. The village that still existed in Strabo's time succumbed to malaria and disappeared in the marshes. Not a trace of Spina remained; no one even knew where the city had stood, for the coastline continued to move forward. The arms of the Po delta constantly shifted; in the swamplands Lake Comacchio formed.

Dionysius of Halicarnassus, who wrote a *Roman Antiquities* at about this same period, deals more extensively with Spina than does Strabo. The Pelasgians, a mythical people he speaks of, may have been Greeks, pre-Greeks, or Etruscans. A migrating folk, they had settled down in Dodona (western Greece) with their relations. "But when they realized that they were becoming a burden to their kin, since the land could not feed all of them, they left the country, in obedience to an oracle which commanded them to sail to Italy, then called Saturnia. They equipped many ships and crossed the Ionian [Adriatic] Sea, intending to land in the nearest part of Italy. But due to the south wind and their ignorance of the region, they were driven northwards and came to one of the mouths of the Po which was known as the Spinetan mouth. There they left behind those of their company who were least able to endure hardships, and left the ships also. They set up a stronghold which would serve them as a refuge if their further enterprises should prove unsuccessful. The people who remained behind at this place built a wall around the camp and the ships, and began to work to maintain themselves. Since everything seemed to be going well with them, they founded a city, naming it after the arm of the Po (Spina). Of all the inhabitants of the coast of the Ionian Sea they were the most fortunate, for they dominated the sea far and wide and sent the tenth part of the profits of their voyages to the god at Delphi. Theirs were, indeed, the most splendid gifts of all. Later, however, they abandoned their city, since a horde of neighboring barbarians went to war against them. These barbarians were later expelled by the Romans."

The twentieth century ushered in an irrigation project that was to disturb the millennial sleep of Spina. Dikes were built and canals dug. New farmland was created,

and when the farmers dug deeper, they encountered
graves thousands of years old. In this way the necropolis
of Spina was discovered; it was the custom in ancient
times to situate the cemetery outside the town. Now the
lake is being drained, and the city buried and forgotten
for so many centuries is to be brought to light once more.
The necropolis has already furnished a preview of the
rich finds awaiting archæologists. The museum of the
neighboring city of Ferrara owns a magnificent collection
from this necropolis: splendid Greek vases and more
primitive ceramics from native workshops, gold and silver
ornaments, glass and amber.

Chance is said to have guided archæologists to the
area. A hiker, the story goes, became lost in the region
around Comacchio, wandered into the marshes, and was
saved from sinking in over his head only because he
poked his walking-staff into a tremendous urn of pure
gold, which supported him until help came. An urn of
pure gold sounds like an exaggeration; nevertheless, newspapers report that the finds now in the museum at Ferrara are valued at more than one million dollars. The
inhabitants of Comacchio are still poking around in the
swampy ground with long sticks in the hope of more
treasures. They work at night, with shaded lanterns, for
Italian law of course prohibits such grave-robbing.

The silting of the Po delta and the consequent reces-
sion of the seacoast, with the land becoming swamp and
a breeding-ground for malaria, destroyed not only Spina.
A good many coastal cities suffered a similar fate. One
of these cities may be mentioned, for, though it survives
only in the sleepy provincial town of Atria, it gave its
name to the Adriatic Sea itself.

Diomedes, king of Argos and one of the bravest of the
Greek heroes in the Trojan War, is said to have founded

the city. One classical author, Justinus, maintains that it
was actually of Greek origin; Livy calls it an Etruscan
colony. These varying accounts suggest that it was a trading city like Spina and within the sphere of influence of
both peoples—founded by Greeks but occupied by Etruscans. In its vicinity, however, dwelt the presumably Illyrian people known as Venetians, who much later gave
their name to the city of Venice.

Atria was once an important city and, like Spina, noted
for its wealth. It was connected with other heroes of
myth besides Diomedes, for Phæthon was said to be
buried there, and also the artist Dædalus, who built the
labyrinth on Crete for King Minos and who with his son
Icarus ventured man's first flight. An anonymous book,
De mirabilibus auscultis, speaks of them: "On the Amber
Islands which lie in the corner of the Adriatic Sea there
are said to be two statues, one of tin, the other of bronze,
both executed in an ancient manner. These are alleged
to be works of Dædalus in memory of the time when he
came to this region from Sicily and Crete in the course
of his flight from Minos."

It is not certain that Dædalus ever really lived, but
archæologists have a good knowledge of the appearance
of the many statues ascribed to him. These were crude,
primitive, obviously very early work. "Early," at any rate,
for Europe—that is, for the peoples of the Indo-European
linguistic family, who were outright barbarians when
they first entered the sphere of Mediterranean civilization.

Atria is also mentioned by Aristotle in his *On Animals.*
"Adriatic hens are small," the philosopher writes, "but
they lay every day. However, they are ill-natured and
often kill their chicks. They are of various colors. Many
domestic hens even lay twice daily, but those who lay

too much soon die." This seemingly insignificant note
adds a new dimension to our knowledge of the city. We
see the city as harboring not only peddlers, merchants,
and stout aldermen, customs officials, slaves, dock workers, soldiers of the mercenary troops and of the militia,
sailors, thieves, and prostitutes—such as constitute the
population of every port city. Evidently rural life flourished in the midst of the urban community. Wealth and
a rich cultural life did not, in the fifth century B.C., ex-

GREEK FREIGHTER.

clude the probability that behind every burgher's house
was a dungheap where the good citizen went to relieve
himself, unless he simply used the street. (Both customs
are mentioned by Aristophanes, the great writer of comedies, as characteristic of Athens.) The burgher slept on
the floor wrapped in a blanket or in his cloak, and if he
had no slave to follow him through the streets and bear
his money purse, he occasionally carried his small silver
coins in his mouth.

For the beginning of the Christian era we once again
have Strabo's report on the city. He speaks of Atria as
suffering the same evil as Spina, a retreating coastline.

At Atria, however, ultimate doom was fended off for a while. "Atria and other such small towns are less threatened by swamps, and are connected with the sea by small canals. Atria is said to have once been a considerable city, from which the Adriatic Sea received its name."

The town once more entered history during the struggles that shook the Roman Empire after the overthrow of the Emperor Nero. In Ravenna the marines of Vitellius, who was briefly emperor, mutinied. The commander of the fleet, Lucilius Bassus, was put under honorable arrest and brought to Atria on a light warship (the canals were evidently still passable), and there was placed in custody by the cavalry commandant, Vibennius Rufus. He was released from his chains, however, when an emissary of the later Emperor Vespasian intervened in his favor.

Thereafter we hear nothing of this once powerful seaport. On a Roman road-map dating probably from the end of the second century A.D. it is not marked, unless (this is an unsettled question) the town of Radriani represents an altered form of the name Atria. The gloom of the barbarian migrations and the Dark Ages falls upon Atria. Today a town of Adria once more exists, with 15,700 inhabitants; it is some twenty miles from the Adriatic Sea.

When Jason sailed forth to fetch the Golden Fleece, he was accompanied by fifty of the foremost heroes of his age, among them Heracles, Theseus, Castor, and Polydeuces. The goddess Hera lent them protection on their voyage, and in gratitude they erected altars and sanctuaries dedicated to her at various points along their way. One of these was on the coast of the Campania where the River Silaros (the modern Sele, some fifteen miles south of Salerno) flows into the sea, making a good harbor.

The legend of Jason stems from very ancient times, when no one worried about geographical realities. For on a voyage from northern Greece into the Black Sea, Jason could not very well have touched the coast of Italy. Nevertheless, Greeks did cross the sea from their over-populated homeland and settle on this hospitable coast.[2]

Such colonies did not spring up at hazard. When the founders consulted an oracle, the priests of the oracular god usually possessed sufficient knowledge of geographical, political, and economic facts to guide intelligently the stream of Greek emigration. Seafaring merchants would already have explored the coasts of Italy and have established relations with the native population before a Greek city or league of several cities sent out a small fleet. Often such a new settlement had to be defended against the natives or against other Greek colonists. Consequently, the support of older colonies was needed. In this case it was the city of Sybaris that undertook to protect the new arrivals at the mouth of the Silaros.

It was around the middle of the seventh century B.C. that the small settlement won a foothold and immediately began trading with the barbarians of the hinterland. The site was extremely favorable. Here came the farmers of the fertile coastal plains as well as the people of the mountainous interior. They brought their agricultural products, leather, and wool, and gladly bartered these for the strange things borne across the sea in the Greek vessels.

----

[2] The Greek geographer Strabo speaks of the founding of this city (V.4.13). His statements have been variously interpreted by modern scholars. Our account follows chiefly the arguments of Amedeo Maiuri in his *Saggi di varia antichità* (Venice, 1954), pp. 79–96.

Sybaris,[3] the luxury-loving city on the Gulf of Taranto, had just defeated its rival Siris and was now feeling strong enough to extend its power from the Ionian to the Tyrrhenian Sea. The first two stations on the way were the Campanian towns of Laos and Skidros, the next stage the settlement on the Silaros. There the Sybarites erected a wall to protect the port from barbarians, and so the little town became its colony. Under this ægis, commerce flourished; the citizenry grew prosperous and looked about for a more easily defended dwelling-place. The site on the riverbank was comfortable, but it was far too exposed to enemy attack. Therefore, the people of the town moved some seven miles farther south, where a kind of natural terrace of travertine rock offered a splendid setting for a proper city. The sanctuary of the goddess Hera was left behind at the fortified mouth of the river.

The rocky terrace in the heart of this fertile land had already been inhabited for many thousands of years. After futile resistance the natives retreated into the mountains. A good many, however, probably accepted the new order and adjusted to it. They might well be content, for life in the new city was extremely pleasant. It was called Poseidonia, in honor of the god of the sea. Guarded by strong walls, it soon had splendid temples, an agora, and a theater, like every other Greek city. And Poseidonia burgeoned.

From Miletus in Asia Minor merchant ships sailed into the Gulf of Taranto to Sybaris. From there caravans of donkeys crossed the wooded mountains of Lucania and what is now the barren wasteland of mud and stone on the border of Calabria and Basilicata, and made their

[3] Whence the adjective *sybaritic.*

way to Poseidonia on the Tyrrhenian Sea. There goods
were transshipped for Etruria.

When Sybaris was destroyed in the year 511 B.C.—the
story will be told in a later chapter of this book—this
important east-west trade route was abandoned. At about
the same time Etruscan expansion into the southern part
of the Italian peninsula ceased. These two factors dealt
a severe blow to Poseidonia. But the city gave refuge to
many citizens of razed Sybaris. These fugitives were by

YOUNG SHEPHERD WITH FLUTE, AFTER A VASE PAINTING.

no means only the poor; perhaps Poseidonia owed a good
deal of its wealth to the wave of refugees from Sybaris.

The fame of the city, however, rested not so much
on its riches as on the fact that it was the home of many
Pythagoreans, a religious-political group of philosophers
who believed in reincarnation and shared their property
communally. A citizen of Poseidonia named Parmenides
won a race in the 78th Olympic Games (468 B.C.). The
Doric temples that make the city a place of pilgrimage
today were erected: the temple now called the "basilica"
around the middle of the sixth century B.C., the "Temple
of Neptune" about a hundred years later. Both temples
were in actuality dedicated to the same fertility goddess,

Argive Hera. The third of the still-preserved temples, likewise Doric, is generally called the "Temple of Ceres," but was in fact consecrated to Pallas Athene. It was built toward the end of the sixth century. The erroneous names for these sanctuaries were conferred upon them in the eighteenth century.

The impression these temples make upon a modern observer has been described by Curzio Malaparte in his book *The Skin:*

"When, at dawn on September 9, 1943, Jack had leapt from the deck of an L.S.T. on to the beach at Paestum, near Salerno, he had seen a wonderful vision rising before his eyes through the red cloud of dust thrown up by the caterpillars of the tanks, the explosions of the German grenades and the tumult of the men and machines hurrying up from the sea. On the edge of a plain thickly covered with myrtles and cypresses, to which the bare mountains of Cilento, so like the mountains of Latium, provide a background, he had seemed to see the columns of the Temple of Neptune. Ah, this was Italy, the Italy of Virgil, the Italy of Aeneas! And he had wept for joy, he had wept with religious emotion, throwing himself on his knees upon the sandy shore, as Aeneas had done when he landed from the Trojan trireme on the sandy beach at the mouth of the Tiber, opposite the mountains of Latium, with their sprinkling of castles and white temples set amid the deep green of the ancient Latin woods."

In the end the wealth of the merchants of Poseidonia proved too much of a temptation to the city's neighbors. In the struggle of the native Samnites and Lucanians against the Greek cities, Poseidonia was one of the first victims. Her troops and those of her allies were defeated and the city taken. The Lucanians were not content with pillaging; they kept the city permanently occupied, and changed its name to Paistom. The lot of the Greek inhabitants was a sad one, as we are informed by a pupil of Aristotle, the musician Aristoxenos of Taranto:

"The people of Poseidon have become complete barbarians. They have changed their language and their entire mode of life. They continue to keep only one of the Hellenic festivals. At this occasion they come together, recollect their old names and customs, and when they have finished telling one another their woes and have ceased to weep, they go away again."

The Romans came as liberators from the Lucanian yoke, and remained in the country. In 273 B.C. a Latin colony was established in the city, which thereafter called itself Pæstum. The Greek agora was transformed into a Roman forum. Streets were paved, sewers dug, the fortifications improved. The city retained its pentagonal form, which sprang from the nature of the terrace site. In each of the four principal directions there was a strongly fortified gate.

Roman rule evidently was not felt as a burden by the inhabitants of the city. They adhered loyally to Rome when the Punic soldiery occupied the countryside and many of the cities of southern Italy defected to Hannibal. After the disaster at Cannæ the people of Pæstum brought some of the golden treasures of their temple to Rome, to offer them to the Senate. The Senate thanked them, as it did the Neapolitans, who were prepared to make a similar sacrifice, but did not accept the gold—whether out of Roman pride or out of fear of the gods whose temples had been stripped, tradition does not say.

Throughout the Punic Wars the citizens of Pæstum continued to demonstrate their loyalty. In 210 B.C. they supplied ships, and in the following year soldiers. Twelve

of the thirty Roman colonies refused to send their troops
into the field against Hannibal; the other eighteen declared their readiness to supply the requested contingent
of men, and more if need be, and to do anything else
the Roman people required. With pride and gratitude
even after two hundred years, Livy in the twenty-seventh
book of his history records the names of these loyal cities.
Along with Brindisi, Rimini, Piacenza, and Cremona,
Pæstum is named.

As the reward for such fidelity, the city received the
right to strike its own bronze coinage. Splendid buildings were erected: baths, more temples, an amphitheater,
a senate house, a double-columned arcade flanking the
forum on three sides. The forum itself was at least in
part paved with slabs of marble. Pæstum remained a trading center, a market for cattle, oil, grain, honey, and
vegetables. The violets and privet and especially the roses
of Pæstum, which bloomed twice a year, were praised by
the poets Virgil, Propertius, and Ovid. The satirist Martial mentions them so often that it would almost seem as
if no Roman youth could laud a girl's red lips without
mentioning the roses of Pæstum. But alongside these trib-
utes we must place the dry comment of Strabo: "The
river in the vicinity, which seeps away into marshes,
makes the city unhealthful."

Perhaps the slow subsidence of the coast, as at Puteoli,
prevented the river from flowing straight into the sea,
thus creating marshes. Or perhaps the river itself blocked
its outlet with its own deposits. The question is still de-
bated by modern geologists. But there is no argument
about the fact: the short but sometimes torrential river
Salso, which flowed by the southern wall of the city,
reinforcing the defenses and carrying away the city's
sewage, transformed the meadows all around into insani-

tary, mosquito-breeding marshland. Malaria made its
appearance, driving away many of the inhabitants. The
city became more and more depopulated.

The people who remained transformed the so-called
temple of Ceres into a Christian basilica by closing the
spaces between the pillars and tearing down the wall of
the cella. Soon, in fact, they were forced to live in this
basilica, for it was the highest point in the city and everything else had been flooded by the river, whose waters
broke in through the southern gate. The pavement of the
main street, which led to the forum, and even the forum
itself were covered with standing water. These pavements gradually became coated with a layer of lime. The
water continued to press farther and farther. Out of
fragments of the tumbledown buildings the last inhabitants of the city constructed low embankments so that
they would be able to walk dry-shod from house to
house. But the water, the malaria, and finally the incursions of the Saracens along the entire Tyrrhenian coast
drove away the last of the citizens of Pæstum.

Pæstum remained dead and forgotten. Its fate was that
of most of the Greco-Roman cities of Italy: plundering
of the remains of the old buildings and ultimately a re-
birth out of the ruins, if not as a new city, then as a
shrine for tourists. But here, in this city of magnificent
temples, destiny operated on a grander scale than elsewhere. The Italians of the Middle Ages did rob the
abandoned buildings to adorn their own. But Pæstum
still had her protectress of pagan days, Argive Hera. Her
ancient temple at the mouth of the Siaros was the first to
be seized on by the temple-robbers; from it were taken
the building materials for the Cathedral of San Matteo in
Salerno and the Duomo of Amalfi. Both these cities continued, under Lombard and later under Norman rulers,

to pursue the wealthy, cosmopolitan existence of ancient Poseidonia, with its vigorous intellectual life and its trade with the Orient.

In Pæstum, meanwhile, shrubbery grew up around the Doric pillars. The city was not "rediscovered" until the eighteenth century, when Bourbon King Carlos III of Naples had a road built which cut through the amphitheater of Pæstum. This road runs through the city proper; the railroad passes by somewhat to the east. The city walls have once again been exposed and stand fifteen to twenty feet thick, capped by imposing towers. The city gates can also be seen, and inside the city the vicinity of the forum has been excavated, as well as the shells of many buildings, the senate house, treasury, shops, baths, and some sanctuaries. Above all this stand proudly the three great Doric temples, calm and grave, the most beautiful temples on the Italian mainland. The place is comparatively unvisited; the broad, shadeless plain between the sea and the mountains of Basilicata, far to the east, is not nearly so inviting as the splendid rocky coast near Salerno, Amalfi, and Sorrento, or as the sights of Naples and Capri. Grass and low bushes grow around the temples; lizards scurry across the paths. All is still in the sacred realm of Argive Hera. But twice a year the awe-inspiring, somewhat stern beauty of the scene is quickened to gaiety: when the roses of Pæstum bloom.

During the second millennium before Christ, when the Hellenes were first penetrating into Greece, peoples of the same Indo-European linguistic family moved across the Alps into Italy. Little is known of their struggles with the earlier Mediterranean peoples. In historic times they formed a native population in most parts of Italy, a strong, rough folk of peasants and shepherds, industrious, tena-

cious, taciturn, with few cultural achievements to their
credit, without a script, without a kingdom or even sizable cities. These people were split up into many tribes.

On the wooded slopes and in the fruitful plains of
Campania lived the Oscans, though how long they had
been there we cannot even approximately tell. Their beautiful country, however, held a constant attraction for
strangers. In the coastal plains, especially, cities sprang
up, which the Oscan peasants at first regarded with mis-
trust. But later they were happy to visit the cities in
order to exchange the products of their land for the
wares of the entire Mediterranean world.

These cities were the homes either of the Etruscans,
who had extended their dominion from their original seat
in northern and central Italy into parts of Campania, or
of the second foreign element in southern Italy, the
Greeks. These Greeks were often partners of the Etruscans in trade and their adversaries in war.

Greek settlement of the coasts of southern Italy goes
back at least to the eighth century B.C. In connection
with Pæstum we have heard of Jason and the Argonauts;
a little farther to the north Heracles was the mythical
founder of cities. The tenth of the famous twelve labors
had taken the god to Spain to fetch the red oxen of the
giant Geryon. The Greek writer Apollodoros relates:
"During his journey through Tyrrhenia a bull in Rhegium
broke loose, plunged into the sea and swam over to Sicily.
The adjoining land, through which the bull had come,
was therefore given the name Italy, for bull in Tyrrhenian
is called *italos*."

There is a speck of truth within this myth. In Greek
there is no letter V, so that the Greek word *italia* might
stand for a Latin *vitalia*, meaning "cattle land," for in
Latin *vitulus* means "bull calf." As late as the first cen-

tury B.C. the Oscans called their country Viteliu. It was
the Greeks who first applied this name to the entire
peninsula, which had formerly been known to the Etruscans as Tyrrhenia, or as Saturnia, after an old god of
the harvest. The bull, however, was the sacred animal of
the entire Mediterranean world, and its worship is very
ancient indeed, as is indicated by the Stone Age cliff-
paintings in the Atlas Mountains, wall-paintings in Crete,
and the cult of the bull in Egypt. Even the bullfights of
Spain and southern France derive ultimately from this
worship.

To come back to Heracles: "When he had settled his
affairs in Spain and his fleet returned safely to Italy, he
sacrificed to the gods the tenth part of his booty and
founded at the spot where his fleet anchored a small city
to which he gave his name. This city, now inhabited by
Romans, still lies between Naples and Pompeii, and has
a harbor dependable at all times of the year." Thus writes
the Greek historian Dionysius of Halicarnassus. At this
same time, around the birth of Christ, Strabo wrote of
the same city: "In the vicinity of Naples lies the Citadel
of Herakleion [in Latin, Herculaneum], which has a
promontory extending into the sea and is laved so won-
derfully by the south wind that it is a salubrious place
of residence. This city and neighboring Pompeii, on the
River Sarnos, was in the possession of the Oscans, later
the Tyrrhenians [Etruscans] and the Pelasgians, and
after them the Samnites; but these latter, too, were driven
away from the region."

At the beginning of the sixth century B.C. the Oscan
village of Pompe and its harbor were practically dominated by the Greeks of Kyme (Cumæ) and Naples, who
held maritime control of the coast and the islands off
Campania. In Pompe they erected a temple in the Doric

style, the foundations of which may still be seen. This
seaside village was of particular importance to them; it
served as a valuable storage place and mart for the whole
of the Sarno valley and the villages and towns of the interior, which were under Etruscan rule. At this time the
relations between Greeks and Etruscans were governed
by treaties designed to further their mutual commercial
interests.

Around 539 B.C., however, mercantile competition between the two peoples grew sharper. The Etruscans
formed an alliance with the Oscans and the Samnites,
who occupied the mountainous country above the coastal
plain. They seized the harbors in southern Campania,
occupying, among others, Herakleion and Pompe. Their
interest in these towns was purely political and commercial, however; they made no attempt to establish
colonies of their own people, to increase the size of the
towns, or to fortify them more strongly.

The naval battle at Cumæ in 474 B.C. turned out badly
for the Etruscans. They had to retreat deeper into the
interior, leaving the coastal towns to the victorious Greeks.
Now the Greeks went to considerably more trouble to
hold what they had just won back. They systematically
built up the towns, provided them with a regular network of streets, and erected strong walls and gates.

Nevertheless, within a few decades the area fell to the
Romans. Swift as was their success in the political realm,
it took centuries before they were able to penetrate the
region culturally. The Etruscan language died out rather
soon, but Greek continued in use, especially among the
wealthier classes of the population. The mass of the people continued to use the Oscan-Samnitic dialect they had
spoken before the Roman conquest. Plays, too, were performed in the Oscan tongue throughout Campania, and

even in Rome itself. These dialect plays were pitched on a gay, popular note. Full of coarse jokes and farcical situations, they were called "Atellan plays" after the city of Atella, where they had their origin. (The ruins of Atella are near Aversa, nine miles north of Naples.) In the beginning these were extemporaneous plays. At a later period, however, they followed a written script, but much room was left for impromptu jokes.

The village of Pompe had meanwhile developed into a small city, and had acquired a Latin form of its name: Pompeii. Long before Rome it possessed a stone theater of considerable size; some five thousand seats were arranged in a semicircle on the Greek model, rising by steps. This theater had been built into a natural hollow in the slope of a hill in the southern part of the city. Beyond the building that housed the stage the spectators had a splendid view of the hills of the Sorrento peninsula. The performance of Greek tragedies and comedies on festival days was sponsored by rich citizens, but the whole populace took part in supporting the Oscan farces, and young men considered it an honor to be allowed to appear in these as actors. The characters of the farces were always the same. There was Pappus, the absurd old man who still insisted on going a-wooing; Maccus, whose name possibly lives on in macaroni; the glutton Bucco; and Dossennus, who was always hunchbacked, clever, miserly, cunning, and lascivious. These characters were tremendous favorites and clung to life long after the plays in which they had figured had been forgotten. Maccus, Bucco, and especially old Pappus found their way into the Italian *commedia dell'arte* and thereby stole into the comedies and comic operas of modern times.

When Hannibal and his Punic army entered Italy in the third century B.C., Pompeii stood aside, refusing to team up with the many cities of Campania which opposed the Romans. But about a hundred and twenty years later, when the peoples of southern Italy once more revolted against the power of Rome, Pompeii threw in her lot with them. This struggle is known in Roman history as the Social War; it ended with the victory of Rome. Pompeii, too, after a stiff fight was forced to yield. Cornelius Sulla, later dictator of Rome, in person conducted the assault upon Pompeii. The city walls between the

A CHARIOT OVERTHROWN IN PASSING THE GOAL AT THE CIRCUS,
FROM A TERRA COTTA.

Herculanean and Vesuvian gates in the northwest of the city still show the scars made by the siege machines.

A small neighboring town suffered more from the war than did Pompeii. This was the resort town of Stabiæ. On April 30, 89 B.C., Sulla destroyed the town—so thoroughly that Stabiæ never fully recovered. The populace scattered to the near-by slopes of the mountains, and to villas and farms of the vicinity. There, and in all likelihood among the ruins of the city, life went on; the fertility of the soil held the peasants here, and the sea drew the fishermen, while the wonderful situation of the town on the Gulf of Naples attracted inveterate city-dwellers.

Rich Romans and the patricians of Campania liked to spend vacations in and around Stabiæ.

The grapes that flourished in the neighborhood of ruined Stabiæ produced a highly esteemed wine. The sea supplied excellent fish. The slopes of the hills near the town provided fine and healthy pasture for cattle, so that milk cures in Stabiæ were recommended by all physicians, from the great Galen in the second century A.D. to Cassiodorus in the sixth century. In fact, the mountain above the town of Stabiæ was known as Mons Lactarius (now Monte Lattaro), the "milk mountain." Still more important for the town as a health resort were the warm springs, whose waters alleviated the sufferings of the gout-ridden.

Altogether, Stabiæ was a pleasant vacationland and a delightful retreat for convalescents like one Marcus Marius, who had a country estate there. It was situated on the brow of a hill, with a splendid prospect over the chestnut woods, the coastline of the Sorrentine peninsula, and the entire Gulf of Naples as far as the promontory of Cape Miseno. This Marcus Marius was a friend of Cicero, who wrote to him: "I do not doubt that you in your bedroom—with its lovely loggia overlooking the Gulf—are spending the morning hours these days with edifying reading while we unfortunates who had to return to the City are sitting sleepily in the theater. The rest of your day you may employ for pleasures which you have arranged for yourself according to your own tastes, while we must endure what the authorities think good for us."

The destruction wrought upon Stabiæ by the Social War did not, then, affect its popularity. Herakleion— or Herculaneum, as it was now called—had been conquered by one of Sulla's generals during this same war.

It lost all of its former autonomy and became an ordinary Roman provincial town, but remained as wealthy as it had been. Oscans, Greeks, and Romans lived together peaceably. The beautiful and at the same time economically favorable site by the sea, as well as the fantastically fertile soil, made it a city that had everything desirable. The streets were laid out in a regular grid and paved with the characteristic trachyte of the region, or sometimes with limestone. Lanes were narrow, but there was

OXCART, FROM AN ANCIENT ALLEGORY OF AUTUMN.

little wagon traffic. The sidewalks were frequently roofed over, since the upper stories of the houses (supported by pillars) jutted over the streets. Land was dear, and so the city grew vertically, with houses of two and even three stories. Public wells were placed at intersections. Herculaneum was a conservative small town, with few factories and workshops but a great many arts and crafts. The poor lived mainly by fishing.

The development of Pompeii during this period was altogether different. In 80 B.C., Sulla had settled a number of deserving veterans there, in order both to reward them by giving them expropriated houses and estates, and to establish a reliable core of Romans in this predominantly Oscan-Greek city. The government of this veterans' colony, and of public affairs in the conquered city, was placed in the hands of Publius Sulla, the dictator's nephew. During the early days there was a good deal of friction between the natives and the immigrants. Disputes arose, for example, over the voting for the town council, and over certain zoning regulations in respect to new building which the Romans were unwilling to observe.

When, in 63 B.C., Consul Cicero exposed Catiline's conspiracy, it was charged that Publius Sulla had also participated in the plot and had incited the inhabitants of Pompeii to rebel against the Roman Senate. But Sulla was able to afford the two best lawyers in Rome, Quintus Hortensius and Cicero himself, who happened to need money because he wished to buy a house in the noblest quarter of Rome, on the Palatine Hill. With the aid of these great advocates, Sulla was acquitted.

The dissension between the old settlers and the new citizens in Pompeii was of short duration. The veterans of the Roman army had seen enough of the world to recognize the opportunities open to them in this new city, and to understand how important it was to live in peace. Consequently, they endeavored to do their part in making the city prosper and grow.

Since Samnite days there had been a palæstra, an athletic ground for the aristocratic youth of the city. In Greek fashion it had a hall and a pillared courtyard and even a splendid statue, the "Spear Bearer," a copy of one of the most famous works of the sculptor Polycleitus. Aside from the theater, which has already been mentioned, the city also boasted a large public bath. Between the men's and women's divisions were the gigantic furnaces, and both sections followed the classic floor plan of all thermæ: an anteroom, a disrobing room with niches for clothing, a domed room with round pool for cold baths, then a lukewarm pool and a steam room. In addition there was an athletic field open to the sky, surrounded by a loggia, tub baths, and a large communal latrine—for the Romans were fond of company and talk even while relieving themselves. The brothel on the side street near by, on the other hand, contained many small single rooms. Here specialization went so far that a painting above every door showed the particular mode in which the complaisant lady within could give pleasure to her visitors.

Pompeii was already a town of considerable luxury. But now, under Roman administration, there was much new building. Besides the large theater a second, smaller one was built; it contained only fifteen hundred seats, but these were roofed over. This theater was not used for plays, but for musical offerings, singing, dancing, pantomimes, and readings.

Near the forum a second public bath was erected, smaller than the first, but with several of the rooms much more beautifully decorated. The same chief magistrates, Valgus and Porcius, who had erected the small theater at their own expense during their term of office from 80 to 75 B.C., presented the city with an amphitheater located in the southeasternmost corner of town. This was one of the earliest amphitheaters of its type in Italy. As yet it was unequipped with underground rooms; the arena was at a level lower than the street, and the balustrade in front of the first row of seats was also low. True to the old Etruscan tradition, gladiatorial fights were the main spectacle; animal-baiting was less well known. Had there been much use of animals, a higher railing would have been needed for the protection of the audience. There were some thirteen thousand seats, and on the top row were three thousand places for women to stand: they were not supposed to come too close to the bloody games. Altogether, the amphitheater held more people than the total population of Pompeii. The reason for this was not anticipated growth of the city but the fact that many came from neighboring towns and villages to attend performances in the amphitheater.

The building of the amphitheater relieved the pressure on the forum. Hitherto this market place had served (as it had in Rome and other cities) not only as the center of trade and traffic but also for the public games, with the spectators either standing around or sitting on hastily erected wooden stands.

The great slave rebellion under Spartacus (a gladiator who had fought in such amphitheaters) in 73 B.C. began in Campania and affected Pompeii and Herculaneum also; but otherwise these cities had little share in the rapid events of those decades. The peaceful period after the civil wars was favorable to both commerce and agriculture; the cities grew bigger and richer and, in fact, outgrew their fortifications. Where, after all, was there an enemy? There seemed to be no need of walls.

In Pompeii the old forum was triangular in shape, enclosed on two sides by porticoes with Doric columns and on the third by the ancient temple built in bygone times by the Greeks. Here visitors to the near-by theater met; here the citizens repaired for their evening promenade when they wished to enjoy the view of the mountains to the southeast of the city. Since pre-Roman times, however, there had also been a larger, rectangular forum. There stood temples, public offices, and courthouse; there, too, were the market stalls. Now the forum was partly

repaved. The portico was renovated, and fine public
buildings were erected on sites formerly occupied by
private dwellings. To supplement the supply of water
from the public wells, a water line was installed; from
a high tower a network of lead pipes distributed water
through the entire city.

Near the big theater, a portico that had previously
served the audience as a place of refreshment after the
performances was rebuilt into a barracks for the gladiators of the amphitheater. The gladiators lived well; there
were sixty rooms for one hundred and twenty men.
Alongside the amphitheater was a tremendous palæstra,
an athletic field measuring some 460 feet on each side.
Within the encircling wall ran a shadowy portico; in the
center of the field was a swimming pool.

The whole city profited from the many strangers who
came to Pompeii for the gladiatorial combats. Innkeepers
and merchants welcomed the visitors, but once there was
an unpleasant incident. "About the same time" (A.D. 59),
Tacitus relates in the fourteenth book of his *Annals*, "a
trifling happening led to frightful bloodshed between the
inhabitants of Nuceria and Pompeii, at a gladiatorial show
sponsored by Livineius Regulus. . . . With the unruly
spirit of provincial townsfolk, they began to throw abusive
language at each other; then they took up stones and at
last weapons, the advantage resting with the populace
of Pompeii, where the show was being exhibited. And so
there were brought to Rome [as proof of the outrage] a
number of the people of Nuceria, with their bodies mutilated by wounds, and many lamented the deaths of
children or of parents. The emperor delegated the trial
of the case to the Senate, and the Senate to the consuls,
and then again the matter being referred back to the

Senators, the inhabitants of Pompeii were forbidden to have any such public gathering for ten years."

This was a harsh penalty, and not alone for the citizens of Pompeii. Life in the city went on, however. Then, upon the hustle and bustle of the Pompeiian merchants and into the contemplative peace of Herculaneum and the upper-class holiday life of Stabiæ fate suddenly, incomprehensibly, laid a merciless hand.

MARKET SCENE, AFTER AN ANCIENT VASE PAINTING.

Toward noon of February 5, A.D. 63, a fearful earthquake shook the Campanian coast. The tremors rolled like waves from east to west, from Vesuvius toward the sea. The temple of Jupiter in the forum of Pompeii collapsed. So did the old temple of Apollo, the sanctuary of the Egyptian goddess Isis (for this port city had been receptive to many Oriental cults), one of the city gates, and many private dwellings. The theaters, the baths, the water tower, and the lead-pipe water lines were severely damaged. Herculaneum and Stabiæ were likewise hard hit, and even Naples was affected. A fissure in the earth

which yawned suddenly in an open field was said to
have swallowed a herd of six hundred sheep.

The Roman Senate wondered whether it would be wise
to rebuild cities in so obviously imperiled a situation.
When, however, the decision to undertake repairs was
finally made, the Emperor Nero personally contributed
a large sum, for the resources of the cities themselves
were, of course, insufficient. In the same spirit, Nero had
given his people financial assistance after the fire at Rome.
These wise and generous measures show him as a different sort of ruler from the one painted by his enemies,
who after his death charged him with so many misdeeds
that until a few decades ago he was even thought to be
the author of the great fire. In reality, his acts of madness
affected only a small group. As far as the rest of the
Empire was concerned, his reign, like the reigns of other
and often equally maligned emperors of this era, was a
peaceful and constructive period. Thus, in the cities struck
by the earthquake, everything possible was done to repair the damage. Of course the new buildings were in the
pompous style of the period; Pompeii lost much of its
mellow Greco-Samnite charm and acquired the rather
stereotyped look of other rich provincial towns of Italy.

One of the first buildings to be repaired was the temple
of Isis in Pompeii. The costs were paid by private do-
nations. Even before all of the wrecked buildings, including those of the forum, had been restored, the building of a third public bath was begun. This was situated in
the center of the city and was provided, in accordance
with new notions of hygiene, with spacious, airy rooms
illuminated by large apertures in the walls, with a gym-
nastics area and a swimming pool open to the sky.

The new baths were not yet finished, the old ones on
the Stabiæ road not yet repaired, and only the men's

section of the baths at the forum was usable. At this point a lady named Julia hit on an idea both lucrative and public-minded. From her father, Spurius Julius Felix, she had inherited a splendid villa with a number of outbuildings, including a private bath. The whole complex occupied an entire block on one of the main business streets of the city, in the quarter in which the amphitheater was located. This quarter was visited by many strangers, since the ban on gladiatorial games had meanwhile been rescinded. Julia Felix had alterations done on her private bath and upon the servants' rooms. These buildings were then walled off from the rest of her property, and Julia had a large sign written: "For rent on the property of Julia Felix, daughter of Spurius: a delightful, elegant bath, shops, alcoves, and living chambers; from the middle of August, on a five year lease."

The living-chambers were in the top story; they could also serve as rooms for transients when strangers came to Pompeii for a few days for the games. Moreover, the big palæstra was near by; as soon as this was rebuilt, the athletes would certainly flock to such conveniently situated baths. The baths themselves were calculated to satisfy the most refined taste; they possessed, in addition to the usual rooms, grounds for more open-air games and a swimming pool. Naturally, the place was not nearly so large as the other thermæ; consequently, visitors often had to wait until they could be accommodated. In order to divert them, and turn a pretty penny at the same time, a kind of bar was set up next to the waiting room, and a small open-air café. The owner reserved for herself the elegant main dwelling in the block of houses, for which she had a special entrance on a side street built. In addition she retained a pretty ornamental garden with a pool and fountain, and a huge orchard.

This entire establishment was dug up about two hundred years ago. But the excavators of the time merely removed a few marble columns to the Naples Museum and then covered everything over again. Only in recent years have house, baths, and gardens been once more brought to light in all their ancient splendor.

Since Herculaneum is closer to Vesuvius, the earthquake did even greater damage there. The town was wealthier, however, and reconstruction proceeded faster, both on the private dwellings and on the theater, whose twenty-five hundred seats could hold about half the population of the town—an indication of the Herculanean's intense interest in art. The rebuilding of the temple of Cybele, the Phrygian (Asia Minor) "Mother of the gods," was largely subsidized by the Emperor.

During the years after the earthquake Herculaneum became even more beautiful than it had been before the disaster. Many prosperous people from Rome and Campania had chosen the town as a place of retirement, in order to enjoy the beauty of the gulf and the refreshing summer breezes. Of course these people did not build along the shore, amid the smell of fish and the shouts of sailors, but on the slope of the promontory that Strabo mentions.

A good view and fresh air were the chief desiderata of these houses; they were designed accordingly. For all the marble and mosaics, murals and statues, the aim of the builders was to display the panorama of the gulf. Living-quarters, pavilions, loggias, and porches all looked out over it. Seen from the sea, this portion of the city presented a charming sight; the entire shoreline was a cluster of porticoes and loggias.

The one public bath in the city did possess the rarity of a glass window, but was apparently somewhat outmoded; it was not connected to the new, still incomplete water line, but drew its water supply from a well. In any case, it was too small. Consequently, a second public bath was built on the steeply sloping shore. In part it was cut right into the rock; the anteroom received its light from a vertical shaft. The roof was supported by four pillars, and all the rooms were richly furnished.

SILENUS ASTRIDE A GOATSKIN BAG FILLED WITH WINE,
FROM A BRONZE FOUND AT HERCULANEUM.

In Stabiæ the peasants fixed their farmhouses as best they could after the earthquake. Some of the rich owners of villas settled elsewhere—as did some cautious citizens of Pompeii and Herculaneum; but the majority had the damage repaired and continued to enjoy the pleasant region, the curative thermal waters, and, according to taste, the milk or the wine.

Stabiæ also possessed an institution unusual in the ancient world: a sanatorium. It was, however, not open to the public, but reserved for the foremost aristocrats and courtiers of Rome. In fact, it was really the private property of the imperial family, which had the means to erect buildings of such vast proportions and such logical arrangement in so choice a situation that a stay there was bound to benefit the patients.

To assure a pleasant temperature at all seasons, the winter garden of the sanatorium was built where it would receive the most intense sunlight, on the slope of one of the promontories of Mons Lactarius, but protected from the wind. The usual peristyle surrounded this winter garden, but had a unique feature: the columns were not fluted vertically, but displayed spiral-shaped channeling —a hypermodern form of decoration in the first century A.D. Precious paintings, similarly novel and breaking with tradition, adorned the walls, fine mosaic the floor. Adjoining this garden was the summer garden, shielded from the sun by tall trees, and situated somewhat farther down the slope. But instead of steps there was a ramp leading down to it, for the ease of patients.

The thermæ, with walls ducted for heat, could satisfy even the most spoiled epicures of Rome, but they were still considered inadequate. Parts of the adjoining rooms were sacrificed in order to enlarge the peristyle around the swimming pool.

Between corridors lay the lobby. In size it echoed the generous proportions of the rest of the institution: more than thirty-five feet wide by sixty-five long, with large windows opening toward the northwest. Only the world-famous spa of Baiæ, twenty-five miles distant across the Gulf of Naples, could offer a view of comparable beauty. From this lobby the convalescents at the sanatorium could look out over the rows of chestnuts and oaks on the slope to the narrow gold strip of coast and across the blue sea with its silvery foam to the promontory of Miseno. And above all this arched the blue sky of Campania.

The internal struggles after the death of Nero had scarcely touched Campania, and the fearful earthquake sixteen years before was already half forgotten. In Pompeii the statue of the Emperor Titus was being raised in the imperial temple, and the finishing touches were being put to the work of reconstruction. But suddenly, in the middle of August in the year A.D. 79, fresh earthquakes shattered the peace of the fruitful region around Vesuvius. The sea grew restless, though no wind was blowing. Cattle and dogs seemed to sense disaster, and a feeling of unbearable tension hung in the air.

Half of the Roman fleet was stationed at Miseno. A seventeen-year-old boy, accompanied by his mother, was visiting his uncle there. The boy was later to become the famous writer and jurist Pliny the younger; his uncle Pliny the elder was commander of the Roman fleet and also the foremost scholar of his time. The story of this uncle's experiences on the fateful day was later recorded by Pliny in one of his *Letters* to Tacitus:

"On the 24th of August, around the seventh hour [about one in the afternoon], my mother requested him to observe a cloud of very unusual size and shape. He had just taken a turn in the sun, and after a swim and light luncheon had gone back to his books. He immediately arose and went out upon a hill whence he might get a better view of this very uncommon sight. A cloud, from which mountain was uncertain at this distance (but it was found afterwards to come from Mount Vesuvius), was ascending. I cannot give you a more exact description of it than to liken it to a pine-tree; for it shot up to a great height in the form of a very tall trunk, which spread itself out at the top into branches, as it were. This shape was caused, I imagine, either by a sudden gust of air, the force of which decreased as it advanced upwards, or by the cloud's being itself pressed back again by its own weight. It appeared sometimes bright and sometimes dark and spotted, according as it was either more or less impregnated with earth or ashes.

"This phenomenon seemed, to a man of such learning as my uncle, extraordinary and worth further looking into. He ordered a light vessel to be got ready, and gave me leave to accompany him if I liked. I said I would rather go on with my work; as it happened, he himself had given me something to write out. As he was coming out of the house he received a note from Rectina, the wife of Tascus. She was in the utmost alarm at the danger which threatened her. Her villa lay at the foot of Mount Vesuvius, and there was no way of escape for her except by sea. She earnestly begged him to come to her assistance. He, accordingly, changed his first intention, and what he had begun from a scientific, he now carried out in a noble and generous spirit. He ordered the galleys to put to sea, and himself went on board with the intention of assisting not only Rectina, but the people of several other towns which lay thickly strewn along that beautiful coast. Hastening then to the place whence others fled with the utmost terror, he steered his course directly to the point of danger, and with so much calmness and presence of mind as to be able to make and dictate observations upon all the aspects of that dreadful scene.

"He was now so close to the mountain that the cinders, which grew thicker and hotter the nearer he approached, fell into the ships, together with pumice stones and black pieces of burning rock. They were in danger, too, of being run aground by the sudden withdrawal of the sea, creating shallows where none had been. Vast fragments rolled down from the mountain and obstructed all the shore. He stopped to consider whether he should turn back, as the pilot advised. Then he said, 'Fortune favors the brave; steer to where Pomponianus is.'

"Pomponianus was then at Stabiæ, on the other side of the bay. He had already sent his baggage on board a ship; for although he was not yet in actual danger, he was determined to put to sea as soon as the inshore wind died down. This same wind, however, was favorable for carrying my uncle to Pomponianus, whom he found very troubled. My uncle embraced him tenderly, encouraged him and urged him to keep up his spirits. The more effectually to soothe his fears by seeming unconcerned himself, my uncle ordered a bath to be made ready. Then, after having bathed, he sat down to supper with great cheerfulness, or at least with every appearance of it.

"Meanwhile broad flames shone out in several places from Mount Vesuvius. The darkness of the night rendered these even brighter and clearer. But my uncle, in order to soothe his friend's fears, assured him it was only the burning of the isolated farms, which the country people had abandoned to the flames. After this he retired to rest. And it is certain he was so little disquieted that he fell into a sound sleep. For his breathing, which on account of his corpulence was rather heavy and sonorous, was heard by the slaves outside.

"The court which led to his apartment was by now almost filled with stone and ashes, so that if he had remained there any longer it would have been impossible for him to make his way out. He was therefore

awakened. He came out and went to Pomponianus and
the rest of his company, who were feeling too anxious
to think of going to bed. They consulted together
whether it would be wisest to trust to the houses—which
were now being rocked from side to side with frequent
and violent concussions, as though shaken to their very
foundations—or fly to the open fields, where the calcined
stones and cinders, though light, yet fell in large showers
and threatened destruction. In this choice of dangers
they resolved on the fields. While the others were hurried
into this decision by their fears, my uncle embraced
it only upon cool and deliberate consideration. They then
went out, with pillows tied upon their heads; this was
their sole defense against the storm of stones that fell
round them. It was now day everywhere else, but there
a deeper darkness prevailed than in the densest night.
However, it was to some degree alleviated by torches and
oil lamps. They decided to go farther down upon the
shore, to see if they might safely put to sea, but found
the waves still running extremely high and boisterous.
There my uncle, laying himself down upon a sail-cloth
which was spread for him, twice called for cold water,
which he drank.

"Flames and sulfurous vapors drove away the rest of
the party, and compelled my uncle also to rise. He raised
himself up, with the assistance of two young slaves, and
instantly fell down dead—suffocated, I conjecture, by the
noxious vapors. He had always had a tendency toward
asthma. As soon as it was light again, which was not
until the third day after, his body was found without
any marks of violence upon it, in the dress in which he
fell. He looked more like a man asleep than dead."

Thus the commander of the imperial fleet met his end

in a manner worthy of a Roman and a scholar, having retained to the last his courage and his common sense. Stabiæ lay buried under a layer of ashes and pumice; the sinister clouds had banked up against Mons Lactarius and deposited a large part of their burden. Some clouds, however, were driven a good deal farther. They buried a portico of the ancient temple of the goddess Hera on the River Sele, forty miles southeast of Vesuvius. Some ash fell in places as far off as Egypt and Syria.

Vesuvius had long been considered an extinct volcano. Its slopes were planted almost to its peak with crops and vines. No one imagined that it represented the slightest danger to the flourishing cities of the vicinity. But the volcano was far from dead. Steam pressure building up inside it had long been seeking an outlet; this pressure had caused the earthquake of A.D. 63 and had now gathered enough strength to rend the rock above it. The hole where the eruption first burst forth rapidly became a fiery crater; the explosion hurled ashes and pumice into the air, where the clouds were caught by the northeast wind. The rain that suddenly began, together with the streams of water pouring from the volcano and the masses of material ripped from the brink of the crater, combined to form a tremendous avalanche of mud, which rolled down the slope of Vesuvius from the old wall of the crater, now unsealed and gaping. It rolled toward the sea—and Herculaneum.

Mud rushed into the streets, rose higher, entered houses and temples, flooded them, filled them from wall to wall, pressed through doors, windows, and sagging walls and roofs, until at last it covered everything to a depth of thirty, forty, and even fifty feet. The wave of mud pushed on toward the sea and piled up in a shoal reaching 650 feet into the water. In spite of the darkness, the inhabitants could not fail to recognize the danger from the moment the avalanche of mud began to roll. Most of them fled toward Naples as fast as possible. They left everything behind, saved nothing but their bare lives. But they did save these; there were relatively few dead in Herculaneum.

Pompeii was somewhat farther from Vesuvius than Herculaneum. After the first ground tremors in the morning the Pompeiians had seen the mountain suddenly split down the middle, its substance rising into the air like a cloud and slowly spreading. At first the people hoped the disaster would not directly affect their city. Then, when the rain began to fall, mingled with ashes and small stones, they sought refuge in their houses and public buildings. This was their doom; the rain did not slacken. It grew steadily heavier. Lapilli as large as eggs and larger, mingled with fine dust and ashes, fell upon the entire city, building up on the roofs until these collapsed under the weight. Streets, squares, and interior courtyards were soon covered. The rainwater and ash together formed a clinging mud that impeded movement.

A good many of the citizens were wise enough to jump on their horses and make their getaway. Some called for their slaves, and if these in their terror did not come quickly enough, they themselves hitched up the mules, placed wife and children in the wagon, and headed for the open country. Even those who without delay fled on foot were able to escape.

In the mud-coated streets many fugitives slipped, fell, and could not rise again. At the gates of the city, vehicles piled up; people had to clamber over the bodies of fallen horses. Walls collapsed, pillars crashed to the ground.

Everywhere, tiles slid from the roofs, the dust and ashes obscured vision, the torrents of rain extinguished the lamps. Nevertheless, the only safe place to be was in the open.

A great many people did not realize this in time. Children who had been playing in gardens sought shelter under the roof overhangs until the roofs collapsed, burying them. Women hastened to their living-quarters to gather up a few articles of value; men weighed themselves down with purses of money and precious household gear; slaves tended to their sick masters; doorkeepers would not leave their posts—and all perished. In the top stories of the houses, which collapsed first, but also in rooms lower down and in solid vaulted cellars, death caught up with those who had not grasped the nature of their danger. The fine dust crept through every crack, and sulfurous vapors suffocated the unfortunates.

With the fire belching from Vesuvius and the ashes raining from the sky, with the populace stricken by horror, a Jew remembered the destruction of cities recorded in the book of Genesis: "Then the Lord rained upon Sodom and upon Gomorrah brimstone and fire from the Lord out of heaven." That disaster had been a punishment for the sinfulness of the people. No special vices could be attributed to the inhabitants of Pompeii, but had not Titus, the new Emperor of the Romans, destroyed venerable Jerusalem and carried away the sacred implements of the Temple? Was it not possible that at this hour the entire Roman Empire was being destroyed; was not Pompeii only a prelude to the destruction of the whole world? God was punishing the unbelievers as he had punished them once before. So the Jew, remembering the names of those cities whose doom should have been a warning to all ages, wrote on the wall of a house in the ninth district of the city, in which he was trapped, the words: SODOMA GOMORA.

Thirty-four people and one goat died in the lower chambers of one of the most elegant villas of Pompeii, just beyond the walls of the city. They were evidently the family and the servants of the master. He himself was heading for the garden gate with a sack full of gold coins, perhaps to see whether escape toward the sea was still possible. Death struck him at the threshold of the house, together with the slaves who were carrying the household's silver utensils.

In the gladiators' barracks there were sixty-three fatalities. Two convicts in a dungeon cell, who had not been released from their leg irons, perished as wretchedly as the chained watchdogs in the houses.

Those who remained in the streets and observed the deadly layer of stone, mud, and ashes steadily rising could not doubt that the whole city was doomed. Those who had the strength had to climb over the bodies of suffocated victims, had to leave their stumbling friends behind, if they would escape with their own lives. Once successfully past the western gate of the city, they hurried toward the sea, anxiously seeking a ship. But most of the ships had already lifted anchor and were now far out to sea, fighting for life, for the earthquakes had raised towering waves. Those which remained—cargo vessels and fishing boats, even the last leaky rowboat—were crowded with fugitives. They tried to push off from shore and were held back by those who desperately hoped to wedge themselves in, until at last the boats sank under their burden or were swallowed up by the raging surf.

People, dogs, and rats had plunged in blind terror into the water, hoping to swim to safety. Their bodies were later washed up on the beach. Dead fish and birds lay among them on the sand—a ghastly, horrifying sight in the flickering light of the torches. Seeing the doom by the seashore, some people tried to make their way back to the city. But they could not get through the steady stream of fugitives and wandered about on the beach until their strength gave out.

In a tomb on the highway that led to Herculaneum a family had gathered for a funeral when the rain began. The people were lying on the couches set out in the anteroom of the burial vault, about to begin the funeral supper. Perhaps they did not think it right to cut short the ceremony immediately, and before they could finish, it was too late. Suffocated in the tomb, they followed the newly deceased member of the family into death.

CARICATURE OF A PAINTER'S STUDIO, AFTER AN ORIGINAL
FOUND AT POMPEII.

Women found themselves unable to escape from upper-story rooms where they had gone to hide or save their jewels; the stairs collapsed, and then the roof came down on top of them, so that they lay with broken bones amid the ruins, helplessly awaiting slow death by suffocation. Some slaves hid in the cellar vaults of a house on the outskirts of the city. Another took refuge in a windowless room in the interior of the house. All of them suffocated. The gods of the mystery cult represented in a fine mural in one of the rooms in this building were unable to protect the inhabitants against their doom. The lucky seal-ring brought no luck to the man who wore it. Not even Isis could safeguard her priests; one of them died on the street, having delayed his flight to collect a sackful of religious utensils, sacrificial vessels, and coins. Two other priests of Isis fled from the temple on the old triangular forum; they were killed by collapsing columns. Others died inside the temple itself. The crash of falling buildings and the patter of falling lapilli drowned out the cries of the dying. Darkness shrouded the city.[4]

When Vesuvius quieted down on the morning of the third day, when the wind scattered the clouds and the sun broke through once more, white ashes fifteen to twenty-five feet in depth, lay like a funeral shroud over the city and its environs.

---

[4] A description of the rediscovery and excavation of Pompeii and Herculaneum, interesting as the story is, would be inappropriate within the limits of this book. Professor Amedeo Maiuri, Director of the Naples Museum and of excavations in Campania, has published a number of works on the subject. Readily available are the guides issued by the Italian Ministry of Education: *Ercolano* (3rd edition, Rome, 1946) and *Pompeii* (5th edition, Rome, 1953). The story of Stabiæ is well covered by an article by Maiuri in the magazine *Atene e Roma*, Vol. I (May–June 1951).

PART TWO

GOLD

◻ GOLD WAS FOUND MANY THOUSANDS OF years ago: in the valley of the Nile, along the upper reaches of the Indus and the Satadru rivers, in Asia Minor, on the island of Thasos, in the Pyrenees, and in countless other places. At first, no doubt, gold was an object of pure pleasure; easily worked, it made pretty jewelry. It reflected the light of the orb of day, whose color it was; it did not corrode, and was therefore assumed to be the metal of the sun. Thus, it acquired religious significance, becoming the attribute of everything mighty and supernal.

It was fairly late, around the middle of the history of mankind as we now know it, that the ever shining and beautiful metal was stamped into coinage. But it never congealed into a mere symbol of value; it remained value in itself. Ever and again people of all ages and climes sought after gold. They went forth in ships to fetch it from distant shores—sometimes shores with legendary names whose locations we seek to this day. They sent sea captains out over the waters the earth in the unadmitted hope of discovering lands of gold. Seeking for gold, they explored the world; in pursuit of gold they subjugated foreign peoples, killed strangers, burned cities to the ground, and rummaged among ruins, graves, and tombs. . . . The sudden appearance of cities from nowhere when gold had been discovered, and their abandonment and subsequent decay when the supply became exhausted, was not a phenomenon only of the nineteenth century in California, say, or Alaska; for in all ages men were impelled by the passion for profit and wealth. To those lucky centers where goods were shunted from place to place, and where easy profits beckoned, traders poured throughout the centuries; and if a few decades later a new sea route was found, a new city that promised quicker profits would be established. The earlier one became depopulated, its streets grew still; impoverished, finally it fell to ruin. So a city passed away. Gold as the symbol of commerce and economic life raised innumerable cities to the heights, made them beautiful and rich, and took itself off again when the sources of wealth dried up. As long as gold reigned, violence was of little avail. Time and again cities were rebuilt on sites most favorable for commerce. But if commerce took another course, neither siege nor assault was needed to make a city fall to ruin.

IV

COINED GOLD

A DESERTER. THE TOWER OF BABEL AND THE HANG-
ING GARDENS. THE ASS FROM THE MOUNTAINS AND
THE ASS FROM THE SEA. MURASHU & SONS. DARICS
AND SHEKELS. HIT SONGS, BOXING MATCHES, AND
BARBECUES. WHAT HAPPENED TO DOCTORS WHO
MADE MISTAKES. ALEXANDER AND BABYLON. THE
METROPOLIS BECOMES A HUNTING PRESERVE. PAL-
MYRA, THE CITY OF GREAT BEL. THE BLACK-EYED
QUEEN. CITY OF BISHOPS AND EXILES. THE BEDOUINS
HAVE THE LAST WORD.

ONE DAY in the year 479 B.C. the guards upon the
watchtowers of Babylon, which was being besieged by
the Persians, saw a man ride toward the city from the
enemy camp. He kept looking back, as if afraid of pur-
suers; his horse wore rich trappings. The guards guessed
him to be a deserter from the camp of Xerxes I [1] and
opened a gate to him. When he stopped before them, they
started in horror. For the man had no ears; his head
was shamefully shorn, and instead of a nose his face
showed nothing but a horrible, blood-encrusted wound.

[1] The following tale has probably been embellished with legendary
elements by Herodotus or his source. Herodotus erroneously tells the
story in connection with the subjugation of Babylon by Cyrus, which
occurred sixty years earlier.

The stranger was led through the long narrow corridor between the gate towers. No attacker could have passed through alive, even if he had succeeded in battering down the brazen gates, for everywhere stood Babylonian archers, and the narrow passage offered no escape from the deadly arrows. Now, however, the soldiers lowered their weapons and permitted the foreigner to pass through. He was brought before the Council. There he gave his name: he was, he said, Zopyrus, one of the noblest of the Persian princes. He had advised the King to abandon the hopeless siege, and for this advice he had been so cruelly disfigured. "And now," he went on to say, "my coming to you, Babylonians, will prove the greatest gain that you could possibly receive, while to the Persians it will be the severest loss. Verily, he who has so mutilated me shall not go unpunished. All his counsels are known to me."

The frightful wounds vouched for the genuineness of his motives. The Babylonians recognized the advantages of having on their side a Persian prince who must harbor an immoderate hatred for the King, and who was, in addition, an experienced general. They therefore placed a sizable contingent of troops under his command. On the tenth day after his arrival Zopyrus undertook a sally against the besiegers from the gate named after the great queen Semiramis. He achieved a significant victory; a thousand of the enemy were left lying dead upon the battlefield.

The Babylonians rejoiced; this was their first success in months. The double walls of the city were strong, protected by a moat and towers and so thick that they could serve as roadways for troops if it were necessary to bring reinforcements swiftly to a danger spot; but, on the other hand, the Babylonians were in terror of Xerxes. Now, grateful to the Persian Zopyrus for his aid, they entrusted him with still more soldiers for his next sally. This time he ventured out of the Nineveh gate and won an even greater victory, killing two thousand of the besiegers. Twenty days later Zopyrus, at the head of Babylonian troops, destroyed four thousand of the enemy in front of the Chaldean gate. In every case they had encountered poor and ill-armed detachments of the Persian army, but the Babylonians were wild with joy over their victories. Accordingly, they entrusted the Persian prince with the supreme command of their entire army. Thus, he was in charge of the fortifications as well.

The whole city was brimming with confidence. No one suspected that Zopyrus was a secret agent whose mutilations were self-inflicted to give credence to his tale. Each step of the great betrayal had been worked out beforehand with Xerxes—that was the secret of the successful battles.

On the twentieth day after their last defeat the Persians moved up from all sides for a general assault upon the city. While the Babylonians fought from the walls, Zopyrus opened the Belian and Cissian gates and admitted picked Persian troops. The Babylonians who saw them enter fled to the temple of Baal; the rest remained at their posts until they, too, realized they had been betrayed by Zopyrus. Thus Babylon fell into the hands of the Persians. Xerxes had the walls razed and the brass gates removed. Three thousand of the leading citizens were crucified. As the reward for his feat, Zopyrus was given the government of Babylon for his lifetime.

Thus the city at last came into the possession of the Persian Empire—Babylon, the metropolis that had been great even in the third millennium B.C. It had assumed the heritage of Sumerian civilization, had fought its neighbors as well as the barbarians of the north and east, and had repeatedly contested with the Assyrians the hegemony of the Mesopotamian world.

Babylonian was the language of international communication through most of Asia Minor. The influence of Babylonian script and culture extended for great distances. King Hammurabi (*c.* 1700 B.C.) was renowned throughout the world for his power, for the peace and prosperity of his kingdom, for the building of canals and the furthering of agriculture, for the burgeoning of literature under his rule, and for his great codification of laws. More

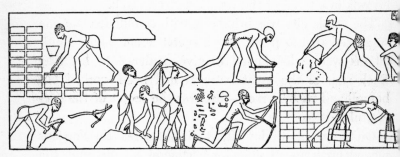

BUILDING A BRICK WALL, AFTER AN ANCIENT EGYPTIAN
REPRESENTATION.

than a thousand years later, after invasions and temporary domination by Hittites and Cassites, after the oppression and destruction of the city by the Assyrians, Babylon had risen once more; it flourished economically, politically, and militarily under Nebuchadnezzar until the new world power of the Persians appeared upon the stage of history.

The ancient temple of Baal, restored by Nebuchadnezzar—famous from the Bible as the "Tower of Babel"—fell once more into decay. But at the time of the Persian conquest the Hanging Gardens of Semiramis still existed and were counted among the Seven Wonders of the World. These were irrigated, terraced gardens laid out one above the other in the northern part of the city, between the royal palace and the processional avenue that started at the gate of Ishtar. The trees and shrubs towered above the city wall, visible to anyone approaching the city. Around the middle of the fifth century B.C., Herodotus could still say of Babylon that "in magnificence there is no other city that approaches it."[2]

Babylon's political role was played out, but the city still possessed its old importance as a communications and trade center, and as the capital of an extraordinarily fertile region.

Primitive though Oriental agriculture now seems in those areas where its methods have scarcely changed for thousands of years, it was the height of modernity when the Semitic nomads were adjusting their customs to the older Sumerian civilization. They turned over small areas with the hoe, larger fields with the plow. This frequently had only a stone instead of an iron plowshare, but a rudimentary form of grain drill had already been developed. The Babylonians also knew the use of the flail and employed it along with that simpler tool which the Romans later called *tribulum*: a wooden disk with sharp stones on its undersurface, which was drawn across the grain by an ox. The simplest and most common method of threshing, however, was to spread the grain out on a threshing-floor and drive oxen or asses over it until their hoofs separated the chaff from the grain.

The land was also extremely productive in vegetables, which were screened by fruit trees and date palms from wind and excessive sunlight. In addition, animal husbandry, and especially dairy farming, flourished. Great herds of sheep and cattle were pastured, guarded by shepherds with dogs, and occasionally by archers, against robbers and predatory beasts. The Babylonians raised

[2] Herodotus I.178; for the conquest, III.151–60.

water buffalo and humped brahman cattle imported from India; the bison were already almost extinct. The commonest domestic animal, employed equally as draft animal, mount, and beast of burden, was the ass. In fact, the horse was called "mountain ass" and the camel "ass from the sea." The camel remained the chosen beast of the Arabian nomads and was purchased from them when a journey across the desert was planned. The horse of the mountain peoples of the north and northeast had become well acclimatized in Mesopotamia, and the Persians gave a great impetus to horse-breeding. The satrap of Babylon, holding as he did the richest governorship in the Persian Empire, allegedly owned a herd of eight hundred stallions and six thousand mares. The animals were kept in stables only in winter, of course; most of the year they grazed freely, their ownership indicated by brands. Horse-stealing was severely punished.

Thousands of years before, the Sumerians had already learned how to make the steppe soil fruitful. There is scarcely any rain in Mesopotamia; the growth of crops depends upon irrigation. Canals were dug up and down the country, conducting the water of the rivers into the plain and at the same time protecting the flatlands from flooding. These canals received, distributed, and stored for the dry season the huge quantities of water produced by the melting snows and the spring rains in the mountains of Armenia, where the Tigris and Euphrates have their sources. The canals were of the simplest construction: the excavated earth served to build up the side walls, from which channels could easily be run if water were needed for fields or gardens. Bridges of boats or ferries provided passage from shore to shore.

These canals also served as fisheries and water highways. Traffic moved over them in barks that were rowed or, more frequently, punted with long poles. The cargo vessels also had sails, but usually were drawn by animals that walked on tow paths. These ships were not especially large and were of shallow draft; between thirty and eighty bushels of grain was the usual load.[3]

For Babylon, the broad, deep, and torrential Euphrates itself was the most important trade route. The river also fed the moats around the fortifications and the canals. It flowed through the middle of the city, dividing the newer western part from the older quarter with its royal palace and temple tower. When the city was fortified, the river also was lined with walls, so that it too could be defended. But there were many gates, of brass like the big gates in the city walls; wherever a street led down to the river, these gates permitted access to the shore. On the walls of the quays the peasants offered their produce for sale; the Babylonian word for quay, *karum*, means the place where offices are found. The market, stock exchange, and customs office were all located by the river, the principal artery of trade.

Up the Euphrates from the Persian Gulf came goods from India; down the Euphrates traveled wares from Asia Minor and Syria, and from Egypt via Syria, though for this latter commerce the caravan route along the edge of the desert was sometimes preferred. We can say what goods were traded in Babylon, and at what prices, more easily than we can for periods of European history far closer in time. The reason is that writing-materials were

[3] The archæological evidence for these statements may be found in the four-volume *Manuel d'archéologie orientale*, by G. Contenau (Paris, 1927). The same scholar has written a highly readable book, *La vie quotidienne à Babylone et en Assyrie* (Paris, 1950), on which we have drawn for many valuable insights.

cheaper in Babylonian days. Consequently, a great deal was written down, and, since the material was more permanent, much was preserved.

We even know the names of the largest commercial houses. As early as the beginning of the second millennium B.C. the Assyrian firm of Pushukin was established in the Cappadocian city of Kültepe (eastern Asia Minor) and was reaping high profits in this virtually virgin territory. In the fifteenth century B.C. the family of Teheptilla operated in the Assyrian city of Nuzi, two hundred miles north of Babylon. The details of its business affairs and real-estate speculations can be followed closely in the firm's archives. In the period of Persian dominion over Babylon, the business of the firm of Murashu and Sons was flourishing in Nippur, fifty-five miles southeast of Babylon. The Murashu family were Jews whom Nebuchadnezzar had led into the notorious Babylonian Captivity in 587 B.C., after the destruction of Jerusalem. The Murashus had done so well in exile that they did not return to their native land when they were given permission to do so by Cyrus, the Persian King, after the first conquest of Babylon. Their archives were still kept in Babylonian cuneiform script, though the language of the country had long since become Aramaic.

The original standard of value had been barley. Gradually silver took its place, but only as a weight, not as a coin. The countries of the eastern Mediterranean did not possess a gold coin until Darius I struck the coin known after him as the *daric*. The government used it primarily for paying the army and navy; but most of the gold reserves were not struck into coinage. Alongside the daric, the Biblical silver *shekel* or *siglos* (8.4 grams) remained in common use.

For historians and economists it is fascinating to compare the shifting purchasing power of silver, and the prices of specific goods, at different periods. The value of gold vacillated between fifteen and eighteen times an equal weight of silver. Far below silver in value was lead, then copper; iron from Cyprus was of better quality and consequently far dearer than iron from Lebanon. Dates, which had once equaled barley in price per unit

PROCESSION OF ASSYRIAN MUSICIANS.

weight, rose under Persian rule to double the price they had fetched under Nebuchadnezzar. Barley became still dearer. It is almost impossible, however, to estimate the average income of a Babylonian; we know only that two soldiers of the temple guard received 34 shekels of silver for twelve days' service. An ox cost, on the average, 20 shekels, an ass 30, a goat 2. Under the Persians land became more expensive. Slaves, too, rose in price—perhaps as the natural consequence of relatively peaceful times, since fewer prisoners of war would be brought to the slave mart. Under Nebuchadnezzar an average slave cost 40 shekels—as much as two oxen. Under Cyrus the price rose to 60, under Darius to 100, and under Xerxes to 120 shekels (2 minas or slightly more than 2 pounds of silver). Slaves, incidentally, were not badly treated. The rights of their masters were clearly delimited. Slaves could engage in trade, not only for their masters, but on their own account. We know of a slave named Ribat who rented a fishpond from one of the sons of the banker Murashu.

That trade was so important in the life of Babylon, and of the whole Near East, need not surprise us. Goods were unevenly distributed throughout this region, and the needs of a highly developed civilization were naturally extensive. Egypt possessed gold, but little wood; for the cedars of Lebanon she exchanged perfume, articles of luxury, and other finished goods. Mesopotamia also needed wood and imported it from Syria. Metals had to be purchased in Armenia and Asia Minor; spices and incense came from southern Arabia. In return, agricultural produce was exported. In Borsippa, the city nearest to Babylon, there were large linen mills.

Linen, flax, purple-dyed wool, sesame oil, wine, foodstuffs, clay and metal vessels, jewelry, tools—practically anything could be bought in Babylon along the banks of the river or in the great roofed market places, which were veritable bazaars. Most artisans plied their trade right on the street. The noise of potters, weavers, and smiths mingled with the cries of peddlers who offered cloth, jewelry, and perfume for sale, and of bakers who sold cakes for consumption and for sacrifices. Bats, incidentally, were eaten as a great delicacy in Babylon.

Even the texts of sacred and profane songs were sold on the street. A whole catalogue of favorite songs, arranged according to first lines, has come down to us. These lines suggest that the songs were certainly colorful, if not at times off-color:

"Your love, O Lord, is like the perfume of the cedar. . . ."

"O gardener of the garden of dreams!"

"Come into the garden of the king, there where the cedars stand so thick. . . ."

"Ah, how she shines in all the abundance of her beauty. . . ."

"I saw two courtesans down below on the street. . . ."

Georges Contenau, to whom we are indebted for these details, remarks that life in this part of the Orient scarcely altered in any fundamental way from around 600 B.C. down to the invention of the automobile. The motor car has, he adds, introduced a certain restiveness into the region.

A number of excavated reliefs show clearly that boxing matches were immensely popular. And on a good many of these sculptures we can clearly see, standing behind the fighters, a man with a gong! No less surprising are the social sidelights gleaned from the famous half-reliefs of Khorsabad near Mossul. One of these shows us a banquet: richly dressed dignitaries are sitting around a table, and all have their right hands, holding drinking vessels, raised. It is obvious that they are about to drink a toast. Curiously enough, their seats are like high bar stools, so that the legs of the drinkers are dangling.

Somewhat less modern were certain regulations governing the practice of medicine. Hammurabi says in Paragraph 218 of his famous code: "If a physician inflicts a severe wound with a bronze operating scalpel, thus killing the patient, or opens a sore with a bronze operating scalpel and destroys his eye, the physician's hands shall be cut off." With such penalties hanging over him, the doctor's fee of ten shekels, established in the same paragraph, does not seem excessive.

The streets of Babylon were wide and partly paved. Some were very straight, but many others were narrow and twisting. There were no sidewalks and no sewers. In noise, dirt, and smells Babylon did not differ from present-day Oriental cities. The streets were not even level; if a building collapsed, its successor was built upon the ruins—no one bothered to clear the ground for a new foundation. Some houses were of several stories, with almost windowless walls facing the street. There were inner courtyards, roof terraces, little furniture, and a great many vermin. Not only bedbugs, ants, cockroaches, beetles, lice, and spiders infested these houses; scorpions and snakes were also frequent guests, as was inevitable in the climate and under the prevailing living conditions.

Nevertheless, Babylon was a beautiful city. Its long processional street was eighty feet wide, lined by high walls. Reliefs in brilliant colors adorned these walls from far outside the city all the way to the Ishtar gate on the north side. Other splendors of Babylon were the royal palace, the tremendous temple tower, the golden statue, the golden throne, and the golden altar table of the god Baal. Darius wanted to carry off these treasures, but did not quite dare. In 479–8 B.C., when Xerxes defeated the rebellious Babylonians, he destroyed the temple tower and carried off the golden statue of Baal, with which the tradition of an independent native kingship was linked.

For two centuries Babylon was one of the most important cities of the Persian Empire. Darius III, after his severe defeat at Issos (333 B.C.), seized his opportunity while Alexander the Great was in Egypt and assembled at Babylon troops from all parts of his Empire: Medes

and Persians, Hyrcanians from the shores of the Caspian
Sea, Parthians, warriors from the mountains of Pamir and
Turkmenistan, Scythian cavalry, and Hindus with fifteen
war elephants. Darius also had two hundred war chariots
equipped with deadly sickles. Naturally, Babylonians, too,
served in his army.

But Alexander made short work of this mighty host.
Defeated near Gaugamela, the Persian general, Mazaios,
fled back to Babylon with the remnant of his troops. But
neither he nor the Persian garrison could consider a
serious defense of the city, for the ancient fortifications
had never been wholly rebuilt. The victorious Macedonians advanced from the north; Alexander placed his
troops in battle order—and Babylon surrendered uncon-
ditionally.

The walls were lined with people who wanted to see
the great Macedonian king. Others hastened forward to
hail him and bring him presents. The priests sang hymns,
bands played, and the nobility of Babylon rode out on
splendidly caparisoned horses. The streets were strewn
with flowers, wreaths hung everywhere, altars were set
up, and the air reeked of burning incense. Alexander
entered the city and the royal palace not on horseback,
like a warrior, but standing in a chariot like a king.

Next day he inspected the treasures and the magnificent appointments of the royal palace. Alexander displayed the utmost consideration for the religion and
customs of his new subjects; he performed the royal sacrifice to Marduk, the god of the city, and ordered that
the shattered temple tower be rebuilt. Ten thousand men
are said to have worked for two months just to clear
away the rubble. For thirty-four days Alexander's soldiers
enjoyed the delights of Babylon, reveling in wine and
women, and then moved on to further conquests. The

Roman historian Curtius Rufus chides the Babylonian women for their loose conduct, and the Babylonian men for their tolerance.

Harpalus, the friend of Alexander's youth, established himself in the royal palace at Babylon. He was officially charged with supervision of the treasures and with the transshipment of supplies to the army; but the greater the distance that Alexander placed between himself and Babylon, the bolder Harpalus became. He soon began holding court with great pomp. He had the Hanging Gardens planted with Greek ornamentals; as it happened, most of them took nicely, only ivy being unable to stand the climate.

Along with the plants, Harpalus had imported two famous hetæræ from Athens. One of them, Pythionice, died and was given a splendid tomb; the other, Glycera, insisted on being treated like a queen. Harpalus continued to draw freely upon the treasures entrusted to him until his King returned from India in the spring of 324 B.C. Then Harpalus fled Babylon—taking five thousand talents with him.

In the fall of this same year, 324, Alexander's dearest friend, Hephaistion, died. A tomb for him was to be erected in Babylon, of a size equal to the former temple tower but surpassing it in beauty. The architect Dinocrates of Rhodes (who had wanted to transform Mount Athos into a statue of Alexander) was given the commission. Twelve thousand talents were appropriated, but the plan was never carried out.

When Alexander returned to Babylon in the spring of 323, the Chaldean priests warned him that if he entered the city, it would bring him misfortune. Perhaps they themselves believed in their own prophetic gifts, for which they were noted throughout the Orient, or perhaps they were merely afraid of accounting for the money he had entrusted to them for the reconstruction of the temple. Alexander would not be frightened off, but deemed it best to enter Babylon by detours.

En route he was met by emissaries from all parts of the known world: from Scythia and Etruria, Carthage, Spain, and Ethiopia. That there were Romans among these envoys was asserted by some classical historians, but contested, with good reason, by others.

The King's next goal was a campaign against Arabia. A gigantic harbor was to be built for Babylon; the cypresses of Babylonia would supply wood for the building of a new fleet, and the city was to become a naval base and center of commerce between Egypt and India. Tremendous hosts of troops camped round the city. There were grand sacrifices and farewell festivities, and the day of departure had already been fixed when Alexander fell ill after a banquet. He lay in the royal palace with a raging fever. The soldiers were unwilling to march off without him. Finally they forced their way past his bodyguard and into the palace. Man after man marched silently by his bed to bid their great commander farewell. The evening of June 13, 323 B.C., Alexander died in Babylon.

During the struggles among Alexander's successors, Babylon was fought for and conquered several times. Ultimately the wealthy city fell to Seleucus, one of the generals. On the Tigris, about thirty miles north of Babylon, the new royal residence of Seleucia was built. This city was granted all possible privileges and the full support of the King. It became the heart of the Seleucid Empire. The caravan routes now intersected at Seleucia; envoys and traders came thither. Henceforth, Babylon lay in the shade.

Possibly the enormous area of the city had never been fully occupied. For military reasons the houses were not permitted to abut on the city walls, and in earlier times there had been grainfields within the walls so that in case of siege the city would be amply provisioned. Now, with declining trade, the cultivated area increased from year to year, while the residential area shrank. The wealthy moved to the glittering cities of Seleucia, Antioch, and Susa. The merchants left a city to which profits no longer flowed. There remained only the peasants and a few astrologers, for as the seat of Chaldean prophecy Babylon still had some small reputation.

The decline continued throughout the period of the Seleucid Empire and under the Persian rule that followed. When, in the second century A.D., the Roman Empire reached its greatest extent under Trajan, Babylon was also included within the Imperium. But the city was beyond reviving.

With the spread of Christianity the Chaldean astrologers found no further call for their services. In the fifth century A.D. the Parthian kings used the walled-in wastes of what had once been Babylon as a game preserve, and under Arab rule the name of the city completely vanished from history. A small village named Babel slept away the years until the excavations begun in the nineteenth century revealed something of the bygone glories of what had been the largest city of the ancient world.

On the northern rim of the Syrian desert lies a parched steppe, crossed by age-old caravan routes that touch the few oases. One route, from the Armenian plateau to the Red Sea, intersected another, leading from the Mediterranean coast to Mesopotamia, at the Bedouin village of Tadmor. There are good springs in this vicinity, and the oldest settlement on the spot may well be three thousand years old.

The city that was later called Palmyra arose in this favorable climate, was nourished by commerce and secured from enemy attack by the desert, and was doomed to destruction when Roman logistics solved the problem of moving sizable bodies of troops across the desert tracts. Now, on the spot where Palmyra flourished for three centuries, nothing has survived the tempests of time but the ancient Bedouin village of Tadmor: a few huts and a caravanserai sheltered from sandstorms by mighty ruins.

"And it came to pass at the end of twenty years, wherein Solomon had built the house of the Lord, and his own house, . . . he built Tadmor in the wilderness," says the Old Testament (II Chron., viii, 1, 4). The name Palmyra was given by the Greeks; the first reliable accounts of the city have come to us, as is so often the case, from the Romans.

In 41 B.C., Mark Antony was trying to raise money for his troops in the eastern part of the Roman Empire, which had been assigned to him. Palmyra seemed worth a *coup de main.* After his first meeting with Cleopatra, Antony sent his cavalry to Palmyra to plunder the city. The Palmyrenes, however, had been warned; they moved their possessions across the Euphrates and, armed with bows, took up positions on a hill. Antony's cavalry did not engage them in battle, but merely searched the deserted city and returned without any booty.

This story is the first mention of Palmyra in classical literature. It must have continued to grow and prosper, for about a hundred years after these events Pliny the younger mentioned it in his *Encyclopedia:* "The city of Palmyra is famous for its site, the richness of its soil,

and its good water. All around it lies sandy desert. It
possesses tillable fields, an exception in this region; it has
its own destiny between the two great empires of the
Romans and the Parthians, and in war is always the
first concern of both sides."

Growing by stages, without any unified building plan,
Palmyra spread steadily eastward from the ancient settlement on a hill. In appearance it resembled the Roman

SETTING UP A MILITARY CAMP, FROM A ROMAN RELIEF.

towns of Syria. The new city received the name of
Hadrianopolis after the Emperor Hadrian visited it in
A.D. 129, but the old name clung. So did the antique
character of the oasis town. The caravan routes continued to be the dominant factor in its life.

The residential quarter was in the north. Above the
mud huts with their almost windowless walls there soon
towered the mansions of the merchant princes with their
elegant porticoes. Among these buildings was a small
temple that had been dedicated to the god Baalshamin
in A.D. 131. The public buildings were south of the main

artery—the caravan route, which followed a wadi. Gates opened onto the market squares.

The intersecting caravan route to Damascus bisected the city in the other direction, marking off the western quarter. Here, during the third century A.D., the permanent camp of the Roman garrison was built up. A triumphal arch with four gates on the caravan route formed the beginning of a magnificent colonnaded street that ran approximately southeast. Some 375 columns may still be counted here; of these 150 are still standing. They led to the agora and then on past the theater and the thermæ, and were topped with statues in honor of important ctizens. This street terminated in a triple gate. Southwest of this gate stood a temple, facing south and surrounded by Corinthian columns—an overwhelming revelation of the glory of Greek architecture for the primitive desert-dweller, and a pleasantly familiar sight to the visitor from the Mediterranean world. For the inhabitants of Palmyra itself this was only a temple of the second rank, however. For if they continued down the newest portion of the colonnaded avenue beyond the gateway, they would come to the propylæa of the most famous of the city's temples.

The temple of Bel is not old. A sanctuary of this god had probably been established on this spot for countless centuries, but none of the splendid edifices of the oasis city was built before the age of Augustus. Two centuries of builders labored on this temple, and, in spite of all the classical Greek elements, the fundamental outlines are curiously reminiscent of ancient Assyrian or Hurrian prototypes. On April 6, A.D. 32, the temple was dedicated to the Palmyrene trinity: Bel and his companions, the sun god Jarhibol, and the moon god Aglibol.

Who inhabited this strange metropolis without kingdom or empire, this city dropped in the middle of the desert?

First of all, of course, there was the Roman garrison, not numerically large, but the hard core of authority for the entire region. Accompanying the Romans were a few Greeks as teachers and merchants. All the rest of the population were Orientals: the native Arabs, Phœnician and Jewish tradesmen, a scattering of Babylonians, Persians, and Egyptians. Certainly the scenes in the splendid avenues and the markets of Palmyra were colorful enough: gaily dressed desert-dwellers, caravan leaders, and peddlers in picturesque Parthian costume swarming about the proud, aloof Romans who strode about with weapons clanking.

No less colorful was the babel of languages in the markets of Palmyra. (The city was, after all, not too distant from the Babel where, according to the Bible, the building of the tower was rendered impossible by the confusion of tongues.) The language of the courts and of government was Greek, as was the case throughout the eastern part of the Roman Empire. The garrisons spoke the language of their commanders, Latin, and the natives of the city employed a dialect of Aramaic enriched by numerous Latin and Greek loan-words. In the outlying districts Aramaic inscriptions are found even on the gravestones of Roman soldiers.

The architecture has remained as the lasting testimony of a hybrid civilization. From it we can still form a reliable picture of the atmosphere in which the propertied citizens of Palmyra lived.

The temples, catacombs, and private houses were adorned with murals. We may, if we wish, see it as a sign of decadence that around the time of the birth of Christ the classical Greek artistic tradition gave way to a new primitivistic trend. Examples of this art have been preserved in many hunting scenes. The artists, for the most part, bore Semitic names. On the whole, we may say that Palmyra developed a Mesopotamian art that took in Greek, North Syrian, and Babylonian influences.

Undoubtedly it was tremendously expensive to conjure all these magnificent buildings out of the desert at a spot where for thousands of years there had been nothing but the most humble settlement for camel-drivers. Palmyra's wealth came from commerce; the city was the link between Egypt and Mesopotamia, and the gateway to the great Roman Empire. A lucky find has given scholars a great deal of information about life in this peculiar corner of the earth. This find is an inscription from A.D. 137 which proved to be nothing more nor less than a customs-and-tax list, divided up into categories of goods. Thus the principal wares traded in Palmyra are known to us.

The list is headed by slaves. Then come foodstuffs, and purple-dyed woolen fabrics from Phœnicia. From India, Mesopotamia, and Hadramaut came scents, the legendary "perfumes of Arabia." For the ladies of Roman society these were shipped in little pots of metal or onyx. For the wholesalers who sold the perfumes in the less elegant quarters of Rome, goatskins sufficed. Bronze statues, we learn, were taxed not on the basis of their artistic value but on their sheer weight. Camel hides passed free; apparently they were used as packing-material.

From the trade and transshipment of these wares wrapped in camel hides and goatskins an entire city lived, and lived not badly. Hundreds, perhaps thousands of camels must have swayed in and out the great gates, for a hundred camels carry no more than the load of a single freight car. Moreover, Palmyra profited from the caravans themselves, as well as from trade and customs. Caravans coming from the Mediterranean had to outfit themselves for the passage across the desert. When caravans had come across the desert, the animals would be worn out and the men exhausted. Palmyra was a place to rest; the traders might be prevailed upon to sell their wares on the spot, and would certainly wish to enjoy the city's ladies of easy virtue—whose popularity was such that it was worth while imposing on them the same tax Caligula had introduced in Rome: a monthly payment of their fee for a single visit.

Palmyra also provided armed protection for the caravans against the bandits of the desert—levying a specific tax for this purpose—and drew additional profits from the salt mines to the east and southeast of the city. Handicrafts flourished; the artistic leatherwork of Palmyra swiftly became famous. Proximity to the sources of raw materials, Oriental resins and fragrant oils, favored the perfume industry. Its reputation vied with that of the Palmyrene goldsmiths.

A rich city needs order. The merchants and landlords, the proprietors of workshops, and the owners of caravans adhered strictly to the class stratification by wealth. A fortune had to be of a certain size to entitle its owner to citizenship and a voice in public affairs. Inscriptions on graves inform us of two men named Worod and Hairanes, both of whom were surpassed in fame by Odenathus, Hairanes's son. Intelligent, very strong, and remarkably courageous, he had the rank of a Roman senator and commanded the troops of the city.

For centuries the Roman Empire had been so large that it was prone to trouble. Generals in the more distant provinces had the habit of crowning themselves emperors, but within Odenathus's realm such rebels had no success. He defeated a number of these usurpers, fought against the Persians, against the Goths in Asia Minor, and extended the power of the city-state of Palmyra over Syria, Mesopotamia, and Arabia as far as the Red Sea. The open commercial city of Palmyra became a fortress; between the funerary towers, which became bastions, Odenathus had strong walls erected, and now he himself assumed the pompous Oriental title "King of Kings." Before long the onetime village had developed into the most powerful military city in the Near East. Within the Roman Empire it bore the honorary epithet *metrokoloneia* —that is, chief or mother colony.[4]

Once walls are erected around a city, its growth is cut off and a phase of its evolution comes to an end. Expansion had reached its high point, but an essential element was still lacking from the life of Palmyra. Odenathus had, with the increase in his prestige, gradually adopted a complex and pompous court ceremonial, but Palmyra was still a city of merchants and soldiers. There was little of the cultivation and artistic life that enhance the glory of powerful rulers. Conscious of this lack, Odenathus called one of the greatest scholars of the day from Athens to Palmyra: Cassius Longinus, who was dubbed by his contemporaries "the itinerant university."

It is not certain that the warrior-king Odenathus was actually thinking of the good of his city when he sent for Longinus. Perhaps he merely wanted his youthful

[4] The details on the buildings of Palmyra are drawn from *Palmyre*, by J. Starcky (Paris, 1942). For the history of the city: *Essai sur l'histoire politique et économique de Palmyre*, by J. Février (Paris, 1931), and an article, "Palmyra," by C. Watzinger, in Pauly-Wissowa: *Realenzyklopädie der klassischen Altertumswissenschaft*. The credibility of the classical biographers of the rulers of Palmyra is subject to much dispute.

second wife, Zenobia, to acquire a little learning so that
she would do him honor. And so it became Longinus's
principal task to instruct the beautiful queen of the *dux
Romanorum*. We do not know whether she was Syrian,
Arabian, or Hebrew; she is described as dark-skinned,
with radiant black eyes, a lithe body, and a vibrant,
rather mannish voice. She was considered one of the most
beautiful women of the age, and accompanied her husband on his hunts and his military campaigns.

Unexpectedly, Zenobia found herself raised to the seat
of power. While Palmyra's soldiers were fighting Gothic
tribes in Asia Minor, Odenathus was slain in Emesa. At
almost the same time Odenathus's son was assassinated.
Perhaps the powerful ruler and his son were eliminated
on orders from Rome; perhaps Zenobia herself instigated
the murders in order to establish her own children as
Odenathus's successors. In any case, the black-eyed
queen assumed the rule of Palmyra and its dependent
territories as regent for her minor children. Her chief
adviser was the philosopher Longinus.

If a historic situation can ever be described by the
word *fascinating*, this was the word for the situation
around A.D. 270. The Roman Empire was engaged in warfare on almost all its borders; its hands were tied in
regard to Palmyra. The Goths had invaded Greece, conquered Athens, pillaged Sparta and Corinth. Out of these
upheavals there rose on the fringes of Mediterranean
civilization a new empire whose center was an oasis in
the desert and whose ruler was a young woman: Queen
Zenobia. Her troops defeated the Roman army. She conquered Egypt and forged an alliance with Persia.

At the moment of her greatest power Zenobia made a
conciliatory gesture toward the Romans. The coins she
had struck, the symbols of her power, bore on one side

the portrait of her son Waballath, whom she also called "King of Kings," and on the other side the head of the Emperor Aurelian. Zenobia was wise, or at least well advised: she appealed to Rome to recognize her son as a king owing allegiance to Rome. Similar coins were struck in both Syria and Egypt. But Aurelian did not accept the offer; in his own coins of the year 270 he threateningly calls himself *Restitutor Orientis* (Restorer of the Orient).

Apparently Zenobia decided that she had done all within her power, for her reply to Aurelian's coins was a new issue in which her son Waballath bears the radiant crown and the imperial mantle that had been reserved for Aurelian on the earlier coins. And on the reverse we find, instead of Aurelian, the young Queen Mother Zenobia herself. She now called her son Augustus and herself Augusta; from a conciliatory spirit she had swung to pride and defiance.

It is a remarkable development: three hundred years after its first mention in Roman accounts this commercial city without any military tradition had suddenly become Rome's mightiest adversary. With the rise of Palmyra the whole of the subjugated Orient seemed to spring to new power and prestige. Roman, Hellenistic, and Persian customs formed a unique compound at Zenobia's court. Table manners and court ceremonial were Persian; anyone admitted to an audience with the Queen had to fall to the ground before her and touch the earth with his face. But when the Queen appeared before the populace, she wore the male dress of a Roman emperor.

Zenobia spoke Egyptian and Aramaic fluently, Greek very well—she read Homer and Plato—and Latin poorly. But, for all her attainments, she was woman enough to love display. For her hoped-for victorious entry into Rome she had a magnificent chariot built. Her mode of life is described as chaste and moderate, but she was also said to be capable of drinking the Persian and Armenian envoys at her court under the table.

Even at a distance of seventeen hundred years we can feel something akin to sympathy for Palmyra and its ruler. It is sympathy for the weaker, for a city that possessed no class of experienced soldiers or statesmen. Yet, with the naïve rashness of suddenly acquired wealth and power, this city had dared to challenge the Romans. It was soon to be taught its lesson.

The following year, A.D. 271, Egypt, the granary of the Roman Empire, fell to the Roman general Probus (who later became emperor). Meanwhile, Aurelian advanced across Asia Minor against Palmyra itself. Zenobia's strength lay with her archers and heavy cavalry. But Aurelian was the superior tactician; a clever maneuver with light cavalry in the course of a river crossing gave him a victory. Then he waited. The march across the belt of desert protecting the oasis city involved great risks. Only after he had persuaded a number of desert tribes to guard his supply lines did Aurelian venture to push on to Palmyra.

Zenobia negotiated desperately with Shapur I, the aging King of the Persians, but obtained little aid. Her Saracen and Armenian allies proved unreliable. The siege of the city began.

Hungry fugitives poured into the city. The once humming markets were deserted, and more and more Roman firebrands shot over the walls. When food supplies began running short, Zenobia secretly left the city, accompanied by only a few attendants. Mounted on the swiftest of the royal dromedaries, she set out for Shapur's court to appeal for troops. She reached the Euphrates and was just about to board a ship when she was caught by a Roman patrol.

When word of the Queen's capture reached Palmyra, the peace party within the city seized control and opened the gates. Aurelian spared the city, only requiring the temple to surrender its treasures. A cohort of imperial archers remained in Palmyra as a garrison.

Zenobia was taken to Rome. Oddly enough, we do not know her further fate. According to some sources, she refused all food in order not to be paraded through the streets in a Roman triumph, and died of starvation en route. According to other sources, she was pardoned and ended her days in a villa at Tivoli. Her daughters are said to have married Roman senators.

Orphaned Palmyra exhibited little political maturity. The mentality of desert warriors overcame the counsels of prudence. In A.D. 272 the city rebelled against Aurelian, who had treated it so mildly. The satrap and the entire Roman garrison were slaughtered, and a kinsman of Zenobia was placed upon the throne. But before the city could be prepared for defense, Aurelian was once more at its gates, and this time he did not restrain his legionaries. The Romans' wrath was a fearful thing, and their punishment terrible. A letter of the Emperor's describes with soldierly brevity the days that marked the end of Palmyra's brief career of glory.[5]

"Aurelianus Augustus to Cerronius Bassus:

"The time has come for the soldiers to put by their swords. Enough Palmyrans have already been slaughtered. We have not spared the women, have butchered children, throttled graybeards, slain the peasants. To

[5] Letters or speeches quoted by classical historians almost never reproduce the actual original texts. This letter is cited from the biography of Aurelian in the collection *Scriptores historiæ Augustæ,* a work whose historical accuracy has been severely questioned.

whom are we going to leave the land, to whom the city? Those who remain must be spared. For we believe that these few have been brought to reason by the death of so many. I would like to see the temple of the Sun God in Palmyra, which was pillaged by the eagle-bearers of the third legion, restored to its former condition. You have 300 pounds of gold from Zenobia's hoard, 1800 pounds of silver taken from the Palmyrans; you have the royal jewels. Use this money to have the temple restored; you will thereby be doing me and the immortal gods a great service. I will write to the Senate and request them to send a priest to dedicate the temple."

Palmyra's role as a power in the Orient was finished. The Persians took over the trade with India, and Palmyra slowly died. Now and again its name bobs up in history, but as no more than a melancholy invocation of faded glory. At the Council of Nicæa a bishop from Palmyra took part in the deliberations. By A.D. 403, Palmyra had sunk to the level of a place of banishment: the Emperor Arcadius exiled the bishop of Emesa to Palmyra. In the year 13 of the Hegira (A.D. 634), Palmyra was compelled to open its gates to one of Abu Bekr's generals. But the change-over to Islamic rule and civilization did not bring about a revival of the city. The Seljuks reduced the area of Palmyra and threw up a wall around this shrunken city. Clearly, evolution was now speeding in reverse; the former capital was becoming a mere citadel.

In the seventeenth century a Bedouin tribe thought the mighty ruins of the temple good enough to serve as protection from storms. The tribesmen settled down among the walls and columns. The history of Palmyra had come full circle; it was once more a thinly populated Bedouin village in a dry wadi.

In the twelfth century the Spanish rabbi Benjamin of Tudela visited Palmyra in the course of his famous journey to the Orient. Five hundred years later (1693) an oil painting of the city was hung in Amsterdam University. Later travelers copied a few inscriptions, and in 1710, King Charles XII of Sweden actually sent an expedition to Palmyra. (The notes and reports of this expedition are preserved in the library at Uppsala.) In

EGYPTIAN WAR CHARIOT, FROM THEBES.

1902 and 1917, German expeditions worked there, and since 1929, French archæologists have been conducting systematic excavations—for which purpose they have resettled the Arab villagers somewhat to the north.

The museums of Damascus and the special museum newly built on the historic site now contain many valuable antiquities from the old city. In addition, most of the important collections of the world have acquired a sampling. For the Arabs have not missed their opportunity. The caravans that now leave Palmyra contain vases and old household utensils, fragments of statues and

frescoes, all destined for the lusty black market in antiques. Unabashed by the glory of their forefathers and
with no fear of the shades of the dead, the desert-dwellers have gone back to their old game of commerce.

V

GOLD AND GARRISON

ROME AND THE ALPS. CELTIC MINING. PILGRIMAGE
TO THE WAR GOD. CARRUS NAVALIS AND CARNIVAL.
THE SACRED REMAINS SACRED. ÆNEAS LANDS AT
OSTIA. A METEORITE FROM ASIA MINOR. THE GOD-
DESS HEARS CLAUDIA QUINTA. SKYSCRAPERS IN AN-
CIENT OSTIA. EARLY CHRISTIANITY IN THE BATHS.
THE DEAD REST IN THE THEATER. SARACENS AND
POPES. LOVELY BAIÆ. LUXURY AND LOOSE MORALS.
SCIENCE OF WINE. THE CURSE OF A JEALOUS POET.

IN ITALY, the land of calves, the people were still
reckoning in cattle long after the Greeks had round coins
and the daric was accepted currency throughout the
ancient world. In the fourth century B.C. the Romans
used shapeless, heavy pieces of copper for ready cash.
The first silver coins were struck not in Rome itself, but
in Capua.

The Romans did not create a commercial empire, as
the Phœnicians and Greeks had done. Roman senators
were not allowed to engage in trade; as early as 218 B.C.
the Lex Claudia prohibited such base activities. Instead
of bothering with laborious commercial competition,
Rome overthrew her economic rivals with the sword.

Wherever Roman merchants did appear, mercenary

soldiers followed at their heels—and sometimes the order
was reversed. Not that the Romans neglected business,
but they did not trust it as had the early seafaring peoples
who set out from their homes in Asia Minor and established small trading colonies all around the Mediterranean. One by one, the Romans assumed mastery of these
colonies.

In the northernmost corner of the Adriatic Sea lies the
city of Aquileia; it bears the same name today that it did
more than two thousand years ago. In those early days of
Roman power it was inhabited by Latin colonists whose
business it was to keep the restive Istrians in order.
Through this point, between the mountains and the sea,
an important trade route led from Italy to the lands of
the east, and the inhabitants earned a good living by
transshipment of goods. But they were not satisfied with
these profits alone; they also ascended into the mountains,
those Alps which were the home of a mixed population.
The original Alpine population that had inhabited the
mountains since the Stone Age had been swelled by
Illyrian tribes and later, in the course of the last centuries before Christ, by Celts driven out of upper Italy.
By occupation they were peasants and herdsmen, but had
gradually amalgamated themselves into organized political communities. Scattered about the mountains, their
settlements had in some cases grown to considerable size.

With these people and these towns the merchants of
Aquileia traded. The great commercial houses sent their
representatives—usually freedmen, but sometimes slaves
—up into the mountains with whole columns of mules.
Itinerant peddlers also made their rounds. It might be
that all they owned in the world was a mule and the
load on its back. But a peddler who had borrowed the

money for his first venture might well be able to pay
off all his debts by the time his second round of trading
was finished.

The Ambisontians, Halaunians, Ambidravians, Taurisks, and other tribes of the mountains were by no means
sorry customers. For the wine, oil, spices, textiles, and
even objects of art which were brought to them they
traded the products of their rural economy: cattle, hides,
cheese, wood, honey, wax, resin, pinewood for torches.
But their substance did not consist in agricultural products alone. For many centuries they had been skilled
miners. The copper they extracted did not compete with
the rich stores of the Mediterranean world; it was
primarily for their own use. But Noric iron (Noricum
was the general name for the region) was of first-rate
quality and therefore much sought after. They had also
the salt of the Noric mountains to sell. They had gold
and lead. If the demands of trade required payment in
cash rather than kind, that too was feasible. The Noricans
had their own silver and bronze coins.

The habits of the mountain folk may have seemed
barbarian to the cultivated Latins of Aquileia, but as a
people they were certainly not primitive. Proof of this
is found in their mining engineering, in the artistry with
which they fashioned iron weapons, inlaying them with
bronze or gold, and in the plan of their cities. Many of
these cities survived for long periods: Ovilava (Wels in
upper Austria), Aguntum (in the eastern Tyrol), and
Teurnia (in Carinthia). To judge by the many Celtic
royal coins found there, this last must once have been
the residence of a ruler.

Some of the other towns were destroyed or abandoned
in early times. Even their names have vanished. So, for
example, on Mount Gracarca near the southeasternmost

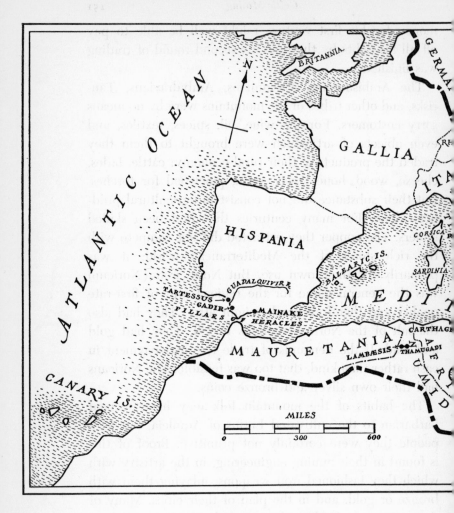

THE MEDITERRANEAN WORLD

SARMATIA

CASPIAN SEA

ALBANIA

DACIA

COLCHIS

DANUBE R.

PANNONIA

MŒSIA

BLACK SEA

DALMATIA

ARMENIA

EPIDAURUM

THRACE

BITHYNIA

PONTUS

CAPPADOCIA

ASSYRIA

MESOPOTAMIA

MACEDONIA

GALATIA

TIGRIS R.

ADRIATIC SEA

EPIRUS

TROY

ASIA

LYCAONIA

CILICIA

EUPHRATES R.

SYBARIS

ÆGEAN SEA

PISIDIA

PALMYRA

BABYLON

MYCENAE

LYCIA

PALESTINA

PYLOS

ACHAIA

CYPRUS

SYRIA

IONIAN SEA

RHODES

ARABIA

CRETE

MEDITERRANEAN SEA

LIBYA

ALEXANDRIA

CYRENAICA

RED SEA

ÆGYPTUS

NILE R.

GUY FLEMING '57

shore of Lake Klopeiner in lower Carinthia (Austria) a
settlement, or at least a castle built around a sanctuary,
existed in the second millennium B.C. It was a fortified
place to which the peasants of the vicinity could repair
in time of war. It fell to ruin in pre-Celtic times, long
before written history began in these parts. We know
nothing about either the date of its destruction or the
cause.

Nor do we know the name of another ancient city
likewise situated on a mountain in present-day Carinthia,
between Klagenfurt and St. Veit an der Glan. And yet
this was no paltry peasant settlement. In the first century
B.C. it must have been the capital, or at least one of the
chief centers, of the Noric kingdom. It, too, had originally been a refuge built around a tribal sanctuary. At
first it had been protected only by two rows of palisades,
the spaces between the rows being filled with stones and
earth. In spite of its high altitude, this fort was watered
by good springs, which made it suitable for permanent
settlement. Later a double encircling wall was built. The
slopes were dug out and earth was heaped up behind
retaining walls, making artificial terraces on which
houses could be erected.

In the course of one of their tribal feuds the Gauls
at one time obtained allies from Germania. The leader
of these allies, Ariovistus (if this is actually a name and
not merely the title *hariofurist,* meaning "leader of the
army"), did not return home after the war. Apparently
he was smitten with the beauty of Gaul and decided to
settle down there permanently. His power grew rapidly.
The Noric king Voccio—whom Cæsar mentions in the
first book of his *Gallic War*—sought a marital alliance
with him. Voccio's sister became one of Ariovistus's two
wives. But where was Voccio's royal residence—in Teur-

nia, Noreia, or this nameless mountain town in what is now Carinthia?

The question remains unsettled. In any case, the town was not only a political and commercial center, but also a religious one. It had a temple to the war god Latobius, with a sacrificial basin standing on a pedestal carved with three human heads in low relief. Pilgrims came here from all the country round about, bringing gifts; even visitors from the Roman Empire paid their respects to Latobius. In gratitude for their good business relation-

SALE OF WINE, FROM A MURAL IN A POMPEIIAN TAVERN.

ships with the Noricans, the freedmen of the prosperous merchant family of the Barbii of Aquileia presented the temple with a precious bronze sculpture, copy of a classical Greek statue of a youth.

The Noric kingdom extended at that time as far as the Danube. Beyond the great river lived the Marcomanni and the Quadi, warlike Germans who were not exactly the most delightful of neighbors. In order to keep them contained, Roman troops established themselves in Noricum in the last century before Christ. They came as allies and did not interfere directly with the internal affairs of the Noric kingdom.

Along with the troops came an ambassador from Rome, who took up quarters in the mountain city in 15 B.C. Gradually, under Roman influence, the city's character changed, for Rome desired magnificent buildings in order to impress upon the mountain peoples the wealth and power of Rome and what a privilege it was to adopt the Roman way of life.

Naturally enough, the Romans chose the warmer southern side of the mountain, below the temple of Latobius and the royal citadel, for their own buildings. Since the slope dropped rather steeply on that side, rock had to be hewed, earth dug out of some places and filled in at others. By these means an open square for a market and assemblies, orations, and theatricals was created—a Roman forum, in other words. It was of considerable area, 375 by 130 feet, open to the south and surrounded by buildings on the other three sides. In the middle of the forum rose a second, smaller terrace, divided from the rest of the plaza by a six-foot-high ramp. Spacious colonnades along the sides gave this terrace the appearance of an inner courtyard. In the middle of this courtyard, on massive foundations, stood a Roman temple with vestibule and two cellæ. Its marble facing and the noble site, visible from a great distance, made it one of the most impressive witnesses to Roman grandeur in this peaceably occupied country.

A hundred feet farther to the west on this plaza, its façade toward the temple and likewise faced with marble, stood the ostentatious edifice of the Roman ambassador. It had a second story reached by marble steps. This building, altered almost beyond recognition, had once been the Noric assembly chamber. Any native who entered it would be vividly reminded of the power of the Empire with which his country was now allied—espe-

cially if he went as far as the dining-halls, the kitchen,
and the storeroom. There the Noric peasant, whose nostrils were generally tickled by barn odors, would encounter the fragrance of Roman delicacies: oysters and
purpuræ, the purple shellfish; olive oil and wine in great
clay jugs. No less awe-inspiring to simple folk would be
the wealth of crockery arranged in rows on high shelves,
dishes of clay and glass and *terra sigillata,* that precious
material which in classical days served instead of porce-
lain.

In order to see all this, however, the visitor would first
have to pass through a number of smaller rooms on the
side of the building facing the mountain slope, then cross
the wide central portion. This last was a sight not only
for the natives; a Roman, too, would scarcely have encountered such rooms elsewhere. This chamber was the
seat of the Noric provincial assembly. Here the Roman
envoy discussed with the deputies from the various tribes
questions of the Empire's domestic and foreign policy;
here congratulatory or honorific inscriptions to Augustus
and his daughter Julia testified to the loyalty of his new
vassals. Behind the platform on which stood the deputies'
seats a mosaic displayed the age-old symbol of the Celtic
war god, a horse in a sort of boat which rests on a sled.
In the Alps the sled takes the place of the wagon. We
know of a Germanic god whose image stood on a boat
placed on a wagon; this boat-wagon (Latin *carrus
navalis*) was paraded about during a spring festival, and
the word possibly survives in our "carnival." [1] Following
Celtic custom, there had been an ancient sacred spring
in the apse of this chamber; but the spring went by the
boards when the floor was raised in order to install a

[1] Another etymology derives "carnival" from *carne vale,* "farewell
to meat."

heating system. For the Romans did not wear long
trousers, like the Celts, and they suffered from the cold
in this mountainous country. An adjoining room, un-
heated but with a fine mosaic floor, contained the archives of the kingdom. These were kept in thirteen niches
corresponding to the thirteen tribes of the Noric kingdom.

Such rooms, with mosaics and murals, plumbing and
drainage systems, were an impressive display of Roman
civilization, just as they were intended to be. The palace
along the southwestern rim of the terrace, however, was
not intended for ostentation alone. It had a splendid
view of the lowlands and the near-by mountains, and in
addition an expensive installation that for the cultivated
Roman was not a luxury but a necessity: a bath. As in
the rich cities of Italy, there were the usual appointments
even here in the wild mountains: vestibule, disrobing-
room, cold, warm, and hot baths, heating through ducts
in the floor and walls, and sunken tiled tubs adorned
with mosaics and heated directly from below.

Thus, within a few decades the whole aspect of the
mountain town had changed radically. Celtic girls married Roman veterans, or freedmen who came in the
retinues of officials or as emissaries from some commercial
house in Aquileia. The town grew cosmopolitan; Latin
and even Greek could be heard alongside the familiar
Celtic tongue. In the wooden houses of the mountain-
dwellers, alongside the dark pottery of their own manufacture, appeared the bright red products of Italian
factories. Romans and Noricans got along well together,
lived comfortably—as far as the climate permitted—and
were not threatened by any foe.

This happy state of affairs lasted only sixty years. The
Roman envoy, originally there as an adviser, more and

more took on the functions of leadership; the Noric kingship steadily faded. In A.D. 45, at the time of the
Emperor Claudius, it came to an end. Without any show
of violence or special stir, Noricum became a Roman
province. A Roman governor arrived to replace the
ambassador. He no longer saw any reason why he should
go the extra distance to the ancient Celtic tribal sanctuary. Virunum, in the lowlands below the mountain,
became his residence. (Virunum was located near the
present village of Maria Saal, north of Klagenfurt, Austria.) This became a beautiful town, with a theater
equipped for dramatic performances instead of the mere
amphitheater for gladiatorial shows and animal-baiting,
as in other Roman towns of the Alpine district. Virunum
also provided a convenient junction. The traders came
to it rather than to the mountain city first because it was
more accessible, and secondly because economic life
tends to seek out the seat of government. The mountainous location of the older town had protected it against
enemies, but now there were no longer any foes to fear.
The remote mountain city was swiftly abandoned. Only
a few peasants stayed on there. For a while, as long as
the temple of Latobius still stood, occasional pilgrims
visited. Then the darkness of the age of tribal migrations
descended.

But once sacred, always sacred, even though the
religion changes. A pilgrim's church was built on the
mountain consecrated to Latobius, and the mountain itself was renamed Magdalensberg after the church. The
bronze statue from the temple of Latobius was found
there in 1502. For centuries thereafter the graves of Romans and Celts on the mountain were the goal of
treasure-seekers. Since 1948 archæologists have been ex-

cavating the ruins of the town with astonishing success.
But the name of the town that once covered the peak of
the mountain has so far not come to light.[2]

By the time Carthage sank into ruins, Rome had long
since become the most important city of the Mediterranean world—but it was far from being the most beautiful, the richest, or even the largest city. The ancient
Greek cities of Syracuse, Massilia, and Pergamon had
preserved enough of their onetime splendor to offer a far
more pleasurable prospect than the defensively strong

SYMBOLIC REPRESENTATION OF THE WAR GOD LATOBIUS.
(*from* Führer durch die Ausgrabungen und das Museum auf dem
Magdalensberg; *Klagenfurt, 1953*)

but old-fashioned, narrow, planlessly built City of Seven
Hills on the Tiber. Greco-Egyptian Alexandria, moreover,
was far larger, and in Italy itself Rome was surpassed by
Capua, in Campania.

Rome needed time to catch up with these ancient
centers of culture. It was reserved for the Roman emperors to make their city outwardly also the crown of the
known world.

Until the last century B.C. the Campanian town of

---

[2] Some attempts at identification by modern scholars may be briefly
noted. It is held that the city may, in spite of serious arguments to
the contrary, have been the Noreia where, in 113 B.C., Cimbrians and
Teutons defeated a Roman army. Or else it was originally called
Virunum and later gave this name to the new town in the plain.
(We are inclined to subscribe to this theory, communicated to us by
Professor Hedwig Kenner of Vienna.) Or, again, it may have borne
the double name of Noreia-Virunum, after a female and male divinity
of the Noricans.

Puteoli had received all the ships bringing cargo destined for Rome; compared to Puteoli, the river port on the mouth of the Tiber was of minor importance. At this river port, according to legend, the forefather of the Romans, Æneas, had landed after his flight from Troy. Ancus Marcius, the fourth king of Rome, was said to have destroyed the one city lying between Rome and the sea, to have seized the intervening forested area from the Etruscans, and to have founded a city in order to protect the mouth (*ostium*) of the Tiber and the salt works of the region. This city was named Ostia.

The story is pure legend; in fact the first Roman colony on the mouth of the Tiber was established around 335 B.C. But the herdsmen and farmers of Rome were proud to have reached the sea. When the first coins were struck in Rome, around this time, they bore the emblem of the bow of a ship. The new settlement of Ostia was far from being a city. As yet it was scarcely a trading center, but was primarily a military base, a primitive citadel, 625 feet long by 405 feet wide, with thick tufa walls over sixteen feet high. The building material was taken from the ruins of the Etruscan-Sabine town of Fidenæ.

Here, in the year 278 B.C., Carthaginian ships landed. At that time the Carthaginians were still Rome's allies in the struggle against Pyrrhus of Epirus. About sixty years later a fleet sent out by Hieron, the Tyrant of Syracuse, landed at Ostia to help the Romans against the Carthaginians under Hannibal. From Ostia, Roman warships and troop transports left for Spain and Taranto.

At the end of this century Ostia witnessed a unique spectacle: aboard a richly bedecked vessel, a goddess was brought to the town. The sufferings of the long war against Hannibal, and an assortment of evil omens, had prompted the Romans to consult the mysterious Sibylline books. They found that the enemy could be expelled from Italy only if the mother of the gods were brought to Rome from Asia Minor. Still perplexed, Roman envoys went to consult the famous oracle at Delphi, which instructed them to turn to King Attalus of Pergamon, the sole ruler of the East who was at that time friendly to Rome. Attalus gave the envoys a friendly reception and led them to the Phrygian-Galatian city of Pessinus in Asia Minor. This was the principal seat of the cult of Cybele, the great maternal divinity of the country. Here a curiously shaped meteoric stone was worshipped as the image of the mother of the gods which had fallen from heaven. The King gave this stone to the Roman envoys, and they brought it by ship to Ostia.

The vessel arrived at the port in 204 B.C. Meanwhile, a whole series of new omens had fed the anxieties of the Romans. Reflections in the air made it appear that there were two suns in the sky. There was a display of northern lights, and a comet appeared. Lightning struck the gates of two towns in Latium. Altogether, there was reason enough for an excited crowd to assemble in Ostia to greet the ship with the image of the goddess.

There was an impressive ceremony, more solemn than anything the little town had ever seen before. Publius Cornelius, a member of the prominent family of the Scipios, was declared worthy of conducting the goddess into the city. Along with him went all the noble ladies of Rome. Among these was the beautiful Claudia Quinta, a woman of the proudest lineage who did not have a very good reputation. A great hue and cry arose on her account. The vessel had come to a halt. The men tugged in vain at the ropes that were supposed to draw it upstream; the ship did not stir. It was a hot day in April; the Tiber was low, so that the keel of the heavily laden ship had struck on a sandbank in the river bed. Word rapidly went round that it was all Claudia's fault: she was not worthy of standing among the honorable matrons; the goddess was refusing to move any farther on her account! Thereupon the defamed woman stepped forth, bent her knee before the goddess, and addressed her: "Sublime Mother of the Gods, hear the plea of a woman who implores your protection. They call me unchaste. If you condemn me, I would as soon die. But if I am free of guilt, bear witness to it, O Chaste One, and follow my chaste hands." Whereupon she grasped the rope. The boat slid off the sandbank and followed her upstream to Rome.

This legend is recounted by the historian Livy, and retold by Ovid in poetry. It is no more nor less credible than innumerable other judgments of the gods. In any case, the day was the greatest the town of Ostia had seen since its foundation.

Obtaining an ample supply of grain was among the chief problems of Rome. Ostia was favorably situated for grain ships, especially for those coming from Sardinia. For this reason the importance of the little military colony steadily increased; gradually it became a city and, in 67 B.C., the principal base of the Roman fleet for its campaign against pirates.

As for so many cities, Ostia's great age came in the first century A.D., when the horrors of the long civil wars were forgotten, the rule of the emperors had been firmly established, and the Empire itself was far-flung and powerful. Rome herself had become a metropolis at last; Puteoli no longer sufficed as a port for Rome because the land

route between the two cities was too long. The old river
port on the Tiber was also no longer adequate. Emperor
Claudius found a way to remedy the situation.

On both ends the port at Ostia was made secure by
dikes and sea walls, and opposite the entrance a protective mole was erected, in spite of the considerable depth
of the water. In order to reinforce this mole, Claudius
sacrificed the huge vessel that had brought the great
obelisk from Egypt. The ship was filled with stone and

PORTRAIT ON COIN OF EMPEROR CLAUDIUS.

sunk along the mole. He also built, on strong pillars, a
tall lighthouse modeled after the famous Pharos of Alexandria, so that ships could find their way even at night.
Twelve years of tremendously difficult and expensive toil
were required before the harbor, proudly named Portus
Augusti, was ready. Claudius himself did not live to see
it completed.

Now Ostia could really flourish. Caligula had built an
aqueduct for the town; Claudius stationed a detachment
of guards and firemen there. A child who had watched
the building of the Claudian port might, as an old man
(A.D. 100–6), have seen new and vast improvements.
Trajan widened and deepened the canal connecting harbor and river (what is now the arm of the Tiber named

Fiumicino) and established, back of the previous basin, a second harbor hexagonal in shape and even safer and deeper than the first.

The new harbor, with the buildings that sprang up around it, did not, however, overshadow the already venerable city. Ostia remained the center of civil and religious life, and of trade and government. The city had a population of some forty-five thousand: Romans and other Italians, Egyptians, Sarmatians, Greeks, Jews, Arabs, Syrians, Gauls, Germans, Berbers, and Negroes—a medley of peoples possibly more complex than in Rome itself. Merchants, sailors, dock workers, slaves, and tourists of a dozen different races thronged the streets.

The religious life of the city was as variegated as the skin color and costumes of the populace. The Romans exhibited a tolerance in religion scarcely matched before or since. The center of the city had been systematically rebuilt and the forum linked with the Tiber by a broad avenue. There then arose on the northern side of the forum the largest temple in the city. It was dedicated to the sacred Capitoline trinity, Jupiter, Juno, and Minerva. Near the theater there stood, upon a common rectangular foundation of tufa, four temples: to Venus, Ceres (the goddess of grain, hence of special significance for Ostia), and the goddesses of Hope and Fortune. Right beside these were a temple to Jupiter and a nymphæum; not far away was a shrine to the Persian god of light, Mithras. The supreme authority in religious matters, however, was the priest of Vulcan, the god of fires and forges, for his cult was the oldest and most important in Ostia.

It was about sixteen miles from Rome to Ostia. The road followed the left bank of the Tiber, passing through areas of brush, woods, cultivated fields, and pastures. Near the city, tombs, monuments, and small mausoleums

lined the roadside. There were also the large vaults of
burial societies, with so many niches for funeral urns
that they were jokingly called "dovecots" (*columbaria*).
Of course there were also graves on the other roads leading to the city, running parallel to the main avenue;
there was even a special road for graves alone. But all
these cemeteries, for both religious and hygienic reasons,
were outside the city proper.

The eastern gate of the city, with its heavy piers of
tufa and the high vault of the archway, was a relic of
the republican period. In imperial times it was faced
with marble, columns were added, and it was finished off
with a splendid statue of Minerva Victoria, copy of a
Hellenistic work of art.

The square immediately beyond the gate at once suggested the special character of the city, and the main
avenue strengthened the impression. This broad, well-
paved street, about a mile in length, cut right across the
whole city and ran down to the sea. The dwellings that
lined it were of a very different character from those of
Pompeii, Herculaneum, or the other prosperous, domestic
cities of Campania. Here in Ostia the houses rose many
stories high; constructed of brick, they contained shops
on the ground floors and had many apartments for rent.
Almost every one of these apartments had its own entrance; the stairs ran down to the street or, more frequently, to courtyards or small gardens. The windows
were rectangular, and were often grouped in twos or
threes. Balconies were common on the upper stories; frequently these were galleries running the whole length of
a wall. The familiar atrium and the elegant peristyle
were rare; the houses of Ostia anticipated modern apartment buildings.

The city had large warehouses for grain, oil, spices,

paper, textiles—for all the commodities the imperial city needed, which came from every quarter of the Empire. But the citizens of Ostia were not content to be mere traders. Trading was profitable, and wealth bred the ambition to live as well as other Romans. The city had several baths; the Emperors Severus and Caracalla, at the beginning of the third century A.D., enlarged the theater built by Augustus until it had a capacity of twenty-seven hundred. The building housing the stage was faced with marble; the entrance was flanked by porticoes and shops; in front was a square paved with travertine, containing two fountains.

Back of the theater lay the most important and interesting square of the city. In its center, upon a high platform, stood a handsome temple, its façade adorned by two columns. All around the sides of the square ran a double loggia, paved with mosaic. The mosaic was at once a work of art and a directory and advertisement, for it gave the names of the owners of the shops on the square. Black stones on a white background spelled out the names of the cities that had official trade missions there. Alongside the names there would often be a picture, in mosaic, of the commodities dealt in, and some symbol of the foreign city—an amphora between two palms, for example, or elephants, or fish, or ships. Seventy cities were represented—famous ones like Gallic Narbo (present-day Narbonne), Sardinian Carales (now Cagliaria), Egyptian Alexandria, New Carthage; less well-known cities such as Sabrata (west of Tripoli); and many other cities obscure to us who know them only from scant mention in literary remains but no doubt well known to the Roman merchants.

The economic crisis in the Roman Empire during the fourth century A.D. did not fail to affect Ostia. But the citizens could live for a while on wealth acquired during the long era of peace. And dealers in food did well even in bad times. The officials in charge of assuring Rome's grain supply still made their residence in the city; moreover, in A.D. 309 Emperor Maxentius had established a mint at Ostia.

Unused warehouses were converted into baths. When new thermæ opened, however, the old ones decayed, and in two such crumbling buildings the young Christian community of Ostia established itself. Ostia's beach also provided the setting for the dialogue *Octavius,* one of the pearls of early Christian literature, in which the author, Minucius Felix, attempted to defend his fellow believers against the numerous charges that were leveled against them. During the persecutions the Ostian Christian community survived; it had its martyrs, and by A.D. 313 had elected its own bishop. In Ostia, too, Saint Monica, the mother of Saint Augustine, died. Augustine himself wrote some of the finest pages of his *Confessions* in Ostia. The old and the new religion continued to exist side by side. As late as A.D. 359—long after Christianity became a state religion under the Emperor Constantine—the prefect of Ostia performed the traditional sacrifices in the temple of the Dioscuri.

When Constantine transferred the capital of the Empire to the east and renamed Byzantium Constantinople after himself, he stripped Ostia of its rights as a municipality. Rome began to decline in importance, and with Rome, Ostia. Abandoned houses collapsed; the precious marble facing was removed from some of the temples; building blocks were carried off. Decay went so far that after a time the dead were buried in the abandoned thermæ and even in the deserted theater.

One of the most likable figures of declining antiquity,

Two eastern towers of the Ishtar Gate at Babylon.
Images of sacred beasts adorn the yard-thick walls.

PLATE XVII

Persepolis: a portion of the rui
the ancient capital of the Achæ
kings. The carved stone doorway
palace depicts Darius, with the
umbrella protecting him from the

Giant Assyrian sculpture of a
bull with the head of a man,
from the king's palace at Nineveh.

PLATE XVIII

The agora at the oasis city of Palmyra, once accounted among the greatest of the ancient world.

PLATE XIX

The limestone funeral bust of a wealthy Palmyrene wo
veiled and bedecked with jewels. The merchants of Pa
built gorgeously decorated sepulchers for themselves, plac
bust of each deceased person over the spot where he was

PLATE XX

The great colonnade and temple of Baal at Palmyra, with the oasis in the right background.

PLATE XXI

Roman bathtub of the first century B.C., found
at the Celtic city of Magdalensberg in Carinthia.

PLATE XXII

Typical house in the prosperous trading city of Ostia,
famed in legend as the "landing-place of Æneas."

PLATE XXIII

The "House of the Round Temple" at Ostia. These
brick houses often rose several stories high.

The public latrine, which was located near the great thermal baths of Ostia.

PLATE XXIV

a corner of the
r of the theater's
quares.

A mosaic floor in Ostia depicts one of the city's main activities: the transshipment of goods from vessel to vessel.

PLATE XXV

A view of the ruins of th
cient resort Baiæ, showin
impressive terraces and
This was the favorite spa
Roman upper class.

Another portion of the baths at Baiæ. Its recent excavation is regarded as
the most important archæological discovery of Roman antiquity since Pompeii.

PLATE XXVI

The Lady of Elche (ancient Ilici), the limestone sculpture
of an Iberian princess from the territory ruled by Tartessus.

PLATE XXVII

View of Tell-el Kheleifeh before the beginning of the excavations, directed by N Glueck, that uncovered the ruins of King Solomon's port city of Ezion-G

Foundations of the outer fortification walls of Ezion-Geber. Here were located King Solomon's great copper-smelting furnaces.

PLATE XXVIII

The brickyard at Ezion-Geber. The fortification walls—thirty feet high and twelve feet thick—were constructed of air-dried bricks.

Grave of the man who may have been the builder of Ezion-Geber's walls.

PLATE XXIX

One of the conical towers at Zimbabwe; the
jaws of kings were preserved as relics in these t

PLATE XXX

The temple and a section of the Valley of Ruins as seen from the Acropolis at Zimbabwe, the ancient royal city in the heart of the Rhodesian jungle.

PLATE XXXI

The parallel passages in the Elli
Temple at Zimbabwe. The tremenc
thick walls were laid without m

The Temple at Zimbabwe. The gaps in the city's walls were
once filled with round mud huts, thus making a continuous fortification to protect the gold mines of the Zimbabwe kings.

PLATE XXXII

the poet Claudius Rutilius Namatianus, passed through Ostia in A.D. 414. A Gaul, he had occupied a number of high offices in Rome and was now returning to his native land. In the poem he wrote describing his journey we can read all the grief of a loyal Roman who sees everything he holds dear going to ruin: the old religion, the Empire itself. A religion he does not understand is

CONSTANTINE THE GREAT, EMPEROR OF ROME,
AND FAUSTA, HIS WIFE.

driving out his gods, while the barbarian Goths are plundering Italy. His comment on Ostia sounds like an epitaph for the city: "The left arm of the Tiber estuary must be avoided; it is silted up and inaccessible. All that remains is the fame that Æneas once landed here."

By the time the reign of the Goths in Italy was over, Rome had become impoverished. The road from Rome to Ostia was neglected. Part of it had been swallowed up by woods. Scarcely a ship sailed up the Tiber. In the ruins of Ostia, malaria raged.

That was the end of a city that for eight centuries

had been more closely linked with the destinies of Rome than any other. The rest of the tale is briefly told. In the ninth century the ruins of Ostia supplied building materials for Gregoriopolis, the fortress city of Pope Gregory IV. Saracen warships passed by Ostia when they pillaged the coasts of Italy and threatened even Rome herself. The combined fleets of Rome, Amalfi, Gæta, and Naples won a notable victory over these Saracens in the "Battle of Ostia." (The scene was painted by Raphael, and the mural still adorns the Vatican.) Pope Leo IV (847–55) blessed his soldiers in the basilica at Ostia, which was named after the Ostian martyr Saint Aurea. Later Pisans and Genoese as well as Saracens pillaged the remains of the city. The Saracens continued to be a danger for many centuries, even after Cardinal Giuliana della Rovere, the later Pope Julius II, built in 1483 a splendid citadel for the city—one so powerful that in 1556 it resisted the Duke of Alba until the defenders ran out of ammunition. But, for all the fame of this fortress, Ostia had only 156 inhabitants in 1765.

Today, Ostia Antica, only a single express station from the coast, has been excavated. For the visitor it is a quieter and more sobering sight than the ruins of Pompeii or Herculaneum. For the luxury tourist there is a hotel, magnificently renovated in 1954, whose arrangements are entirely in the ancient Roman style. It calls itself Lo Sbarco di Enea—"the landing-place of Æneas." Thus, the ancient legend, with which Ostia began its history, remains its abiding glory.

"No coast in the world surpasses that of lovely Baiæ," said the poet Horace toward the end of the first century B.C. He was right; the eastern slope of the chain of hills cutting through the Misenian peninsula, and the narrow coastal strip at their foot, may well be counted one of the loveliest landscapes on earth. The climate is mild and sunny, the land well wooded and watered, and in addition there is the wonderful view over the peaceful blue gulf of Puteoli. On the other side of this bay is a mountain that the Greeks called Pausilypon, "Freer from Cares"; to this day it is known as Posilippo. Beyond, invisible from Baiæ, lies Naples. Vesuvius can be seen, and beyond it the gentle curve of the coast, lined with prosperous, pleasant towns, villas, and excellent harbors.

The Romans appreciated beauty, and were no less fond of comfort. Baiæ had both to offer. The region is endowed with many thermal springs on the hillsides, along the coast, and even in the sea itself. There are magnesial, saline, alkaline, sulfurous, and calcareous waters, some so hot they will cook food. To these waters came the patricians and *nouveaux riches* from Rome, seeking to cure rheumatism and sciatica, gout, stomach ulcers, headaches, even sprained limbs and broken bones.[3]

Baiæ was not only the pleasantest, but the most fashionable of health resorts. Here the rich had their villas built, and not only on the slopes and the beaches; they even built out into the sea itself, on expensive piles and dikes, and provided the houses with loggias, moles, and swimming pools. Building became a passion; the inhabitants of Baiæ manifested a mania for luxury and extravagance, together with a great delight in bathing and entertainment. Licinius Crassus might be the first to own a villa on this coast, with a hot spring out in the ocean in front of it, but the most beautiful house of all certainly belonged to Julius Cæsar. Like a fortress it rose upon the brow of a hill directly on the coast, commanding the

---

[3] Pliny the Elder: *Natural History* XXXI.5, 6. The line of Horace, above, is from Book I of the *Epistles*, 1.83.

beach and offering a wonderful view of the entire bay.

Anyone in the Rome of the republic's last days who possessed name, rank, and money settled down in Baiæ. Even the rough soldier Marius lived there; so did the general Pompey, the orators Cicero and Hortensius, the scholar Varro. Mark Antony had family property at Baiæ. While these great men sought rest and balm from the burdensome affairs of state, the aristocratic youth of Rome came for quite other reasons. For centuries Baiæ enjoyed the reputation of being the most delightful of summer resorts for the young. Here the fetters of convention were loosened, the supervision and criticism of elders were less strict. Along with fishing, hunting, riding, and swimming, the principal occupation of the young folk was love.

Older, more moralistic Romans were shocked. "Not only the unmarried are common property, but older women and many boys also become girls," as Varro put it.[4] When a beautiful woman went to Baiæ, her lover might well burn with jealousy.

"Are you still thinking of me a little, Cynthia, while you walk the road that Hercules trod along the coast of Baiæ? Does there remain in the remotest corner of your heart a small place for me, or has some rival with simulated love already distracted you from reading my poems? Rather go sailing in a small boat upon the Lucrine Lake than waste your time listening to the flattering maunderings of another while lying stretched out comfortably on the quiet beach—that is how unguarded girls habitually fall and forget their vows of fidelity! Do not think I do not know you; your good repute is well known; but in the place where you now are all flirtations are to be feared. . . . Please leave corrupt Baiæ as soon as pos-

[4] *Saturæ Menippeæ*, Fragment 44 in Buecheler's edition.

sible; this coast, which has always been the ruination
of respectable women, will part many more lovers in time
to come. Oh, if only the baths of Baiæ would crumble.
They are a crime against love." [5]

Even to stay in the sinful resort came to be considered
proof of licentious living. Such was the case for young

BATH SCENE, AFTER A CLASSICAL ORIGINAL (CALLED BY
WINCKELMANN "THE ADORNMENT OF VENUS AFTER THE BATH").

Marcus Cælius, and even for his defender, the great Cicero. Nevertheless, and in spite of some danger of malaria,
Cicero loved his country estate at Baiæ. Situated somewhat to the north of the bathing beach, in the direction
of Lake Averno, it possessed a resplendent portico and a
wooded park. Cicero called it "Academia" after Plato's
favorite resort in the grove of the hero Academus at

[5] Propertius I.11. An abridged prose version of the elegy is
given here.

Athens, and he called the philosophical work he composed there *Academica*. Soon after his death a cold spring burst forth in this park. Its waters were considered a cure for diseases of the eye.

The lovely region continued to attract the mighty. In the first century A.D. more and more of the beach at Baiæ was included within the imperial domains. Private citizens had to leave. Where formerly there had been only private villas, there now rose extensive complexes of magnificent buildings for residences, baths, and sports. The entire beach was built over; moles and artificial bays extended out into the sea. There were baths, yachting basins, pools for the cultivation of oysters and fish. Gardens and groves, porticoes, and orangeries extended up the slope to the ridge of the hills, along which ran an aqueduct conveying drinking-water.

Among the megalomaniac building projects of the Emperor Nero was one for a gigantic reservoir that was to receive all the spring waters between Miseno and Lake Averno. It was to be covered over and surrounded with colonnades. This plan was never fully carried out, but what Nero and his successors did create in Baiæ must have aroused amazement and admiration as well as envy and criticism. At the foot of the slope was a basin 120 feet long and nearly 100 feet wide, which gathered the water from the thermal springs. A broad arcaded promenade with several enclosed pavilions surrounded this splendid warm-water swimming pool. Sweat chambers were built into the hill, in order to utilize the hot vapors from the ground. On a terrace was a small theater, almost semicircular and with so sharp a slope that the visibility was perfect from any seat. In the *orchestra*, the level area within the semicircle, was a round pool of water. Here lovely girls performed as nymphs when a mythological play was being given; here ingenious erotic pantomimes were enacted. If music or a serious lecture was offered, the spectators could afterward refresh themselves in this pool. Only a low wall surrounded the theater area, so that there was an unbroken view of the swimming pool farther down the slope, the near-by thermæ, the moles and colonnades, the fish pools, and even the beach some six hundred feet below. There were loggias and terraces on sturdy arches, broad stairs, and gently inclined ramps. The imperial family could offer its guests everything that people trained in luxury and æsthetic appreciation could desire.

Yet this was only a segment of the great complex of buildings. There was another similar complex alongside, separated from this one only by steps and running from the beach up to the brow of the hill. The baths were divided into separate sections, featuring the various types of thermal springs and hot vapors. At the base of the hill all was connected by a promenade running along the beach, and at the top by a sun terrace and gallery pleasantly cool and breezy even in the heat of summer. Unity with variety was the special characteristic of Baiæ.

The terraces with their fine views were popular not only for the beauty of the landscape. Any of the several swimming pools might interest the spectator; bathing suits were unknown, and the thermæ, nymphæa, and social rooms served to shelter all the pleasures a sensual and untrammeled society could devise. There were few inhibitions.

Baths of every desired temperature, soft beds, fresh air, perfumes of Syria and Arabia, and the heavy fragrance of the near-by myrtle woods, dancers, actresses, song, theater, games, witty conversation, sailing along the coast, hunting, fishing, gay festivities with music and flowers—it was indeed a "sybaritic" life. And then there were the pleasures of the table! The cooks vied with one another to offer the rarest dishes and the choicest preparation—food designed to rouse jaded palates. And the wine! Finding the suitable drink for the occasion was both an art and a science, after which came the matter of serving it at the proper temperature.

The mountains of the vicinity bore the noblest grapes, for these flourish on volcanic soil. Circular Lake Averno was an extinct crater, and on Mount Gaurus, close by it, grew grapes that produced a wine of almost matchless quality, strong and viscous and all the more precious because there was not much of it. The lighter *ulbanus* from the district around Cumæ was considered drinkable after aging only five years, whereas the Sorrentine wine was not ready for twenty-five years. The *trebellicus* from Naples, on the other hand, was mild in spite of its heavy body and was held to be good for the stomach. These are just a few of the long list of Italian wines mentioned by the Greco-Egyptian grammarian Athenæus (probably third century A.D.); they are only the kinds grown in the immediate vicinity of Baiæ. But of course the emperor's guests were not restricted to these. The famous Cæcubian, Falernian, and Massician wines came from not too far away, and wines from the Greek islands were imported freely, no matter what the cost.

Anyone who belonged to the select society that assembled at Baiæ for the month-long festivals could well feel that he was sitting pretty as long as his money lasted or his host was cordial. At Baiæ some people took a last fling at life. Martial tells of a Roman lady who was as chaste as the old Sabine peasant women, even more strait-laced than her crusty husband. But when she came to this fabulous resort, bathed in Lakes Lucrino and

Averno, and finally enjoyed the thermæ of Baiæ, she caught fire. She took up with a stripling and abandoned her husband.

Those who lacked the money or the good connections to participate seethed with indignation over the licentious life of the resort. The philosopher Seneca refers to Baiæ in one of his letters as a dangerous temptation to vices of all kinds. In his case we may believe that he passed this judgment out of genuine contempt for the pleasures of the body. But as long as Roman high society had the money, it continued to seek the delights of lovely Baiæ. The Emperor Hadrian died on July 10, A.D. 138, in the imperial palace at Baiæ, which stood on the site of Julius Cæsar's former villa. The Emperor Alexander Severus, a cultivated man with a high appreciation of Cicero and Horace, created new splendid buildings and baths for his mother Mamæa. The economic troubles of the later imperial era resulted in a depopulation of the area, but it still attracted those with sufficient funds. As late as the sixth century Athalaric, the young king of the Goths, grandson of the great Theoderic, was aware of the curative properties of the thermal springs and recommended them to one of his dignitaries.

Or if it was not Athalaric himself who knew, then it was his Roman secretary of state, the learned Cassiodorus, who composed for his royal master the letter in question. It is moving to see in the midst of barbarian rule the persistence of the Roman style of life and the Roman spirit. Cassiodorus vividly describes the enjoyments that awaited a sick person at Baiæ: the beauty of nature there, the sunshine, the disporting of the fish, to look upon which was more pleasurable than fishing itself. Let delight once heal the soul, and the body would soon be well. "In short," he concluded the letter, "anyone who is

favored with a quiet stay at Baiæ imagines that he lives
in the treasure-house of Neptune. The baths are artistically furnished, but nature herself provides the best
cure. Despite Coral Sea and Indian Ocean—nothing surpasses the coast at Baiæ!" More than half a millennium
earlier Horace had expressed the same sentiment.

About a thousand years later, during the period of
Spanish rule, Viceroy Don Pedro di Toledo built a tremendous citadel on the site once occupied by the villa
of Julius Cæsar, the imperial palace, and the tomb of

A CYMBALISTRIA, FROM AN ANCIENT MARBLE.

Nero's mother, Agrippina. Among the vineyards of the
Misenian peninsula were still to be found fragments of
walls from the onetime magnificent edifices. The marble
facings and mosaics were carried off; peasants built their
houses inside the ruins and used the ancient walls as
stables and cellars. In quest of tufa and pozzuolana, the
slopes were dug up and venerable walls demolished.
Three gigantic domes amid the thickets of vegetation
were thought to have been ancient temples.

In 1941 excavation began at Baiæ, but the work had
to be broken off because of the war. Today, under the
direction of Amedeo Maiuri, the work has been pushed
forward under enormous difficulties and at great expense.
Enough of ancient Baiæ has been brought to light and

restored to evoke amazement and enthusiasm from even the most indifferent visitor. Several hundred yards wide and several stories high, the remains of the ancient baths are once more a striking sight.

On September 8, 1953, the soil yielded a work of art of rare beauty, an excellent copy of a masterpiece of the Greek classic period. It is the Sosandra Aphrodite, which has been ascribed to Calamis. A more than life-size, veiled statue of a woman, it presents a curious contrast to the wanton life characteristic of Baiæ when the sculpture was first set up. Ten days later another statue of a god came to light, this time a Mercury. We do not know what other treasures the ground still holds, or what may have been removed during past centuries.[6]

But, much as the archæologists have already done, Baiæ will never again be fully revealed. The foremost strip of coastline to a width of more than five hundred feet has been flooded by the sea; the coast has sunk in the course of centuries, as it did at neighboring Puteoli. If we sail out when the sea is calm, we may discern at the bottom the walls, columns, and arches of sunken buildings. The huge statue of Poseidon that now stands at the amphitheater of Pozzuoli was fished out of the water here.

Thus the curse of the jealous poet Propertius has been fulfilled; the baths of Baiæ have been destroyed as he wished. The pleasure houses have sunk beneath the sea. And should one seek sins to account for such a fate, he will have no trouble discovering that Baiæ was rife with them.

[6] The reader who wishes to know more about Baiæ must turn to the classical authors already cited, and to Amedeo Maiuri's essay "*Scoperta di Baia*," in the *Bolletino d'Arte del Ministero dell'Istruzione*, No. 4 (1951). Aside from this, to our knowledge nothing further has been published about the latest excavations.

VI

SILVER FROM ATLANTIS AND GOLD FROM OPHIR

BIBLICAL TARSHISH. FLOUNCED SKIRTS AND CASTA-
NETS. BARBARIANS DRINK WATER. THE PREHISTORIC
SEAFARERS. INVENTION OF THE BLOCKADE. THE
GOLDEN CITY OF THE SUN-WORSHIPPERS. WHERE
WAS OPHIR? KING SOLOMON AND THE QUEEN
OF SHEBA. RUINS "FROM THE ABYSSES OF TIME."
ANCIENT AFRICAN RUINS. THE MURDER OF THE SA-
CRED KING. SLAVE TRADE FOR HUMANITARIAN REA-
SONS. THE BEAD GAME IN THE JUNGLE. COSMIC
ORDER IN THE KINGDOM OF DRUMS. THE THUDDING
HEART OF BLACK AFRICA.

IN SOUTHERN Spain, about seventy-five miles northwest
of the Strait of Gibraltar, a river flows into the Atlantic
Ocean. The Arabs called it simply Wadi el Kabir, "the
Great River," from which its Spanish name of Guadalquivir derived. In antiquity it was known as the Bætis.
South of Seville, which lies on this river, begins a swampy
region called Las Marismas, which was once a large lake.
Still farther south, on an island in the river, there was
a rich commercial city some twenty-five hundred years
ago. Its beginnings probably go back to Neolithic times.

Shielded from the north wind by the mountains of the Sierra Morena, easily accessible from the sea, drawing an adequate food supply from the fertile Andalusian plain, and enriched by the silver mines at the headwaters of the river—such was Tartessus, mentioned several times in the Bible under the name of Tarshish.

For ships coming from the Mediterranean it was a day's sail from the Pillars of Heracles (Gibraltar) to the Phœnician island city of Gadir (present-day Cádiz). Gadir was the trading partner, rival, and occasionally foe of Tartessus. While it took a full day for a vessel to sail the thirty miles from Gadir to Tartessus, that was the end of the journey. Mediterranean ships scarcely ever sailed farther.

Water birds swarmed on the flat beach; splendid russet cattle and sheep with wool gleaming like gold pastured in the meadows of the river delta. On a peninsula extending far out to sea stood the building that for sailors was the landmark of the city: the citadel of King Geron. Beyond this peninsula lay the principal mouth of the river, seven and a half miles wide, and on the other shore rose the second landmark of the city, the venerable temple of the moon goddess. Vessels had to sail a good way up the broad estuary, for Tartessus was well protected. A narrower arm of the river flowed around the city to the north, making it an island.

The long voyage was always rewarded, for the shipowner as well as for the lowest oarsman. In Tartessus all found what they were seeking. Here bronze was alloyed out of native copper and tin that the Tartessians brought from England and Brittany. Hither came gold from Ireland and from other parts of Spain. But silver, above all, was cheap, for the Tartessians possessed rich mines in the mountains. Precious amber from the shores

of the Baltic was available in quantity. There was heavy
demand for Corinthian vases, olive oil from Africa, wine
from the Ægean islands, salves and perfumes from Syria.
Tartessus was the port of exchange between the Atlantic
coast and the Mediterranean world. Enormous sums of
money could be made in this city—and spent with equal
facility.

Not that food cost much. Grain, fruit, vegetables,
honey, beef, and mutton of the best quality were available at the markets in any amount. Fresh supplies were
constantly pouring into the city on boats and huge cargo

GREEK FIFTY-OARED SHIP.

rafts that were floated down the river. The sea supplied
ample fish.

But the sailors' taverns were dangerous. There sat the
seafarers of many lands: proud Greeks from the motherland and from all the Greek colonies around the shores
of the Mediterranean; shrewd Syrians, Phœnicians, and
Carthaginians; mustached, tow-haired men from the
misty northern seas who sailed down the coast in their
hide boats, and who were rumored to practice cannibal-
ism; cultivated Tyrsenians and rude, red-haired Celts;
belligerent, dark-haired Iberians and cheerful, loqua-
cious Tartessians.

The Tartessians, as a matter of fact, were also considered Tyrsenians. They had at one time emigrated

from their Lydian homeland in Asia Minor, had come to Sardinia, and from there had spread out over Italy; perhaps they were the same people who there were referred to as Etruscans.[1] Others had come here to Iberia, or, as the neighboring Carthaginians dubbed the country, the land of rabbits, I-shephan, out of which the Romans later formed the name Hispania. From gold-rich Lydia the Tyrsenians may have brought the knowledge of mining to this land of silver and copper. But these were old tales, half-guesses that may or may not have been believed. At any rate, the Tartessians thought of themselves as far superior to the native Iberians. They alone among the inhabitants of the Iberian peninsula had a script of their own, possessed written epics and ancient laws, and had a real kingdom.

The Tartessians were wont to tell proud tales of their rulers, especially of King Geron, whose citadel marked the entrance to the harbor. The Greeks knew him, referring to him as the giant Geryon whom their hero, Heracles, had overcome. Cattle like those Heracles had seized and brought back to Greece still grazed in enormous herds on the pastures around Tartessus. They were considered sacred animals, and were used in bullfights. The Tartessians would also boast of King Gargoris, who had invented beekeeping, and King Habis, the father of agriculture. They were as partial to telling tales about their heroes as the Phœnicians and Greeks. Perhaps they occasionally embroidered their legends with borrowed color. For when they described the childhood of King Habis and told of his being exposed and then found again, the Jews in the tavern might well laugh and cry out: "There's nothing new in that story; that is what happened to our Moses!" And when they went on to say

[1] The origins of the Etruscans are still obscure; see note on p. 299.

that a doe had suckled the abandoned infant Habis, the Etruscans could sneer: "Back home we have a small town named Rome whose founder, Romulus, was suckled by nothing less than a wolf!"

The Greeks, too, had their legendary heroes to boast of, and were wont also to tell tales of the great Persian king Cyrus, who was threatening the Greek cities of Asia Minor. That was one reason why so many Greeks came to Tartessus. King Arganthonius received them hospitably and offered them the privilege of settling wherever they liked in his kingdom. But they preferred not to. Some of the refugee Greeks moved to Corsica, some to their colony of Massilia (Marseille), which, like Tartessus, was situated at the mouth of a river and grew rich on the commerce of its prosperous hinterland. However, a Greek colony was also established within Tartessian domains, but not beyond the Pillars of Heracles. It was Mainake, near present-day Malaga.

The Tartessians themselves liked to talk of their bold voyages into the Misty Sea, while Carthaginians and Etruscans in the sailors' taverns would tell of their expeditions to the Isles of the Blessed far to the west. But, tempting as these islands were, the great ocean was a little frightening. It was said that the seafarer Euphemos was once driven far out to sea. There he found many lonely islands inhabited by wild men, red-haired and with tails like horses. When these men saw the ship, they stole silently up to it, lusting after the female prisoners on board. In their terror the sailors finally turned a barbarian woman over to the wild men, who then made sport with her in a highly peculiar fashion.[2]

---

[2] Pausanias tells the story in his *Periegesis* (I.23.7), a ten-volume traveler's account of Greece written around A.D. 175.

The Phœnicians had stories about their King Hiram of Tyre, who centuries ago had sent ships to these waters in behalf of his friend King Solomon. The first ships had brought back so much silver for Jerusalem that the metal ceased to be esteemed there. For these long voyages a special type of ship was developed, the so-called "Tarshish ships," and when these were so laden with silver that they could hold no more, the lead anchor was discarded and replaced by one of silver.[3]

The sailors in the taverns enjoyed such tales, but they were even more delighted when the slender, gracious Tartessian women danced. When they whirled their long flounced skirts, fluttered and clicked the castanets, the sailors went wild and beat time with their hands.[4] Such shows compensated them for the month-long voyages, especially when a belly-dancer appeared, or when men and women danced together, following the custom of the Bastetanic inhabitants of the mountain regions. At such times, as Strabo indicates, the garments of the Bastetani women consisted mostly of flowers.

Many things in rich Tartessus struck a familiar note for the Greeks. For even here, beyond the limits of the Mediterranean Sea, Greek cultural influences had operated. The city was not laid out higgledy-piggledy like Phœnician and all barbarian towns; it followed a clear plan, had broad streets intersecting at right angles, temples, colonnades, and statues. Even the gods were not altogether alien, for the Tartessians worshipped the sun as goddess of war, also the moon, the morning star, a goddess of the sea, and the powers of the underworld—

[3] Narrated by Diodorus in his *Libraries* (V.35.4), a first-century B.C. universal history spiced with anecdotes and curiosa.

[4] Martial (VI.71) and Juvenal (IX.161 f.) indicate that similar responses were the rule in Roman times.

which must have seemed quite reasonable to the Greeks, since the entrance to the underworld was surely situated here in the extreme west, and the word Tartessus always reminded them of Tartarus, the realm of the shades. The hospitality of the Tartessians and their reverence for the aged must also have appealed strongly to the Greeks.

Other characteristics struck them as strange and even repulsive, especially when they left the pleasant city and came into closer contact with neighboring peoples, who were only partly under Tartessian rule. These others were hospitable also, but the Lusitanians, who inhabited the mountains to the north, killed prisoners of war and thought to foretell the future from the twitching of the victims in their death agony. They struck off the right hands of other prisoners in order to offer these hands to the gods. Of course such people were outright barbarians, sleeping on the floor, knowing only a single type of food, drinking water, and washing in cold water.[5]

How old Tartessus is can scarcely even be estimated. In all probability the settlement as a trading center between the North Sea and the Mediterranean goes back to the age of the prehistoric seafarers whose culture has been called the *megalithic,* after the great stone blocks they used for their tombs.[6]

[5] Strabo III.3.7, and 3.6. Compare Diodorus V.31, where similar stories are told about the Celts. The legend, found in Justinus XLIV.4, that Tartessian King Gargoris committed incest with his daughter may indicate that sibling marriage existed among the Tartessians—that is to say, common possession of all women within the family. Strabo (IV.6.4) and Cæsar (*Gallic War* V.14) report similar customs among the native population of Brittany, which was related to the Iberians. Strabo (XVI.4.25) also mentions this in connection with Arabia. Compare the discussion in the following section on brother-sister marriages among the Manamatapa.

[6] Adolf Schulten, who has made enormous contributions to the knowledge of Tartessus, speaks simply of "Pre-Tartessians." He thinks this first (megalithic) civilization of western Europe must have come from the East. Other scholars incline to see the origin of megalithic civilization in the Atlas region. As yet, no really definite conclusion can be

At any rate, the city endured for more than a thousand years, with an Iberian-Ligurian original population, mingled with megalithic, Celtic, and Tyrsenian peoples. For a time it was under Phœnician rule; after the downfall of the power of Tyre (568 B.C.) it became independ-

HORSE KNEELING. AS A SUBSTITUTE FOR THE USE OF STIRRUPS, PARTICULARLY IN THE GREEK COLONIES IN SPAIN, HORSES WERE TAUGHT TO KNEEL AT A COMMAND WHEN THEIR RIDERS WISHED TO MOUNT THEM. FROM A LAMP FOUND AT HERCULANEUM.

ent once more. Always it was wealthy and influential. The Greeks, especially the enterprising Hellenes of Chalcis and Phocæa, were fond of visiting the city. "Now the Phocæans were the first of the Greeks who performed long voyages, and it was they who made the Greeks

drawn. At most we can say that the megalithic culture was not Indo-European, as was formerly assumed. See other remarks on this seafaring people, who have been the subjects of very little research as yet, in our chapter on Atlantis.

acquainted with the Adriatic and with Tyrrhenia, with Iberia and the city of Tartessus," Herodotus recounts. "On their arrival at Tartessus the king of the country, whose name was Arganthonius, took a liking to them. This monarch reigned over the Tartessians for eighty years, and lived to be 120 years old. He regarded the Phocæans with so much favor as, at first, to beg them to quit Ionia and settle in whatever part of his country they liked. Afterwards, finding that he would not prevail upon them to agree to this, and hearing that the Mede was growing great in their neighborhood, he gave them money to build a wall about their town." [7]

But in the long run, so generous, hospitable, cultivated, and unaggressive a city could not enjoy its wealth untroubled, especially when businesslike and greedy rivals like the Carthaginians were at the door. At first the Carthaginians closed the Strait of Gibraltar to the Greeks who wished to sail to Tartessus. The Greeks adopted the recourse of sailing to Mainake on the southeastern coast of Spain, and from there sending caravans over the mountains to Tartessus.

After the Phœnicians of Tyre lost control of the sea, the Phœnicians of Corsica became masters of the Mediterranean, or at least of the western part of the Mediterranean. However, they did not long hold this position. In 535 B.C. a naval battle was fought just off the Corsican town of Alalia between the Greeks and the united Carthaginian-Etruscan fleet. The Greeks won, but at too heavy a cost. Their losses were so great that they had to abandon Corsica to the Etruscans and Sardinia to the Carthaginians. Their voyages to Spain ceased. Their colony Mainake also fell into the hands of the Carthaginians, who imposed a blockade along the entire

[7] Herodotus I.163 (George Rawlinson translation).

coast. Every foreign ship that ventured beyond Sardinia in the direction of Gibraltar was sunk at sight.

This blockade acted as a bronze curtain; the Mediterranean world was ignorant of what went on behind it. It is possible that Tartessus was destroyed by the Carthaginians, but we cannot say when this may have happened. Around 511 B.C., Sybaris was destroyed;[8] in 494, Miletus was conquered by the Persians. Somewhere in this period the third rich commercial city probably succumbed to the military might and the blockade of a superior enemy.

Of Tartessus nothing more was heard. Aristophanes once recalls the delectable eels of Tartessus, and a few historians mention the city, but only as a faraway tale. Other historians confused Tartessus with near-by Phœnician Gadir; still others denied that any such city had existed. In Andalusia, however, many traces of the world of the Tartessians have survived—in the costumes, the lively temperament, and the lithe physiques of the inhabitants. But Tartessus itself vanished utterly, as have few of the great cities of antiquity. When Adolf Schulten in 1922 tracked down the forgotten city, discovered its site, and dug there, he found almost nothing; the groundwater level was too high for successful excavation. In Roman times the inhabitants of a fishing village had used stone from the ruins of Tartessus for their houses. A copper ring with a Greek inscription from the sixth or seventh century B.C. is so far the only tangible witness we have to the great voyages of the Greeks from Tartessus to Asia Minor.

The gates to the underworld opened in the northern Adriatic. In the area where lovely Baiæ was later to be-

[8] See pp. 261–70.

come the Romans' foremost bathing resort, rising vapors from thermal springs had inspired the early Greeks to myths of a battle of giants on the Phlegræan Plain. It was a well-known fact that west of Tartessus, beyond the Pillars of Heracles, the world came to an end in a dense fog bank.

Step by step, sea captains and merchants widened their knowledge of the earth's geography. They saw, marveled, and fetched up myths to rationalize what they had seen. But at bottom it was the steadily growing demand for metals which impelled men to sail their ships out of the ore-poor Mediterranean area to the western ports of the Iberian peninsula, to the Tin Islands in the foggy northwest, and to the south also, where it was hot, where the sun hovered directly overhead and the earth yielded gold.

From the west came ships with silver anchors, heavily laden with the metal that gleamed white as the foam of waves. But from the south came the ships with gold and with black men on whose skins precious ornaments glittered. The watery waste to the west could not, at that time, be explained in any other way than by myths. Africa, however—which Herodotus calls Libya—was "undoubtedly surrounded by the sea on all sides," for Pharaoh Necos had sent out a Phœnician ship to circumnavigate Africa. Moreover, Sataspes, a nephew of Xerxes, had escaped a death sentence by sailing along the coast far to the south until he saw that the land turned eastward. Obviously the country of gold in the heart of the hot continent could not be far away.

The gleam of the noble metal and its apparent nearness lured men for centuries, for millennia. Two thousand years after Herodotus, who personally traveled the Nile as far as Assuan and Elephantine Island, the first Europeans reached the coast of the gold country and entered the port of Sofala, which had for ages been exporting gold. Until then the two great coastal civilizations of the Old World, the Mediterranean and the Indian Ocean, had remained almost independent of each other. On the Indian Ocean there had early developed a vigorous commerce between Mesopotamia, Arabia, the eastern coast of Africa, the Sunda islands, eastern Asia, and the Philippines. Merchants from the north—perhaps Egyptians or Phœnicians—and merchants from the East—Persians, Malays, and Chinese—met in the mysterious gold country of what is now Rhodesia, a land whose cyclopean buildings are bare of inscriptions. Scattered throughout the Rhodesian jungle are two or three hundred ruins, each of which presents us with new riddles.

In the heart of this region lie the most imposing of all the ruins in Africa, the temples and fortifications of Zimbabwe, a jungle city which was perhaps inhabited only by kings and their retinue, and which today is superstitiously avoided by the natives. Only in relatively recent times has any real information about Zimbabwe been amassed.

The sight of these ruins is calculated to give rise to the most fantastic speculations. Out of a jagged hollow overgrown with low shrubbery rises a hill bearing a partly destroyed ring wall. On the hill itself clusters what at first appears to be an utter confusion of ruins of various heights. The tremendous exterior wall, more than twelve feet thick and boldly built close to the edge of a rocky chasm, surrounds the so-called Acropolis of Zimbabwe.

At the foot of the Acropolis hill a dry valley extends from west to east, separating the Acropolis from a second mound on which stands the most celebrated building of these ruins, the Elliptical Temple. Between this temple

and the Acropolis lie several strips of smaller ruins which
have been called the Valley Ruins. The three groups obviously form a unity. They are surrounded by a number
of other, more scattered groups of ruins.

Even today the impression is awesome. The Acropolis
towers majestically above the Valley Ruins, its huge monoliths rising irregularly and mysteriously into the sky.
How could these blocks of granite, some weighing thousands of tons, have been transported up the cliffs? Modern engineering would have difficulty solving some of the
transportation problems involved.

The oldest description we have of the Elliptical Temple is by the Portuguese chronicler De Goes (born in
1501). It is, however, by no means certain that he himself saw the building; he may have based his account on
the stories of Arab merchants. "In the heart of the country," wrote De Goes, "lies a fortress built of huge, heavy
stones. It is a strange, close-joined building which looks
the same inside as outside, since the stones are fitted together without mortar and are not painted. In the stone
above the entrance is a carved inscription so old that no
one knows how to read it. Round about lie scattered other
forts in which the king's subordinates live. As far as we
can judge, all these forts were erected for the protection
of the gold mines. . . . The King of Benamatapa keeps
a rich court, and all who serve him must do so on bended
knee. . . ."

The inscription De Goes mentions has since turned
out to be a ribbon relief of ornamentation which casual
observers (presumably Arabic or Persian) could have
taken for symbols of some foreign script; the ornament
can still be seen above the eastern gate of the wall.

There is a similar detailed description by the Portuguese scholar De Barros (1496–1570), who had, as treas-

AFRICA: GOLD FROM OPHIR

urer for the colonies, access to the journals, letters, and
reports of the early explorers. He flatly characterizes the
towering buildings as the work of the Devil, "since in
view of their merely human strength and their ignorance,
it is not possible that these buildings could have been
built by the Blacks." As we have seen, this idea quite
naturally occurred to men of De Barros's time; the priests
with Pizarro who first saw the Inca citadels on high
cliffs, or the monoliths of Tiahuanaco, made the same
comment.

"In the opinion of the Arab who has seen the buildings, they are very ancient and were erected there in
order to guard the mines, which are also very ancient
and from which no gold has been taken for a very long
time, because of the upheavals of warfare." De Barros
then proceeds to put forward a guess that for centuries,
until quite recent times, led numerous scholars on a false
trail: the guess that even if these buildings had not been
the work of devils, they certainly could not have been
erected by the native Negroes. They must represent, De
Barros assumed, the "Agisymba" of Ptolemy.[9] Since De
Barros wrote the Negro word *Zimbabwe* as *Simbaoe*, the
similarity to Ptolemy's Agisymba must have seemed con-
firmation of his theory.

The Portuguese colonial empire soon lost its original
vigor, and Portuguese travelers ceased to explore. Meanwhile, the buildings at Zimbabwe, which had probably
never been roofed over, disintegrated with extraordinary
swiftness. More than three centuries after the death of
De Barros an American hunter and trader named Adam

---

[9] At the beginning of the second century A.D. a Roman named Julius
Maternus traveled in the interior of Africa. After a journey of four
months he reached the district of Agisymba. The Greek geographer
Ptolemy included this district in his description of the world, but we
are unable to fix its location.

Renders came to the vicinity. The year was 1868, and interest in African ruins was still relatively meager. Moreover, the ruins were so overgrown by vegetation that Adam Renders was unable to form any conception of their size and importance. In September 1871 a German named Karl Mauch visited the ruins, but, on account of ill-health and inadequate funds, was unable to accomplish much more than Renders. He was, however, the first to recognize that the problem was ethnological as well as archæological, and he suggested some probable religious rites that, he believed, had been both state religion and way of life for the forgotten builders.

Since Mauch lacked the knowledge to interpret correctly the fragmentary information he received from an old priest, he deduced that what the natives practiced was some debased forms of Semitic customs. Zimbabwe, he reasoned, had been the residence of the Queen of Sheba, who had brought back from her visit to King Solomon a knowledge of Israelite religious practices, as well as a number of Phœnician architects. Mauch's thesis had a plausible sound, since it answered the two principal questions: was there a connection between the ruins and the ancient gold mines, and how had such mighty stone structures come into existence amid a people whose architecture was limited to conical huts?

The motif of the ribbon relief, which has since been recognized as pure ornament, closely resembles certain figures found on Phœnician coins. A similar figure was also common on Egyptian buildings. As the ancient Egyptian hieroglyph for *water,* it occurs in the account inscribed on the walls of the temple of Der-el Bahri which deals with an expedition for gold sent out by Queen Hatshepsut (1518–1481 B.C.). Moreover, one of the staples of adventure literature was the story of an

African gold city. The popular novels of H. Rider Haggard, *King Solomon's Mines* and *She,* are set partly in Zimbabwe, and millions of credulous readers swallowed their fictions along with their facts. These sundry factors conspired to lead scholars in this particular direction. They began assembling all the evidence suggesting that the ruins of Zimbabwe represented the legendary golden land of Ophir, the country of the Queen of Sheba and the source of King Solomon's gold.

It was soon learned that the coast near Cape Guardafui had been noted for the export of ivory, gold, and spices many centuries before Christ. Commerce across the Indian Ocean may already have begun eighteen hundred years before Christ, when the seafaring tribes of the Yoktans conquered Yemen. Why should not Queen Hatshepsut's expedition actually have gone to the very city of Sofala, which for centuries had been the most important export harbor for gold on the southeast coast of Africa?

Bible societies took a keen interest in this question. The nineteenth century, with its stress on physical science, had robbed the Sacred Book of much of its reputation for reliability. Here was an unexpected opportunity to uphold the historical truth of a number of statements in the Bible which had provided many generations with food for the imagination.

Fundamentalist scholars interpreted Karl Mauch's Ophir theory as follows. King Solomon had built the splendid temple of which his father, David, had dreamed, and a no less magnificent palace, with the aid of Hiram, the King of Tyre, who "had furnished Solomon with cedar trees and with fir trees, and with gold, according to all his desire." In payment "King Solomon gave Hiram twenty cities in the land of Galilee. And Hiram came out from Tyre to see the cities which Solomon had given him; and they pleased him not." Solomon therefore had to look around for fresh sources of gold to pay his debt. He had built good roads and canals in Palestine and was profiting by the transit traffic between Egypt and Syria (horses and iron war chariots were the principal goods traded), but his expenses had been great. In addition, Solomon possessed a port on the Red Sea. This must have been of great interest to Hiram, for from Tyre he could trade only in the Mediterranean—while far higher profits were to be gained in the East. "And King Solomon made a navy of ships in Ezion-geber, which is beside Eloth, on the shore of the Red Sea, in the land of Edom. And Hiram sent in the navy his servants, shipmen that had knowledge of the sea, with the servants of Solomon. And they came to Ophir, and fetched from thence gold, four hundred and twenty talents, and brought it to King Solomon." Such is the account in the Old Testament (I Kings ix, 26–8). No more is known about Ophir. Four hundred and twenty, or, according to another passage (II Chron. viii, 18), four hundred and fifty talents (*kikkar* in the Hebrew text) of gold is almost twenty tons. A country that could deliver so much gold would naturally attract men for centuries. Even Columbus, in sailing westward, hoped to encounter this land of gold, and men have never ceased to speculate upon the location of Ophir.

At one time the idea arose that the Ophir of the Bible may have been what is now called Peru. But that is out of the question; no merchant fleet sailed so far in the tenth century B.C. The Solomon Islands, north of Australia, have also been suggested. But that is pure nonsense; all these have in common with King Solomon is the name, by which they were first called in 1568. Moreover, there is no gold in the Solomon Islands. It is also impossible to equate Ophir with the Spanish port of Tartessus, as a modern church lexicon does; no one who wanted to sail from Palestine to Spain would build his ships on the Red Sea!

Flavius Josephus, the great Jewish historian of the first century A.D., guessed that Ophir was located in Farther India. But India was more interested in importing than in exporting gold.

The search for the famous land of gold has therefore been restricted fundamentally to southern Arabia and the African coast. Arabia, however, is also out of the question. If Ophir had been situated there, as some scholars still maintain, Solomon would not have needed the assistance of the King of Tyre; he would simply have used the ancient caravan routes of the Arabian peninsula.

But along the Blue Nile there is gold. The Egyptians obtained gold there as early as the reign of Amenophis II (around 1450 B.C.). The Romans, too, knew of this source. Moreover, along the Blue Nile there are native Jews whose rites are so antiquated that they may well have been settled there for almost three thousand years. One is tempted to assume that they are the descendants of the very Hebrews who worked the gold mines for Solomon. Against this theory, of course, is the argument that the Egyptians would scarcely have permitted other peoples to exploit their mines so successfully for so many years. For the same reason it seems unlikely that Solomon's and Hiram's fleet should have sailed to Farther India to mine gold there—quite aside from the consideration that some experience in gold-mining would have been necessary to obtain so high a yield.

In 1938, Nelson Glueck began archæological work in

Transjordania. He continued his excavations systematically, year after year, until 1943, all the way from the
Red Sea to the Syrian coast. Many hundreds of formerly
inhabited places, some known and some entirely new,
were examined and their age determined by finds of
potsherds. The most important fruits of these labors
came to light in Tell-el Kheleifeh: copper-smelting furnaces dating from the tenth century B.C.—the age of
King Solomon!

These finds added a hitherto unknown fact to the economic history of Palestine. But more than that, they
supply the missing link in the mystery of the trade with
Ophir. Tell-el Kheleifeh is the modern name of the ancient city of Ezion-Geber, from which Kings Solomon
and Hiram sent out their expedition. Moreover, excavations show the existence of a carefully built harbor and
the remains of a city that had been built swiftly and according to a definite plan in the desert. It covered some
2.7 square miles, was protected by walls of air-dried
bricks—the usual building material of the period—thirty
feet high and up to twelve feet thick. Solomon had set
up smelting furnaces in this city in order to exploit the
copper ores found in the southern part of his country.

Smaller furnaces for smelting iron had been discovered
shortly before by Flinders Petrie in Tell Hemmeh (probably the Biblical Gerar). But we know of no other ancient
smelting furnaces even remotely comparable with those
of Ezion-Geber. The walls of the firebox were pierced by
two rows of wide tubes, about four feet above the ground.
The upper tubes converged in a flue that ran along the
walls on the inside; the lower tubes led through the walls
into the open air. The furnaces were situated in places
where the north wind blew strongest; with suitable fuel,

they could be brought to intense heat. The precise technique for reducing copper ore in them has, however, not yet been solved by the specialists.

The heat of the fire in the smelting furnaces had thoroughly "baked" the air-dried bricks of the walls, and the vapors from the copper had tinted them green. Large ceramic forms have also been found. But where did King Solomon's Hebrews, a people of peasants and shepherds, acquire such astonishing technical knowledge? The probability is that Hiram of Tyre again came to Solomon's aid, out of old friendship and because of the strategic and commercial importance of this base on the Red Sea. From their settlements in Spain and Sardinia the Phœnicians were experienced in metallurgy.

Perhaps the celebrated Queen of Sheba did not come to visit Solomon purely by chance. Perhaps his successes in the export business lured her. She may well have come in order to establish commercial relations and not only, as the Bible puts it, "to prove [i.e., to test] him with hard questions." As a matter of fact, the tenth chapter of the first book of Kings also states: "And she came to Jerusalem with a very great train, with camels that bare spices, and very much gold, and precious stones. . . . And she gave the king an hundred and twenty talents of gold, and of spices very great store, and precious stones. . . . And King Solomon gave unto the Queen of Sheba all her desire, whatsoever she asked, beside that which Solomon gave her of his royal bounty. So she turned and went to her own country, she and her servants."

What Solomon gave the Queen of Sheba "of his royal bounty" was personal presents for the guest. But everything else, "all her desire, whatsoever she asked," must have been export goods, and her hundred and twenty talents of gold were simply the purchase price. Thus the

Bible confirms, though not expressly, the theory suggested by the archæological finds: that the Phœnician-Hebrew fleet shipped copper from Ezion-Geber and received in return the gold of Ophir.

Such a valuable commodity as copper would certainly not have been sent out at random to remote and unknown lands. Therefore Ophir must have been located somewhere fairly near to the Red Sea. Because, as we have seen, the Arabian peninsula may be dismissed as a possibility, and because India was too remote, East Africa remains the probable location of the fabled city.

In engaging in such trade Solomon was cutting into the Egyptian commercial monopoly in those regions. Inevitably he became involved in dangerous antagonisms with Egypt. After the death of Solomon the first pharaoh of the XXII dynasty (as there were no vowels in the Egyptian script, his name is given variously as Sheshonk, Shoshenk, Shishak, Susakim) advanced triumphantly against Israel as far as Jerusalem. In the course of his campaign he destroyed the port on the Red Sea which had been such a thorn in his side. The excavations at Ezion-Geber provided evidence of this destruction.

The profits from these trading expeditions had been enormous. In spite of the cost of building the Temple and repaying his debt to Hiram, Solomon's riches became proverbial. "All King Solomon's drinking vessels were of gold, and all the vessels of the house of the forest of Lebanon were of pure gold; none were of silver: it was nothing accounted of in the days of Solomon."

That first success must have encouraged the Hebrews to undertake similar expeditions even after the death of King Solomon and the destruction of Ezion-Geber—all the more so if Ophir were really in East Africa and therefore relatively close to Palestine for seafarers. This assumption, too, is confirmed by the excavations. In Ezion-Geber five strata have been found, showing habitation at different periods. The later smelting furnaces, however, were not nearly so well built as those of the age of Solomon. Solomon's dominions had been divided into the kingdoms of Israel and Judah, and it was probably King Jehoshaphat of Judah who rebuilt Ezion-Geber a hundred years after Solomon's death. He also restored the smelting furnaces in order to provide exportable copper for a new merchant fleet. "Jehoshaphat made ships of Tarshish to go to Ophir for gold: but they went not; for the ships were broken at Ezion-Geber." [1] Apparently a storm shattered the fleet while it was still in port. King Ahaziah of Israel proposed sending out a new expedition in which he would share. But Jehoshaphat refused. The subsequent period of wars and the extension of Assyrian power crippled Israel's foreign trade. The once profitable sea route was forgotten, and the city of Ophir was visited no longer.

The publication of Karl Mauch's theories came at a time when scientists everywhere were seeking the "cradle of mankind," or at least the "missing link between ape and man." America was considered a "historyless" continent, for the various theories about Atlantis and Tiahuanaco were altogether untenable. Asia and its appendage Europe had virtually been dropped from discussion. For a time Africa became the center of attention. For did not the heart of Africa and the almost unknown Zambezi and Limpopo rivers disclose ruins, an ancient culture, testimony to a long history?

A slew of books came out, the work of pseudo-archæologists overwhelmed by the impressiveness of the ruins and the mystery of the Dark Continent. The earlier the

[1] I Kings xxii, 48.

date they placed upon these ruins, the greater their reputation as scholars. A few thousand years more or less did not matter to them. If they discovered a stone ornament in the form of an oxhead, that sufficed to prove contact with ancient Mycenæan religion. Even serious scientists were deluded by the mighty ruins of Zimbabwe. The terraced arrangement reminded Leo Frobenius of Dravidian buildings. Hardly anyone thought it possible that the tribes scattered about this area, living in mud huts and superstitiously avoiding the city, could themselves have built Zimbabwe.

Amid the romantic ecstasies of all those who thought they had discovered a new ancient civilization, or fresh proof of the radial force of the Mediterranean area, David Randall-MacIver's book *Medieval Rhodesia* (1906) exploded like a shell. MacIver coolly stated that in none of the ruins could he find any archæological evidence that the buildings were more than a thousand years old.

His assertion was passionately contested; educated readers refused to accept it. They had just learned to adjust to the idea that man had not been created but had evolved out of some slack-jawed creature with jutting brow and dangling arms—and now MacIver was trying to tell them that those mysterious gigantic structures had not been erected by whites, but in all probability by the native Negroes. For a short while it was contended that the Arabs had built Zimbabwe; farther north and much closer to the coast Arab stone buildings had been found. But Portuguese records show no relationship between Zimbabwe and the Arabs. Moreover, without firearms the Arabs held no military superiority over the natives. They were tolerated as traders, but their settlements were limited to a few coastal areas; they never could have established themselves deep in the interior securely enough to erect such enormous buildings.

The men who had had the closest contact with the Negroes, who knew their lives most intimately, now spoke up. These were the missionaries. Father Paul Schebesta, an Austrian missionary, had spent seven years in the Zambezi region before he went to Lisbon to study the source material on the Portuguese colonial history of this part of Africa. He soon realized that the reports of early adventurers must be as bewildering to the historian and archæologist as the results of the excavations themselves. A meaningful arrangement of all the available information was impossible without the aid of ethnology. That is, everything that was known about the native tribes who lived between the Zambezi and the Limpopo had to be examined. Once that was done, it became evident that scholars had gone astray for decades—and for centuries, if the work of the early Portuguese was counted—in trying to explain the Zimbabwe civilization as the creation of non-Africans.

In the first place, it developed that Karl Mauch's misleading information was derived not from the traditions of the Bantus native to the region, but from the Lemba tribe. These Lembas are a highly interesting, almost purely Semitic group sprinkled among the Bantu tribes. They live as traders and miners, practice an astonishing number of Semitic customs, and are frequently considered to be related to the Jews and Phœnicians. One of the factors that had confused Karl Mauch was the circumstance that the Lembas do not speak a language of their own; they have adopted the dialects of their host peoples, and consequently could easily be confounded with these.

At the same time, more and more ruins were discovered

—stone structures scattered far and wide over the Rhodesian plain. When, in time, the number rose to nearly three hundred, all of them roofless and of similar construction, one of the principal arguments of the adherents of the Phœnician theory was upset. For they had pointed out that if native tribes had built the stone houses or citadels, there should be more such structures besides those at Zimbabwe. Now it was clear that there were such. Three hundred ruins scattered over such a vast, trackless area in the interior of the continent could very well be the remains of a vanished kingdom but scarcely the offshoots of a Phœnician colony. Zimbabwe had to be recognized as a royal residence, or at least as the center of a cult. Moreover, virtually all the Portuguese sources available in manuscript spoke of a large native kingdom called Manamatapa which covered thousands of square miles between Rhodesia, the Zambezi River, and the Indian Ocean.

The Kingdom of Dar For had, of course, been heard of. It was said to have sent caravans totaling five thousand camels as far as Timbuktu or the coast of the Mediterranean. But since the Negroes had proved to be so helpless in the face of the white colonial masters, these tales of a great ancient kingdom had been generally considered pure legend. As it turned out, the legends, the oral traditions of the tribes of Africa, provided the richest source of information on the vanished kingdoms.

In his introduction to the minstrel tales of the Swahili, Leo Frobenius says: "On that shore the ruins of the palace of King Monsol tower up—wretched columns of clay, but nevertheless like fingers raised accusingly at Fate. On this spot are the deep trenches from which the building materials for a city were taken. This city was leveled to the ground in the fifteenth century. On this hill died the last warrior of the Kingdom of Ghana, when the capital of that kingdom still lay in the north."

There were many kingdoms in Africa. We might mention the old Haussa city of Saria, which Queen Amina surrounded with clay walls five hundred years ago. She was the queen who traveled through her realm choosing a lover in each village and having him killed when she departed. Then there was the kingdom of Lake Chad,

NEGROES FLEEING FROM PHARAOH'S SOLDIERS.

which was founded by Saif, a contemporary of Charlemagne; and the "millennial kingdom" of the Nupe, which collapsed only at the beginning of the twentieth century. El Bekri, an Arab traveler of the eleventh century, tells marvelous tales of the great kingdom farther to the west, around the long-since-decayed royal residence of Ghana, which had been founded about A.D. 300 by light-skinned tribes between Nigeria and Senegal. It was said to be matchless in wealth and barbaric splendor. This kingdom passed into the far more powerful realm that Mansa Musa had won by conquest in the course of many campaigns. Our information on these kingdoms, long unknown to European historians, is derived from Arab merchants and travelers.

Ibn Battuta (1304–1377) was amazed by the matriarchal privileges and the great freedom vouchsafed the tall and often beautiful womenfolk of these native tribes. He felt less admiration for their cuisine; they ate a great deal of dog meat and even carrion. Nor did Ibn Battuta approve of the way the young women and female slaves went about naked.

El Bekri's description of Ghana is marked by fewer prejudices and a more scholarly attitude. He describes the vanished capital as having lain between the present-day villages of Ualata, Nema, and Bassikunu, at a spot equally accessible to caravans from the Berber country and to traders from the valleys of central Nigeria and Senegal. The city had two separate quarters, one inhabited by Mohammedans, who had no less than twelve mosques there, and the other being a kind of government quarter with palaces and dwelling-houses for government officials.

At its height the kingdom of Ghana is said to have mustered an army of no less than two hundred thousand warriors, including forty thousand archers. It is, however, difficult for modern scholars to obtain a clear view of these kingdoms and their history because each of the Arab travelers spells the names of rulers and places in his own peculiar fashion.

Southeast Africa, on the other hand, followed its own law of development. Arab infiltration in this region was limited to relatively narrow coastal strips. Under these conditions the Mohammedans could in no manner superimpose their forms of political life upon the native tribes. The kingdom of Manamatapa, for which so much evidence had accumulated, must therefore have been a purely Negro civilization. Along with ethnology, philology also began producing results. It was discovered that *matapa* meant "taking something out." *N-tapo* signifies a place where gold is mined. Manamatapa therefore meant, approximately, "the master of the gold mines." The Portuguese had named the westernmost point they were permitted to visit *as portas de masapa,* "the gates to the mines." It was situated in the vicinity of what is now called Mount Darwin.

The people who formed the populace and built up the Zimbabwe civilization were probably of the Bantu tribe —genuine Bantus such as are still found in Zambezi. They are brown- rather than black-skinned Negroes. But it was not, strictly speaking, a Bantu civilization. The ruling class was a clan from outside the Bantu country. Its origins are as dark as the first beginnings of the Manamatapa kingdom: a splinter tribe of state-builders, perhaps remnants of an exceedingly ancient people, appeared suddenly as did the Incas in Peru a few centuries later. To be sure, the Zimbabwe civilization was far from attaining the heights and the stagnant perfection of the Inca culture, which could, after all, build upon the foundation of important earlier Andean cultures. But the Zimbabwe culture comprehended a large kingdom with a complex governmental apparatus that functioned for several hundred years.

Neither the ethnologists nor the archæologists have been able to determine who the rulers of this kingdom were. They have only been able to say who they were not. It is established that they could not have been Bantus, Zulus, or Barotse. Tentatively, a few parallels were drawn between the Zimbabwe rulers and Ethiopian ruling families, as well as early kings of Egypt. Possible connections with the ancient Lake Chad kingdoms have not yet been adequately studied. But in the remote Solomon Islands a type of sun-worship has been found among the tribe known as the Araka which is strikingly similar to the cult practices of the Manamatapa kingdom.

At first glance, any such relationships would seem utterly fantastic. Yet fighting in the land of the Picts presented more difficulties for the Romans than would a long ocean voyage for Oceanic peoples. Taking account of this, Father Schebesta promptly seconded the theory put forward by Leo Frobenius in explanation of the Zimbabwe ruins: that an Eritrean cultural sphere had extended far beyond Zimbabwe. Father Schebesta, moreover, argued that this sphere probably included not only the coastal regions of the Indian Ocean but Polynesia as well. A bold hypothesis, certainly; but it was later to be confirmed by archæological finds. This Eritrean culture spread over an immense area within Africa, from the district in which the ancient Egyptian Osiris myth [2] held sway to ancient Nubia (Kaffa) and the regions of Uganda and Unyoro. Still unsettled, however, is the question of where this strain of culture came from and what direction it took. Leo Frobenius, in his thoughtful and often brilliant book *Erythräa*, has obviously been unable to draw any definitive conclusions about this.

Frobenius proposes for this realm a second name that sends a slight chill down our spines. To describe the historical and geographical concept of "Zimbabwe culture" he offers the following: "The lands and times of the ritual murder of kings." As we shall see, this name is as apt as it is arresting. The institution of regicide was, as Sir James

[2] Osiris is the brother and husband of Isis; in his marriage with her he symbolized the generative power of the sun; Isis in this relationship is generally interpreted as Mother Earth.

Frazer has shown, widespread among both primitive and civilized societies. While at first sight the slaughter of the sacred king may seem destructive to the state, the grim practice in actuality served to bolster the political structure. But how did this kingdom come into being? The events that influenced the development and history of the Manamatapa kingdom and of its capital, Zimbabwe, in themselves provide evidence that an Eritrean cultural sphere actually existed. For the rupture of a great dam in Yemen in A.D. 542 affected the African southeast coast, and so did the outbreak of the Great Revolution of A.D. 876 in Canton!

For a long time nothing at all was known about the economic history of this part of Africa (and to this day our schools teach the history of Africa's discovery but not the history of Africa itself). It now appears that Roman commercial competition, combined with the breaking of the great dam at Marib,[3] so weakened the Hymyarites of Yemen that more and more they had to abandon the trade with the African gold regions around Zimbabwe.

As late as the third century B.C. the kingdom of Aksum (the holy city and former capital of Abyssinia) had controlled both the African and the Arabian shores of the Red Sea. The traffic in Zimbabwe gold was open to any merchants who ventured to land on the coast and proceed toward the mines in the interior. Iron and salt, the articles most desired by the natives, were laid on the ground, whereupon the merchants withdrew. Representatives of the people who controlled the mines then emerged from the forest and laid beside the goods the amount of gold they were willing to give. The traveler

---

[3] This dam was the basis of the prosperity of Yemen; its breaking turned large parts of the country into desert and crippled trade.

Cosmas Indicopleustus, the mid-sixth-century traveler, vividly described this procedure. But in his day the trade between Abyssinia and the Zimbabwe kingdom was already coming to an end.

From about A.D. 600 on, trade between Byzantium and China, which of course also touched the East African coasts, passed into the hands of the Persians. In the ruins of Zimbabwe and in their immediate vicinity Chinese coins from the years 713 to 742 have been found, also some from the year 845, and a considerable number of the type of coins in use in China from 1068 to 1086. The latest Chinese coins found at Zimbabwe date from the years 1131 to 1163, but we know that as late as 1480— that is, shortly before the great Portuguese voyages of discovery—a Chinese fleet visited the East African port of Magadoxa, through which a large part of the exports of the Manamatapa kingdom were shipped.

Twice bloody events rent this far-flung network of early maritime commerce. In 876 a revolution broke out in Canton, which at that time was a city of more than 120,000 inhabitants, and already filled with foreigners. In the course of the uprising, the wrath of the populace turned against the Mohammedans, Jews, Persians, and Christians who lived among them. Foreigners were savagely hunted down, and their properties confiscated. Persian trade never recovered from the loss of men and money, and hegemony in the Indian Ocean passed to the Arabian merchant sailors. They held their position until the Portuguese appeared in those waters.

Don Francesco d'Almeida was, in contradistinction to many of the other conquistadors, a truly chivalrous person. In the name of his king he established the first settlements in India and Arabia and prepared the ground for the Portuguese conquests in East Africa. His son

Laurenço lost his life at Bombay; his father avenged
him by a brilliant victory in the port of Diu which opened
the Indian Ocean to Portuguese trade. The following
year, however, in 1510, D'Almeida was killed by a South
African native's spear.

Had D'Almeida's work taken place a hundred years
later, we would have found the ruins of Zimbabwe but
would have been left with scarcely a clue concerning the
kingdom of Manamatapa. For the kingdom was declining
when the Portuguese first settled on the coasts of Angola
—all accounts agree on this point. The gold mines were
no longer worked very diligently, and internal dissension
weakened the once powerful kingdom. For the time being, however, there were no dramatic changes for the
people of Zimbabwe. The Portuguese had been settled
in Zanzibar since 1503, and at various spots along the
coast of Mozambique since 1506, but their principal interest was the trade with India. Although they took possession of the mouth of the Zambezi, they did so without
conviction, rather as a token acknowledgment of the rumors about Ophir. References to the land of gold
sounded good in reports to Lisbon, but the principal
profits of commerce came from ivory, white and black.
(Apropos black ivory, it is curious to note that the high-
minded Dominican Bartolomé de Las Casas put through
so many edicts for the protection of the Indians that a
shortage of labor arose in the American colonies. Hence
there began, with the approval of this true humanitarian,
one of the cruelest chapters in the history of man: the
capture and shipment of strong young Negro men and
women in the close holds of caravels.)

A Portuguese named Diego de Alcacova mentions the
Manamatapa kingdom as early as 1506. He declares that
gold production had slackened off considerably (at one

time it had reached a value equivalent to $450,000 an-
nually). It appears, however, that the Portuguese were
being hoodwinked. They were, of course, ardently interested in the gold trade, but they were at a disadvantage
compared to the Arabs because they dared to penetrate
the unknown interior only cautiously and step by step,
whereas the Arab traders were, so to speak, accredited
at the court of Zimbabwe. This situation was unchanged
by a treaty of 1607 in which the Portuguese acquired a
kind of trading monopoly in return for their lending
armed aid to Manamatapa against rebellious tribes. The
inhabitants of the Manamatapa kingdom continued to
exchange their gold for the shining cloth the Arabian
merchants offered, and for the pretty beads that came
from India, especially the small ones that looked so pretty
sewn on clothes.

Consequently, only a comparatively small part of the
gold of Zimbabwe reached Europe. The Portuguese were
not as bold and brutal as Pizarro. Virtually under the
noses of the new lords of the land, the Arabs shipped
the precious metal to India, where, during these centuries, the magnificent courts were reveling in the most
rampant luxury in Indian history and the demand for
gold was at its height.

The textiles with which the king of Manamatapa at-
tired himself and the three thousand women of his harem
moldered away in the crude stone buildings at Zimbabwe. The innumerable beads, however, defied destruction and, together with shards of Malay and Chinese
ceramics, have provided contemporary archæologists
with much information.

The principal buildings at Zimbabwe stand upon rocky
ground, covered only by a thin layer of earth. Sifted
carefully, this earth should yield artifacts that would

help to establish the date of the earliest settlement. Under the direction of the young English archæologist Gertrude Caton-Thompson, diagonal shafts were dug from the tumbled stones of the buildings down to the rock base. At one point Miss Thompson had a shaft driven under a building; all earth dug out was carried away in sacks.

This earth, mingled with small fragments of rock, was washed and sifted, and everything that remained was arranged and examined with the greatest care. Among the larger pieces of rock two prehistoric hand axes were found. While these had nothing to do with the purposes of the excavation, they did provide proof that the archæologists had now reached the lowest level of settlement; anything found above that stratum should indicate the actual maximum age of the ruins.

The finds were numerous but quite monotonous in character: practically nothing but weapons. There were iron arrowheads, ax and hoe blades, spear tips, felloes—these the detritus of the men of Zimbabwe. The women, however, had left innumerable beads, small ornaments of the most various materials, and potsherds.

There are experts on everything in this world, even on beads. Horace Beck's opinion was sought. He measured and analyzed the tiny spheres and ellipses, the yellow, blue, or opaque green beads, and assigned them their proper place in chronology. Egyptian beads dating from as early as 1500 B.C. are known, and no doubt beads were being made still earlier in Mesopotamia. We cannot discuss the dating procedure in detail, though it once more demonstrates the close ties between all the areas bordering on the Indian Ocean (the largest store of these tiny ornaments hitherto discovered, for instance, is at a deserted Malay village named Kuala Sensing). However, Beck confirmed what MacIver had guessed and Miss Caton-Thompson's other excavations had demonstrated: the oldest ruins were of buildings that in all probability had been erected in the ninth century A.D. It appeared fairly certain that none of the ornaments could be more than seventeen hundred years old. From the third century A.D. back to the time of King Solomon there still remained a gap of a good thousand years. The more that was learned about Zimbabwe, the more evident it became that this city could not have been identical with Ophir. Although the gold mines of the vicinity show traces of having been worked in ancient times, it has not been possible to say how old these mines are. The human remains so far found in the mines and ruins are those of eight different individuals. Every one of them is of the Negroid type, and none has lain in the earth longer than eleven hundred years. All belong to the Bantu stock; neither Arab nor Egyptian nor bushman skeletons have been found.

But if beads and ornaments have taken from us the illusion that what we behold at Zimbabwe are the ruins of legendary Ophir, they instead provide archæological corroboration of the newer but no less exciting concept of an extensive Eritrean cultural sphere. Horace Beck, in his study *Rhodesian Beads,* emphasizes that ornaments of the type found in Zimbabwe are encountered in a vast region whose eastern boundary is marked by Borneo and the Philippines.

Since far more is known about Arabic and Chinese than about Rhodesian antiquities, all matters connected with the trade of the old Manamatapa kingdom can be clarified and dated much more easily than the question of the gold mines themselves. These mines are so numerous, so scattered, and in many cases so well hidden that a major expedition would have to labor for years to obtain reliable data for a history of Rhodesian gold-mining and the gold export trade.

We do, however, know a little more about the kingdom which lived by this gold and which erected the cliff capital of Zimbabwe in order to protect the mines.

Our first source of information is the buildings themselves. Since they had no roofs, it seemed fairly easy to explain them as temples of a sun-worshipping cult; the sacred sun was not to be denied admittance to any corner of them. But as dwellings such buildings could scarcely have been very useful. On the other hand, they had more entrances than one would reasonably expect to find in a fortress; to defend so many gates would have presented quite a problem.

Independently, Miss Caton-Thompson and Father Schebesta arrived at the same explanation: those ruins which were not purely ritual structures were a combination of living-quarters and fortifications. The actual dwelling-units must have been the round huts of wood and mud still used by the natives. Between these, however, stone walls had been erected. What the first investigators took to be palaces were basically nothing but Negro kraals surrounded by stone walls instead of wooden palisades. In place of towers the huts—often in groups of ten or more—filled the gaps in the walls.

There now remained the mystery of the famous building which to this day is surrounded by closed elliptical walls, and in which rise two strange conical towers, one of impressive height and a smaller one that was apparently conceived as a complement to the other; the two together obviously expressed a single architectonic concept. Moreover, all archæologists were struck by the timorousness with which the native Negroes spoke of this structure. They were reluctant to lead strangers to it, and after dark not even the most tempting offer would persuade them to accompany one of the archæologists anywhere near the place. Such behavior suggested that the structure had once been a temple or a place inhabited by ghosts—presumably, therefore, a reliquary or a tomb. Further information on this point was secured only after a detailed study of the Portuguese records and a comparison with the customs of tribes—such as the Uganda and Unyoro—who had formerly come under the influence of the Eritrean cultural sphere and about whom more was known.

In the course of her excavations Miss Caton-Thompson came upon numerous small phallic emblems, so many that they appeared to be quite characteristic of the culture of Zimbabwe. The conclusion was inescapable that the conical towers had been part of the same phallic cult. The larger tower must have symbolized the male, the smaller the female principle. Both towers were apparently reliquary shrines in which the umbilical cord and the lower jaw of each king were preserved. Thus the ghosts of the once mighty kings were made to remain on the spot and protect the mines that represented the wealth of the country and the source of its prosperity. For the tribute of the vassal tribes was limited to cattle and to girls for the king's harem.

According to some sources, the *manamatapa* (king) had as many as three thousand women. Seven or eight of these were his chief wives; most of the others were the slaves of these chief wives, but the manamatapa could raise the slaves to the status of concubines any time he chose. Some of the women were his own sisters; in fact, the queen, who was called *mazarira*, had to be his sister. He regarded his children by his sisters as his proper heirs, since they had no intermixture of alien blood. This familial endogamy was, as we shall see, based on religious ideas, and parallels the practice among the Incas. The subjects, however, were forbidden incestuous marriage on pain of death.

The king himself wore garments of silk; on his brow and chest hung large sea shells as ornaments, while his chieftains, the heads of the vassal tribes, wore a sea shell only on their chests. The insignia of rule were three artistically carved rods. Whenever the manamatapa went out, drums were borne before him. These drums were beaten in the usual fashion, but drums that were rubbed together have also been found; presumably these served some special ritual purpose. Other drums produced a horrifying rattle; enclosed in them was the skeletal hand of a human sacrifice.

For the Manamatapa kingdom the drums had the same significance as flags for a modern state. Certain of the old records declare that whoever took possession of the royal harem and the royal drums became king.

The women practiced agriculture while the men hunted, but the importance of the harem rested not so much in this as in the remnants of matriarchal rights. The dying king might propose one of his sons for his successor, but the final decision was made by the women of the harem. These, and especially the queen mother, had the last word. They decided whether the prospective new king was physically fit for the post. If he were sickly or impotent, they forced him to take poison. In Uganda the kings succeeded at a fairly early period in abolishing this cruel custom. In Zimbabwe, however, the practice of forced suicide remained for a long time, until one manamatapa succeeded in converting death by poison into a mere renunciation of the throne.[4]

The court was rich and numerous, and there were a number of rather curious offices. The manamatapa had a chief steward; a chief drummer, who was in charge of all the drums of the kingdom; and a keeper of salves and medicines, who, according to the Portuguese records, was called the chief fetish man. The sons of tribal chieftains served as pages at the court and had to live celibately during their period of service. When they became of marriageable age, they received an assignment outside the royal city.

The king was constantly accompanied by a bodyguard; the men of this bodyguard also served as executioners. Aside from this work, they apparently had little to do, and would set up impatient cries when they had had no one to execute for some time. The cry they uttered on such occasions was horribly significant; it was *nyam, nyam,* meaning "meat, meat," which suggests that the royal bodyguards indulged, at each execution, not only sadistic but cannibalistic inclinations. The manamatapa seldom resisted their demands. If the sinister cry rang out beside or behind him, he looked hastily around for some subject who displeased him, and tossed one of his rods to the ground in front of the man. Next moment the poor fellow was pierced by the spears of the bodyguards.

Perhaps incidents of this sort were the origin of the

---

[4] In their *Völkerkunde von Afrika* (Essen, 1939) Baumann and Thurnwald point out regicidal rites among other East African peoples. In some groups the king's reign was limited to a fixed period, usually ten but sometimes seven years. Thus the people were assured of a strong and healthy ruler and were spared the internal dissension that might arise from a former ruler's attempting to regain his throne. Usually, as Frobenius indicates, the king was strangled with a cord. The four chief officials, functioning as priests and representing the four points of the compass, and possibly the First Wife also, apparently acted as the executioners.

superstitition that to look the manamatapa in the face
brought bad luck. Those who had anything to do with
him prostrated themselves in the dust before his majesty,
and were happy to escape safely from his presence.

Every good or bad trait and action of the ruler was
imitated, not only by his retinue, but by the entire population of the capital city; to this day, imitativeness is a
marked trait of the Bantus. If the king limped because
he had injured himself while hunting, all the court officials and subjects limped likewise; if he coughed, they
all coughed; if he sneezed, they sneezed. It is easy to
imagine the complications this habit would introduce
into an already involved court ceremonial.

Early Portuguese accounts speak of the city simply as
"very large," so that we cannot even attempt to estimate
its size. The thatched mud huts have disappeared, of
course. Many household utensils were of stone, however, especially of easily worked soapstone. The molds
for gold bars were also made of soapstone; to judge by
the molds, the bars must have looked like a crude H. A
number of the pots that have been found were wound
around with gold wire.

The months were counted from new moon to new
moon, and in each month there were six holidays on
which the king held audience. If for some reason he was
not able to do so, or was not in the mood, the chancellor
would receive the petitioners or plaintiffs in his stead.

In May and in September there were great festivals
usually celebrated with mock battles. The festivities in
May, during which the king himself did not appear,
lasted for eight days. On the eighth day one of the chieftains was killed. Also, whenever a new king took office a
chieftain had to die. In September the king, his women,
and the populace together made a pilgrimage to the

royal ancestors, the dead kings of the past, who dwelt on the Acropolis or in the Elliptical Temple or in both, if the theories of Father Schebesta and Miss Caton-Thompson are correct. On such occasions a medium was assigned the task of establishing communication between the living and one or more of the great dead kings. As soon as the medium fell into a trance, he apparently became one of the dead kings, displaying all his personal traits—which were well engraved on the memory of the people. Then king and people would prostrate themselves to show to the medium the reverence they owed the dead ruler.

This spiritualistic procedure apparently served as a substitute for mummification, the technique of which had reached a high point in near-by Uganda. The idea of survival after death was highly developed. Care was taken that the dead, especially the dead kings, lacked nothing they had needed in life. This led to ghastly human sacrifices: the principal wives were killed over the corpse of the king and the whole group was then enclosed with a wall of mud. More human sacrifices were placed beside this wall, obviously so that they could accompany the king as guards, and then another wall was built around these to keep wild beasts from eating the bodies. Occasionally this custom was moderated so that the principal wives were required only to move into the stone building that housed the body of the king, in order to serve him. Many of these mighty ruins were therefore inhabited only by corpses, a few women, and the guards of the tomb.

Along with this conception of survival in human form went the parallel idea that the dead kings continued to live in the solar creatures, the lion and the eagle. These were held sacred, and hunting of them was permitted only once a year during a grand hunt in which the king himself took part. Reliefs on utensils suggest that hunting dogs were used.

According to Frobenius, the religious idea that for centuries underlay the political structure of the Manamatapa kingdom throws light on early forms of kingship in general, and should provide us with a new insight into the life of the city of Zimbabwe itself. The basic myth of the kingdom united elements of old Nigerian ancestor-worship with court epic. The story was that the first king had been the moon. He had wedded the morning and evening stars. "Among the princesses some followed the example of the chaste goddess of the morning star while others . . . the famous *wassare* had always to be ready to give themselves. The sacred hymn sung during the rain-dance by the men, who otherwise were singularly chaste and delicate about sexual matters, proclaimed with rude forthrightness that if the *wassare* were derelict in their duty, the rains would fail."

Customs that in other cultures must have prevailed thousands of years before survived for centuries in Zimbabwe. "The series of wives was led off by a ceremonial 'First Wife' of the ruler who apparently shared his bed and without exception had to be his sister by the same father and same mother. When this culture was at its height, the consummation of the king's nuptials must have been an extremely solemn affair. It could not take place in any room, but had to be performed upon a platform which in the early stages must have been erected on a kind of tower. Such unions served a religious function and were timed according to the positions of the stars." [5]

[5] Leo Frobenius: *Kulturgeschichte Afrikas* (Vienna and Amsterdam, several editions), p. 162.

The purpose of the granite monoliths on the Acropolis at Zimbabwe, which have generally been viewed as phallic symbols, now becomes clear. Here, close to the sky, the king who still symbolized the god slept with the earth-mother goddess who symbolized the god's sister, the evening star.

Only in the course of the past few decades has the archæological picture been rounded out. Some writers on Zimbabwe still cling to the idea that it is the site of a colony established by early seafarers, presumably Phœnicians. They refuse to recognize the results of archæological and ethnological research. And yet the idea of an African culture flourishing a thousand years ago is far more alluring and interesting than the possibility that we have before us only another offshoot of Mediterranean culture. Miss Caton-Thompson, the indefatigable young archæologist, expresses this feeling when she writes: [6] "The interest in Zimbabwe and the allied ruins should, on this account, to all educated people be enhanced a hundredfold; it enriches, not impoverishes, our wonderment at their remarkable achievement: it cannot detract from their inherent majesty: for the mystery of Zimbabwe is the mystery which lies in the still pulsating heart of native Africa."

[6] The fundamental book on all archæological questions relating to the ruins at Zimbabwe is *The Zimbabwe-Culture,* by Gertrude Caton-Thompson (Oxford, 1931). Father Paul Schebesta has written frequently in technical journals on ethnological questions and the evaluation of Portuguese records (e.g., in *Anthropos,* volume for 1955, pp. 484–545). Highly informative on early trade with East Africa is K. M. Kenyon's *Sketch of the Exploration and Settlement of the East Coast of Africa* (Oxford, 1931). As an introduction to the still little-known history of Africa before the discoveries and explorations, we may recommend Denise Paulme: *Les Civilisations africaines* (Paris, 1953).

PART THREE

WAR

WAR HAS DESTROYED MORE CITIES THAN the wrath of the elements and the strangulation of economic hardship taken together. It is as though war were the great enemy of urban life in general. For many hundreds—indeed, for thousands—of years we see the cities and city-dwellers concentrating chiefly on defense against the onslaught of war. Peoples who have learned to stay in one place, harvesting their crops, building towns, and cultivating a higher form of life, have always aroused the envy of nomads, who surge up against walls and gates and destroy the cities because they do not know what to do with them. Until the threshold of the modern age, nomads of the sea, pirates, threatened settled places on and near the seacoast. They not only pillaged, they burned to the ground these habitations, as though their hatred were also directed against the very walls, which seemed to represent to them a hostile principle.

And so, in fact, the walls did. As soon as the strict order of husbandry and village is abandoned, as soon as urban life begins to unfold, men are overcome by a kind of intoxication for which the word "freedom" has been invented. Personal liberty in the variety of urban activities and opportunities at first makes the cities attractive, and then converts them into hotbeds of unrest. In cities, tyrants are raised upon shields and later overthrown; in

cities, freedom of the individual and democracy have
their birth. Cities and war are as opposed to each other
as security and danger, as continuity and catastrophe.

One principle nourishes itself upon its polar opposite,
and one kills the other. But even if they die in the
process, the cities give their names to the wars. From remote times there still resounds in our ears the name of
that conflict which, in the obscurity of the mythic past,
became the prototype of all wars. Prophetesses warned
against it, and compared it with the struggle of giants
amid the volcanic vapors of the Phlegræan Plain. From
this very city of Troy, Odysseus embarked upon a voyage
through a Mediterranean filled with wonders, across a
sea whose shores were the cradle of cultures. From Troy,
Æneas began his journey to that Carthage which Phœnician Dido founded, whence later Hannibal marched
across the Alps and against Rome.

Heroes marched forth, gained victories, fell in battles;
women waited and uttered warnings; soldiers took rich
cities and founded poor ones; and in every city a wise
old man sat in the sun and wrote down his thoughts upon
sand or clay or parchment. Innumerable such old men
suffered the same fate as Archimedes: their heads rolled
in the sand beside the geometric drawing or the scratched
letters they had hoped would preserve the lesson of
events for the benefit of humanity.

The great singer who with prophetic knowledge first
set forth the theme of war and destruction knew the
whole story almost three thousand years ago. As he said
in the Sixth Book of his *Iliad:*

*Like to the leaves in the forest, so are the generations of
    man;*

*The wind casts the leaves to the earth, but the budding
    woods*
*Shoot forth others in turn, when spring brings revival of
    life.*
So is the race of man; it grows, and then disappears.

VII

HEROES AND SIBYLS

HOMER AND GUESSES. TOLL PASSAGE OF THE DARDA-
NELLES. MYCENÆ AND TIRYNS. LIFE IN TROY. THE
TEN-YEAR WAR. THE OLDEST GREEK SETTLEMENT IN
ITALY. ÆNEAS GOES TO THE SIBYL'S GROTTO FOR AD-
VICE. DIDO FOUNDS CARTHAGE. A NAVAL POWER.
RICHES. RECOVERY. TRADE RIVALS KNOW NO MERCY.

THE NORTHERNMOST coastal region of Asia Minor is the oft-mentioned Troad. Although it lies in ruin and solitude, it occupies an unusual quantity of space in our description. We must, however, request forbearance and ask the reader to blame this prolixity not upon ourselves, but upon those who are so deeply interested in famous and ancient matters. A further reason is the number of peoples, Greeks and non-Greeks, who have dwelt in this country; also the writers who have written a great deal about it, but not always clearly. At the head of these is Homer, who has given rise to many conjectures."

So Strabo begins the thirteenth book of his great compendium of the geographical knowledge of his time. For him, too, Troy was already "ancient." For him the existence of the Homeric city lay further in the past than the time of Charlemagne for us. And yet we must begin even further back.[1]

Urban development began in the Orient around 5000 B.C. From the East agricultural civilization spread westward in search of new land to till, and introduced to the West superior types of grain, the art of pottery, and the sickle. Sparsely settled Asia Minor, occupied only by hunters, was easily penetrated. At the point where the land route from the East to the West intersected with the sea route from the Ægean to the Black Sea there arose, early in the third millennium B.C., the city we know by the name of Troy.

It was inhabited by fishermen, peasants, and herdsmen. They felled trees with stone axes, used stone weapons for hunting and fighting, and fashioned their fishhooks from bone. They made their boats, scraped hides, sewed clothes and built their huts with approximately the same kind of primitive tools which was being used at the same period by the people on the opposite European shore. Occasionally a rich man possessed tools or weapons of copper; these were not as hard as those made of stone, but they were more efficient. The women wore jewelry. The black or brownish clay vessels, pots, bowls, cups, broad, hollow-footed beakers, and urns for the ashes of the dead were ornamented.

For dwelling-place these men had selected a stony hill site between the two rivers that in later Greek times were called the Scamander and the Simois. The situation on a hill was designed to protect the settlement from land

[1] Out of the vast literature on the subject we will mention only the following: volume one of the *Histoire Grecque,* by Gustave Glotz and Robert Cohen (Paris, 1938); Joseph Wiesner: *Vor und Frühzeit der Mittelmeerländer* (Berlin, 1943); Carl Schuchhardt: *Alteuropa* (4th edition, Berlin, 1941); Georg Finsler: *Homer* (Berlin, 1914). On the Hittites, C. W. Ceram: *The Secret of the Hittites* (New York, 1956) contains a summary of the latest research and a full bibliography.

raiders; for fear of pirates the town was not laid out directly by the sea, favorable though such a site would have been for trade. For the same reason, strong walls were erected. Between the round and oval huts the rectangular house of the prince rose proudly.[2]

Around the middle of the third millennium B.C. a second town rose above the remains of that first settlement (we do not know what caused its downfall). The prince now had a regular lord's castle, though it was no more than fifty yards wide. The living-room was far from resembling the great hall of a palace; it was only a fairly large rectangular room with a fireplace in the center and a kind of anteroom in front. Its walls, of stone and mud, were three feet thick. Similar smaller buildings stood beside it; opposite it was a long, narrow structure, the preliminary stage of what was later to become the portico.

Now the potter no longer shaped his vessels with his bare hand alone; he turned them on a potter's wheel. Like his fellow citizens, he owned arms and tools of bronze. Men and women wore a great deal of jewelry, which they stowed away carefully, piece by piece, in small leather purses that were placed in large clay pots. The knowledge of metals—which, like the potter's wheel, had come from the East—represented a new acquisition; pottery vessels still displayed the familiar gourd form, and the women's jewelry still adhered to the early patterns, which had been executed in leather. But now the jewelry was of gold, and the service at the prince's table was also of gold.

With such wealth to guard, the town was strongly

---

[2] It has been argued that the rectangular house, or *megaron*, came from the north, thus showing the existence of a "nordic" population in Troy at so early a date. Recent excavations have disproved this; in Jericho, houses of this sort have been found dating from centuries earlier than the houses at Troy.

fortified. On stone foundations sixteen feet thick a strong wall of unbaked brick was erected. The gates were flanked by square bastions; the narrow passage between them resembled a sunken road. Ships passing through the Dardanelles had to stop at this city to pay their toll; likewise the merchants, who brought a great many metal implements and tools from Asia Minor to Europe. For Greece was poor in metals and needed both raw materials and finished goods.

The prosperous life of this city lasted for a few centuries, perhaps for somewhat more than five hundred years. But eventually the fame of its wealth lured enemies of superior might to its gates. Perhaps the foe was a neighboring tribe, perhaps a homeless people from Europe, a rival commercial city, a nation of seafarers, or a gang of pirates. Or had the masters of Troy preyed on passing ships and thus invited retribution? We do not know. All we know for certain is the outcome: Troy went up in flames.

Trade by land and by sea, fishing, hunting, and farming persisted; more modestly, perhaps, but tenaciously, life resumed after the great disaster. And so the burned-over ruins of Troy were settled again. Time and again small huts of stone, adobe, and wicker, with roofs of reeds and straw, collapsed or were burned, and time and again new dwellings were built on their ruins. For centuries that went on.

Across the Ægean Sea lived equally simple people— herdsmen, farmers, and fishermen. Bands of foreign warriors passed by these shores also; merchants brought wares from the east and the south, from Egypt, Phœnicia, and rich, highly civilized Crete. The princes lived on knolls behind tremendously thick stone walls. Their needs were supplied by the peasants of the surrounding villages, who in turn looked to them for military protection. Whatever else they wanted beyond their simple needs—such as ornaments, table utensils, or slaves—could be obtained by piracy.

The most famous of these princely demesnes was that of the descendants of Pelops—after whom the entire peninsula was called the Peloponnesus.

In the northernmost corner of the fruitful Argolic Plain lay Mycenæ. This citadel commanded the surrounding agricultural country and the highways. Tiryns, the other citadel in the vicinity, lay close to the coast.

In peacetime these mighty fortresses were political and religious centers for the rural population. When war threatened, the people fled to refuge towers attached to the castle proper. The peasants might well feel reassured when they walked up the ramp past high bastions and entered through a tremendous gate. Laboring for decades side by side with enslaved prisoners of war, they had built the walls that seemed to later generations the work of the cyclops, the one-eyed giants of myth.

The prince who lived in such a castle need have no fear of enemies. Inside and out, the castle bore witness to his wealth. He loved gold ornaments, and the women of his court loved them even more; they wore gold in their hair, on their breasts, on their arms, and on their gowns. They drank out of gold and silver beakers. They had private bathrooms supplied with urns of water brought by the slave women from the spring at the foot of the hill. The ruler dined in a splendidly appointed room decorated with fine murals; in every respect he sought to imitate the elegance of the Cretan way of life.

He made sacrifices to the gods and to his ancestors —not only flowers, food, wine, or a stainless heifer, but human prisoners also. He pronounced justice, planned new predatory expeditions that would increase his wealth, conferred on political matters, received foreign envoys or itinerant merchants. In his leisure time he went hunting in a two-wheeled chariot. It was a truly lordly life he led, and when it was over he was buried in a vast tomb, his jewelry and weapons beside him, an artfully hammered golden mask over his face.

The pottery workshops of Mycenæ were located to the

A POTTER, FROM A CAMEO.

northeast of the citadel. Their products were exported far and wide, to Sicily, Cyprus, Ugrait on the Phœnician coast, and of course to the rest of Greece. When the Thessalian expedition of the German Archæological Institute discovered the city of Argissa in the spring of 1955, it found Mycenæan ceramics.

Trading vessels carrying Mycenæan wares visited very distant waters. Their pirate ships may also have ranged as far; the masters of the citadels in the plain of Argos represented a considerable power. To what extent they contributed to the downfall of the Cretan kingdom need not be discussed here. In the course of the second millennium B.C. a number of new powers came upon the scene.

In Asia Minor the Hittite Empire had been formed out of numerous tribal principates. This empire fought against Assyria, negotiated with Babylon and Egypt and also, as we learn from official correspondence and the biographies of rulers, with a people named Ahhiyawa who are considered to have been archaic Greeks. Hittite texts speak of one "Attarissiyas, man of Ahhiyawa." This man was for a time friendly with the Hittites, then fought against them in Asia Minor and sent, along with foot soldiers, a hundred chariots into battle. Perhaps he was that Atreus who is famous in Greek myth as the son of Pelops and king of Mycenæ.

In recent years scholars have obtained considerable additional information on the economic foundations of Mycenæan wealth. The entire Orient obtained oil from sesame seed; precious olive oil came from Crete and Greece alone. It served not only as a food, but as a medicine, a cleaner (for soap was unkown), and for anointing of the body for sports, after the bath, and for burial. In Mycenæ we can still see the cooking apparatus used for heating large amphoræ full of oil together with fragrant herbs. The export of aromatic oil was one of the chief sources of income for Mycenæ.

On the fringe of the sphere of Mycenæan rule lived Nestor, the "horse-breaker," orator, and wise adviser of the Homeric epics. His capital was Pylos in fertile Messenia, the southwesternmost part of the Peloponnesus. The city was situated on the northern end of a bay that had an island athwart it, thus making it the safest harbor in the Mediterranean.

In 1939 the ruin of a lord's castle not inferior in size to the palaces of Mycenæ and Tiryns was discovered in this region. Clay tablets with Cretan script were found there which have changed our knowledge of Greece in the second millenium B.C. Unquestionably it had been the seat of a prince of the Mycenæan age, but had that prince been Homer's Nestor? According to the *Odyssey*, Nestor's palace had been near the coast; these ruins were some nine miles inland. However, in the fall of 1954, American archæologists came upon even more likely remains. These were in fact not far from the coast: a large building, the walls of cyclopean construction, with an extensive inner courtyard. Here, it seems, was where Nestor lived, and lived well: the hearth in his house was even larger than the one in the palace at Mycenæ.

Meanwhile, a new settlement had risen and prospered on the hill of Troy. It was the sixth in the course of centuries, and larger and more important than the earlier ones. Once more a great wall enclosed the city, composed of huge stones with a superstructure of sun-dried brick, and provided with towers and strongly fortified gates. On the hill, terraces had been laid out; wide, straight streets passed between the houses. These were large, often rectangular, and sometimes had pillars supporting the roofs; one house even had a second story. Merchants and farmers came from afar to the market at Troy; the city bustled with life, for it consumed a great deal and also manufactured many articles. The smiths made weapons and tools of bronze; the artists ornamented these products and hammered out jewelry of gold and silver; the potters turned out gray, thin-walled vessels and polished them beautifully in order to keep pace with Mycenæan competitors. At the same time, the city imported from Mycenæ cups, beakers, and jugs of yellowish clay. Along with their fine jewelry the rich Trojan women wore ivory combs in their hair. They led a pleasant life, for there

were plenty of slaves to take care of the housework. But
even for the slaves the city now provided a convenience
absent from the earlier settlements on this spot: there
was a well on the hill itself.

This rich, strongly fortified city could hold off human
enemies, but it was helpless in the face of the forces of
nature. Around 1365 B.C. an earthquake shook the hill.
The huge stone blocks in the city wall were tumbled
from their base; the houses collapsed. At one blow the
city was destroyed.[3]

The disaster dealt a fearful blow to the life of the
city, but did not bring it to an end. The survivors rebuilt
the houses, and moved the cyclopean blocks of the city
wall back into place as best they could. Afterward the
city that scholars call Troy VIIa was smaller than it
had been, but it retained its old fame for wealth in gold
and bronze utensils.

This was the city of which Homer sang. Here, if
we will believe the poet, old King Priam and his wife,
Hecuba, lived in a palace of polished stone, surrounded
by a council of elders. With him lived his sons and daughters; those who were married were assigned to rooms that
opened off the great interior court.

The life of the womenfolk was almost entirely restricted to the home. They took care of the children,
though each child had its nurse and governess. In addition, they plied spindles and looms. The men, even the
nobles, did not despise household work; they lent a hand
where necessary. But their chief occupations were hunting and jousting, spear- and discus-throwing, and boxing. There were pastimes aplenty: draughts, and dice,

---

[3] In regard to the chronology of Troy, which is the subject of much
disagreement, we follow the French scholar Jean Bérard: *Historia*,
Vol. I (1950), p. 351 ff.

and ball games, which the girls played also. But the finest of amusements was dancing in a ring in the open air. This was a pleasure for all, spectators as well as dancers. And when they were hot and tired, they would go to the baths, be massaged and anointed, and then proceed to table.

Evenings, the heroes sat in the men's hall, either at a long table or each with his own small table. Skins or purple blankets were spread over the benches. The hearth fire illuminated the room; for additional light, resinous pine wood burned smokily in pans or, if the King himself were the host, in handsome torch-holders. Although there was a stewardess who assisted the mistress in the conduct of the entire household economy, the master of the house himself supervised the preparation of the meal; this he was honor-bound to do for his guests, and probably he also enjoyed it. Maids brought the meat to table already cut; only the most honored guest received an undivided section and fell to with fingers and teeth. Maids or an attendant then poured water over the guests' hands, so that they could wash; in rich Troy the pitchers were of gold and the basins of silver. Servants filled the pitchers with wine from the big crater, the mixing-bowl, and poured it into the beakers. If the masters were feeling high and downed their wine rapidly, the squires would then simply dip the beakers themselves into the crater. Especially prized was a drink made of tart red wine into which goat cheese had been grated. Roast meat, bread, and wine were the main, but not the only, foods. There were also cheese, fish, oysters, milk, blood sausages, beans, peas, and bacon.

The aristocratic Trojan showed his enjoyment of life in the way he decked out himself and his city. He wore purple or multicolored garments of linen, or of the wool

of black sheep, gleaming with violet tints. Men wore
gold and silver spangles in their hair; the women wore a
netlike hood over the elaborate, high-piled coiffure and
a fillet around their brows, the ends falling over their
shoulders and down to the breast. They also had necklaces
of gold or amber beads.

As a result of their active intercourse with neighboring peoples, the Trojans had developed many crafts. There
were building contractors in Troy, masons and carpenters,
cabinetmakers, turners, wheelwrights, leatherworkers, tanners, potters, smiths, jewelers. It was a city resounding
with the joyous noises of work, mingled with the shouts of
children, the barking of dogs, the whinnying of horses,
and the chaffering of slaves at the markets.

How this life came to an end is well known. Paris, the
King's son, had snatched away a beautiful woman from
the mainland across the Ægean Sea. That in itself was
no cause for excitement; the coastal cities were used to
pirate raids. But Paris had violated the laws of hospitality,
and the woman was, moreover, the wife of a prince or a
king. This man appealed to his brother, the principal king
of the Achæan Greeks. Agamemnon, the son of Atreus
of Mycenæ, summoned all the princes of Greece to participate in the punitive expedition. But, beautiful though
Helen might be, she was not the sole reason for the war.
The city of Troy promised rich booty, and its trade
had long been interfering with the export of Mycenæan
wares. Its key position on the strait enabled it to obstruct
sea traffic. And so warships were launched not only in
Mycenæ and the other cities on the coast opposite Troy;
warriors flocked to the cause from Pylos also, the home
of Nestor, and from Crete, Rhodes, and the Greek islands
such as Ithaca, where Odysseus ruled.

King Priam knew he faced a stern test. He assembled

soldiers from all the districts of western Asia Minor around Troy, and even Thracians from the Greek Mainland. Merely landing on the coast cost the Greeks heavy casualties. When at last they were able to set up their camp on the beach outside of Troy, they could fight only in the open field; siege machinery was unknown to them. In addition, they did not have the forces for a full encirclement of the city. In order to obtain supplies they preyed on the coastal cities of Asia Minor, taking food, gear, and women for their camp. Their persistence

THE FIGHT FOR THE BODY OF PATROCLUS.

was at last rewarded; after ten years of bitter fighting Troy fell into their hands. The city was plundered and went up in flames; traces of the frightful conflagration can still be detected in the ruins.

Schliemann, the famous discoverer of Troy, thought he had found Priam's city in rich Troy II. Then for a long time great Troy VI was the favorite candidate. There were no traces of fire in Troy VI, but the English clergyman W. J. Phythian-Adams had an ingenious explanation: the earthquake that destroyed Troy VI, he argued, had overthrown the walls and thus permitted the Greeks to take the city after their long, vain siege. The Trojan Horse would then have been merely a thank-offering to the god Poseidon, the Earth-Shaker.

Today Layer VIIa—it was excavated by the American Carl William Blegen, of Pylos fame—is definitively recognized as Homeric Troy. The cuneiform-script tablets of the Hittite Empire possibly throw additional light on the historical fate of the city. The tablets mention an Alaksandus ("Alexandros" was an honorary name borne by Paris) who was ruler of Wilusa around 1300 B.C. Wilusa may have been the Hittite name for Ilion (Troy). Troy was in fact rebuilt after the fire by the surviving Trojans; impoverished, they nevertheless clung loyally to the cultural tradition of the city. The next stratum is called by scholars "Troy VIIb 1." The conquerers of Troy VIIa departed, just as the Homeric legend declares that Agamemnon's warriors did.

Not until we reach Troy VIIb 2 (around 1250 B.C., the beginning of the Iron Age) do we find traces of a new, foreign population. This period was also the beginning of a new era in the eastern Mediterranean. Rude warriors poured into the region from the Balkans; these were the so-called "battle-ax men." At the same time other peoples began migrating. The old settlers were overrun and their cities annihilated. Into Greece came the Dorians, simple herdsmen from the mountains to the north. The castles of Mycenæ, Tiryns, and Pylos and even the palaces of Crete were destroyed. Barbarism triumphed.

Like the Achæans before them, the Dorians now assimilated the old Mediterranean culture and brought it to new heights in Greece. At that time the cities still existed on a modest scale: Tiryns as a place of pilgrimage, Mycenæ because of its favorable site, and Troy for the tourist trade.

Eusebius, the father of Christian historiography, calls Kyme in Campania the oldest Greek settlement in Italy;

he avers that it was founded in the second millennium B.C. Modern archæologists do not, of course, take this statement seriously. Syracuse must have antedated Kyme, and the shore of the Strait of Messina, as well as the island of Ischia, was settled earlier by Greeks in order to secure the sea route back to their homeland.

Excavations of the past half-century have shown, however, that the castle crag at Kyme had been settled before the Greeks came. Even in prehistoric times a native Italic tribe had lived there. In fact, it would be surprising if this naturally fortified point, the steep hill rising sharply out of a fertile plain so close to the sea, had not attracted people very early.

True urban life, however, came to the region only with the Greeks. The natural terraces of the hill were widened and temples were erected on them. Streets were built, and fortified gates. The city spread out and reached into the plain below. It became rich and mighty. Its dominion extended south and southeast over the Misenian peninsula with its splended natural harbors. Its population carried trade deep into the completely unexplored hinterland. From these Greeks the inhabitants of Italy learned the alphabet.

The population increased. But the Greeks were averse to having their cities grow indefinitely. They clung to the tried and tested ideal of the *polis eusynoptos,* the "surveyable city," and preferred founding a new city, *nea polis,* before the old one swelled to unreasonable size. Thus Naples came into being.

The sixth and fifth centuries B.C. saw Kyme at the height of its glory. It must have been a splendid city, though little has come down to us from that period. Its wealth was as proverbial as that of neighboring Capua and Sybaris. The Kymeans wore gold ornaments and garments embroidered with flowers. The most important buildings of the city were situated on the terrace south of the acropolis (the citadel), which ran almost parallel to the line of the coast. Fortification walls crowned the rims of the hills, especially toward the sea. There were broad streets, a market place, a gymnasium, statues, gateways—altogether it was a beautiful, happy, and prosperous city.

It was trade between the coast and the peasant population of the hinterland that made the Kymeans rich (as it did the inhabitants of so many other Greek cities on the Mediterranean). Their ships sailed the entire Tyrrhenian Sea, thereby running afoul of the economic and political interests of the Tyrrhenians, who dominated the region from the Alps as far as Rome and also ruled in part of Campania. These Tyrrhenians, as the Greeks called them—the Romans used the name "Etruscans"—had hitherto been virtually unlimited masters of the western coast of Italy, and at this time still ruled over Rome.

The Tyrrhenians joined forces with the native peasants, who were perhaps dependent upon them, and took the field against the Greek colonists. But Hellenic military tactics proved superior. The Kymeans engaged the enemy in a region so cut up by lakes and ridges that superior numbers were ineffective. The Greeks won an overwhelming victory. This battle took place in 524 B.C.; it is the first sure date in the history of Kyme, and one of the first definite dates in the history of Italy.

The victorious general, Aristodemos, was a favorite of the common people of Kyme. When he became aware that the rich were not well disposed toward him, he had his bitterest opponents executed, confiscated their property, and became dictator—or, as the Greeks called it, *tyrannos.*

Aristodemos' death—he was assassinated—marked the beginning of Kyme's decline. Although the city won a naval victory over the Etruscans in 474 B.C., it did so only by enlisting the aid of the other Greek cities of Campania and Sicily—especially Syracuse, then under the mighty tyrant Hiero. Subsequently, Syracuse took Kyme's place as the dominant Greek city of the West.

As yet, however, Kyme was still important. It coined its own silver coins, and frequently received envoys from Rome, who came to buy grain. But then the Italic tribes rebelled against their foreign rulers, both Etruscan and Greek. Toward the end of the fifth century they defeated the Kymeans in a pitched battle, besieged the city itself, and finally took it by assault and thoroughly pillaged it. Many Kymeans fled to Naples; those who stayed were reduced to slaves of the new masters, the Oscans and Samnites. The rude herdsmen and peasants of Campania were much taken with the well-formed Greek girls, Strabo relates, but he also notes that even in his time Kyme displayed many traces of Greek manners and institutions and had also preserved its worship of the Greek gods.

About a hundred years later the Romans conquered Campania. Thereafter, Cumæ—as the Romans called the city—gradually became a quiet small town. Neighboring Puteoli replaced it as a trading center, while aristocratic Romans preferred near-by Baiæ and Miseno as vacation resorts. Twice, however, the city was shaken out of its placidity. The first time was when a Roman architect named Cocceius decided to tunnel through the citadel hill of Cumæ. Behind this event lies a long story.

In one of the last phases of the frightful civil wars of the first century B.C., Pompey commanded the sea and Octavian (who was later to be Augustus) had to raise a fleet to oppose him. However, he was without a base for his fleet. Agrippa, one of his generals, found a solution. Ships were built on the quiet, legend-haunted shores of Lake Averno in Campania. The ancient forests of the near-by mountain slopes supplied the wood for the vessels. Lake Averno was then connected by a canal with Lake Lucrino, and the latter lake with the Gulf of Puteoli. Puteoli, Baiæ, and especially Miseno were developed into naval harbors. Two mountains, however, obstructed the highway that was to run to the western seacoast. Therefore the experienced architect Cocceius cut two tremendous tunnels, like the one he had already dug at Naples. One ran from Lake Averno to the plain of Cumæ, the second right through the Cumæan hill.

During the Augustan peace that followed these troubled times Cumæ again became the quiet town it had been, and under the successors of Augustus it remained a nostalgic refuge for poets seeking to escape the noise of the metropolis. Fine villas, the country estates of aristocratic Romans, sprang up everywhere, and the wines of the vicinity were praised by connoisseurs. As in Naples and Puteoli, a Christian community was soon flourishing in Cumæ; the ancient temples of the city were transformed into Christian basilicas during the fourth and fifth centuries. An inscription still preserved honors St. Maximus, the foremost martyr of the Cumæan congregation. In fact, for a time this congregation had a bishop of its own.

The tranquil life of the city was interrupted for the second time during the age of the great migrations, the *Völkerwanderung*. How the Ostrogoths, who had occupied all of Italy, behaved in Cumæ, we do not know. On the whole, their rule was an orderly one; in some places they pillaged, but, on the other hand, we learn that an Ostrogothic officer was executed for raping a Roman girl.

In any case, an army of liberation arrived; the emperor at Constantinople attempted to restore the old Roman Empire. In 536, Byzantine soldiers appeared at Cumæ and occupied the old acropolis, which was considered, aside from Naples, the most important position strategically in all of Campania.

The Byzantines liked Cumæ as well as had the Goths. They left the inhabitants pretty much in peace, and were themselves let alone for six years. Then Totila, king of the Ostrogoths, drove the Byzantines out of central Italy, besieged Naples, occupied Cumæ, and in his turn developed a liking for the citadel—probably less on account of its beauty than its situation and natural fortifications. He had gathered treasures from all of Italy and, as a protection, had buried some of these in the bed of the River Ticino in northern Italy;[4] the rest he stored at Cumæ and set a strong garrison under the command of his brother in the fortress. Once more Cumæ enjoyed ten years of peace in the protection of an occupying power.

The clash of arms rang once more when Narses, the Byzantine general, besieged the fortress. This was during the years 552–3. The cruel and clever King Teia feared for the treasure his predecessor, Totila, had deposited at Cumæ. Evading the Byzantine troops sent to meet him, he reached Campania and relieved the fortress. Fortune, however, turned against the Ostrogoths, and Teia was killed in a great battle at Mons Lactarius. His brother in the fortress of Cumæ held out for more than a year, and surrendered to the Byzantines only to join forces with them against the Franks and Alamans, who were pouring into Italy.

[4] Treasures buried in this way appear frequently in Teutonic legend, as in the Nibelung saga. This particular incident, however, is related by the Byzantine historian Procopius.

The Byzantines repaired the damaged walls and gates. To what extent they also contributed to a rebuilding of the city is unknown. The Lombards were the next enemy. In 717, about a hundred and fifty years after their arrival, a duke of Naples conquered Cumæ. Two hundred years later it was taken by the Saracens. The city was devastated, and it never recovered; Cumæ remained as a fortress, however, and became a hiding-place for pirates who operated so successfully in the Tyrrhenian Sea that a Neapolitan fleet was finally sent out against them. In 1207 the Neapolitans destroyed the former acropolis for good and all. Forest and marsh spread; malaria reigned. Only occasionally was the quiet of the region disturbed; then hunting horns sounded, dogs barked, hoofs thudded. For the kings of Naples were fond of hunting in the great woods.

That would have been the end of the old city if it had been no more than one of many pearls among the Greek cities of Italy. But Cumæ meant more than all the others that had suffered a similar fate. While Rome was still only a small town on the edge of the Etruscan domains a Cumæan sibyl was already famous. There were many sibyls in Greece, in the Orient, even in Sardinia. These sacred, prophetic women were considered to be very ancient, survivals of the mythic age. But the most famous of them was the Cumæan sibyl. To her came the hero Æneas, son of the goddess Venus and ancestor of Julius Cæsar, after he had left shattered Troy and was seeking a new home. The sibyl gave him information about his future destiny and led him to the underworld. That is how Virgil tells it, and the poet also describes the abode of the sibyl in the cliff at Cumæ: a tremendous cave with a hundred entrances, a hundred doorways through which the voice of the oracle could be heard giving answers.

In the Virgilian epic the memory of the sibyl survived the end of the ancient world. When Cocceius's tunnel was found in 1925, and cleared in 1926 and 1930, it was at first thought that this had been the sibyl's cave. Or, rather, the strategic purpose of the tunnel was known, but it was thought that Virgil had used it as a model for his poetic description of the cave. Anyone who enters the tunnel will understand the reason for this assumption.

On the west side of the cliff, the side that faces the sea, a gigantic dark maw gapes. High above it looms the wall of the cliff, gashed by numerous cracks. The outworks of the entrance have been destroyed; probably they were smashed during the Byzantine siege in the sixth century A.D. But deeper within the tunnel handsome supports and strong pillars can still be seen; a good part of the walls are faced with marble. After about thirty steps across a straight vestibule we enter a rectangular chamber, its ceiling arching more than sixty-five feet above the floor; the walls are full of niches and carvings of tufa. Rooms open out to the sides; there are burial vaults, well shafts, and cisterns.

An eerie atmosphere such as we might easily associate with a sibyl's cave hangs over the place. In the main shaft the floor is slippery; toads hop across our path, bats swoop about our heads. And there is the strange sense of being inside the mountain. Far above, separated from us by incalculable tons of rock, stands the temple of Apollo on the acropolis. We go on, round a bend, and ahead of us daylight gleams again. We have walked straight through the cliff of Cumæ.

In a prolongation of the line of this great tunnel lies

the second tunnel built by Cocceius, which pierces Monte Grillo. It is the most magnificent underground roadway produced by antiquity. Somewhat more than half a mile long, it runs in a perfectly straight line and is so wide that two carts can pass each other. Vertical and slanting shafts all along the route provide light; in Roman times a water conduit also passed through the tunnel. This tunnel leads to Lake Averno. When it was being built, and at the same time the fleet for Octavian was in construction on the lake, the whole region must have been bustling with life: the woods were being cut down, construction workers, ship's carpenters, and soldiers ruled the roost. Now another highway leads past Lake Averno. The burgeoning vegetation, the country houses, and the radiant blue sky combine to form a scene of utter loveliness. But in the past, from mythical times to the first century B.C., the tranquil lake in its extinct volcanic crater, the dark water, the shadowy woods, and the vapors of a thermal spring on its shore confirmed the impression that here was one of the entrances to the underworld. The sibyl had not far to go in order to lead Æneas into the realm of the shades.

In May 1932 the great event that stirred admirers of Virgil throughout the world occurred: the actual cave of the sibyls was found. Earlier quarrying had buried the entrance, and gravel had filled the interior. But by now the entire complex of caves has been almost completely restored. A long, perfectly straight, perfectly even shaft leads into the mountain. Its roof is narrow, for the walls slope sharply inward. Side shafts open out from this one; we enter a chamber, and our flashlights reveal niches, other rooms, cisterns. The shaft has been carved right out of the rock. But when, by whom? The walls are smooth; there is no sign of supporting masonry, nothing but naked rock on both sides and the ceiling about fifteen feet above. At last, after more than three hundred feet, we reach a large rectangular chamber with vaulted ceiling. This was the inner sanctuary of the grotto; here the sibyl lived.

"Fate she announces, writes the symbols and words upon leaves," says Virgil, and he describes how the sibyl left her prophecies arranged in order in front of the grotto. There the inscribed palm leaves lay, but when a special door was opened, a wind blew in and scattered them—for it is not well that men should know the future precisely. Today we no longer see doors, but the holes in the rock for the hinges can still be discerned. And such holes are found not only at the entrance to the sanctuary; everywhere, at various heights, and especially between the principal shaft and the rooms off it, we can find these eye-shaped holes into which wooden door frames and doors were fitted. Virgil's "hundred doorways" existed; the whole long shaft could be closed and plunged into total darkness if the sibyl wished. Or else, certain rooms could be opened up and light admitted to them. The principal shaft runs parallel to the western slope of the cliff; the side shafts penetrate the wall of the cliff, admitting light and air.

This grotto is more than twenty-five hundred years old at the least—all scholars agree on that—but exactly how old it is, none can say. Passageways and shafts of the same type lead to graves belonging to distinctly prehistoric times. In fact, one such has been discovered at Cumæ. There are a great many of them in Etruria and in the Cretan-Mycenæan region. Consequently, we are inclined to believe that the sibyls actually date from the second millennium B.C.

The ruins of the city of Cumæ have been only partly

excavated. Remains of many tombs dating from the ninth century B.C. down to the imperial age of Rome are scattered about the vicinity, in the plain and on the slopes of the hills, overgrown by shrubbery and vines. A path leads up the mountain that was once crowned by the acropolis. We walk up ancient steps, over ancient pavements of great stone slabs that still show the furrows made by iron-rimmed wagon wheels. We can see gateposts with holes for the gate hinges, thresholds, abutments, remains of the mighty walls that reinforced the natural fortification the mountain itself provided. Finally we reach a terrace on which stand the foundations of the temple of Apollo.

We walk on for some minutes, ancient pavement underfoot again, among hedges, vineyards, and holm oaks, until we arrive at the highest terrace of the acropolis. It bears the remains of a temple presumably dedicated to Zeus (Jupiter). Legend has it that this temple was erected by the same Dædalus who built the labyrinth for the Minotaur on Crete. The temple was so often rebuilt that little of the Greek foundations can be recognized. The tremendous baptismal font, however, is almost undamaged; this three-tiered font was, of course, placed in the temple when it was rededicated as a Christian basilica.

The view from here is magnificent. To the north the eye can follow the line of the Campanian coast. To the south the famous island of Ischia can be made out, and the Misenian peninsula with the dune, lined by trees and dense shrubbery, that separates Lago Fusaro from the sea. From this dune a narrow strip of sand runs toward the acropolis; it looks sunny and friendly against the forest of dark holm oaks and the impenetrable undergrowth that in classical times was dreaded because

of roaming wild beasts. This, then, was the coast where
Æneas was said to have landed.

In Virgil's account Æneas, before that landing, had
gone astray many times. From Sicily's coasts contrary
winds had driven him to North Africa, to the spot where
another refugee had just founded a city—Dido, the
princess who had fled her native Tyre after her brother,
Pygmalion, had slain her husband. The land for her
new city had been obtained by cunning; she had asked
a Numidian prince for as much land as an oxhide would
enclose, and when this was granted her, she cut the
hide into thin strips and so ringed a goodly area. For all
her cunning, however, Dido could not hold Æneas; he
set sail for Italy, and Dido killed herself for grief.

Various pre-Virgilian versions of the legend do not
mention the Trojan hero. As a matter of fact, the Trojan
War took place early in the twelfth century, but the
founding of Carthage probably took place in the eighth.
At about 800 B.C., moreover, Tyre was ruled by a King
Pygmalion.

The Berbers, who had inhabited the region "where Dido
landed" since time immemorial, possessed royal citadels
with surrounding small settlements, but nothing that could
legitimately be called a city. Actual cities began to develop
only after the Phœnicians established naval bases on the
North African coast in order to secure their sea route to
Spain. One of these bases was on a peninsula so favorably
situated for defense and for trade that it gradually developed into a city. *Quart hadasht* (New City) it was called
to distinguish it from the old Berber settlement that had
been located there. The Greeks transformed this name
into *Carchedon* and the Romans into *Carthago*.

For centuries Carthage had to pay tribute to the

neighboring Libyans. For a long time it also sent voluntary or forced gifts to the temple of Melkarth, the chief Phœnician god, at Tyre. But when Tyre fell under Assyrian dominion, Carthage gradually acquired supremacy over the Phœnician settlements in the western Mediterranean and was even able to establish settlements on the Pityusæ (the "Pine Islands" off the eastern coast of Spain).

When Tyre was conquered by Nebuchadnezzar in 586 B.C., the Carthaginians also found themselves facing a new enemy: the Greeks. But commercial and military conflict with the Greeks did not obstruct cultural contact. Greek works of art, Greek architecture, Greek literature were known and even imitated in Carthage. Nevertheless, the Carthaginians remained thoroughgoing Orientals. They dispensed with their nose rings, but their language remained Phœnician, and their dress likewise. The men wore voluminous garments with long sleeves, and topped their heads with little round caps; the women used jewelry and perfume to excess. They performed obeisance to the mighty by falling on their faces, ate no pork, and offered human sacrifices to the gods.

The city lived by and for trade. Consequently, the harbor was the most important part of it. There was a shallow bay in the southwestern part of the peninsula on which the city was situated. This bay, sheltered from the west and northwest winds, had early served as an anchorage. Later the bay was further protected by a mole four hundred feet long by one hundred feet wide. When this, too, no longer sufficed, two additional basins were dredged out to the southeast of the citadel. These basins communicated with the bay by a wide passage that in time of peril could be blocked off by chains.

Here the merchant ships of Carthage and of cities friendly to her anchored. Goods were piled high on the quays that surrounded the harbor, and in the adjoining warehouses. Walls shut the harbor off from the city proper; customs duties had to be paid on anything passing through the city gates.

Here, in this international port, chaffering and cheating, buying and selling, the extension and withdrawal of credit went on in all the dialects of the Phœnician language, and in Greek, Aramaic, and even Latin as well.

Like the passage for the ships to the south, there was an equally wide channel to the north which gave access to the naval base. This was surrounded by a wall. No stranger was ever permitted to look into it. The occasional spy who managed anyhow must have been amazed. What he saw at first glance resembled a portico around a circular basin, in the center of which lay a perfectly round island. On this island stood a splendid building for the commander of the navy. It was very tall, in order to afford him a clear view of the sea. The island and the rest of the harbor had broad quays providing two hundred and twenty slips for warships. In the armories back of these slips the war materials were stored, and in front of each door stood two Ionic columns.

A large, well-equipped, and well-maintained navy was vital to Carthage. Merchant ships had to be protected from pirates, trade rivals eliminated, and new markets and sources of raw materials opened up by voyages of discovery. As has been mentioned, Phœnician seafarers in the employ of Pharaoh Necos had circumnavigated Africa, starting from the Red Sea, around 600 B.C. Around 500 B.C. two Carthaginian fleets set out simultaneously on similar explorations.

One of them, under Himilco, sailed northward beyond the Pillars of Heracles with the intention of reaching the land whence the two most dangerous trade rivals of his native city—Tartessus (in southwestern Spain) and Massilia (Marseille)—obtained tin and lead. Tartessus communicated with Britain directly by sea, Massilia overland through Gaul. There are indications that Himilco, either driven off his course or with another destination in view, came close to discovering America two thousand years before Columbus; he is supposed to have turned back after reaching the Sargasso Sea. The second fleet, under Hanno, turned south. It sailed along the west coast of Africa, probably in successive stages rather than in one voyage, and may have reached Cameroon.

According to Strabo, the city of Carthage had a population of seven hundred thousand.[5] This figure is certainly exaggerated, but undoubtedly the Punic city was one of the most populous in the Mediterranean area.

The citadel of Carthage was situated on a plateau about seventeen hundred square yards in area. On this plateau also was situated the temple of Eshmun, whom the Greeks identified with their god of medicine, Asclepius. The Phœnician word for citadel was *byrsa,* which in Greek means a flayed oxhide. This chance phonetic resemblance may have been the origin of the story of Queen Dido's trickery.

The harbor quarter was a separate section of the city, as was the constantly expanding "new city." In the old city around the citadel, where space was limited and ground expensive, the houses rose to a height of six stories. As there were no springs inside the city, the population was dependent upon drilled wells. But these supplied only brackish water. Consequently, almost every house

[5] Strabo XVII.3.14, 15. On Necos: Herodotus IV.42. In general, we have followed the accounts of Carthage given in Pauly-Wissowa: *Realenziklopädie der Klassischen Altertumswissenschaft,* and by Julien in his *Histoire de l'Afrique du Nord* (Paris, 1951); also the *Historischer Atlas* of Bengtson-Milojcic (Munich, 1954).

had a cistern for catching rain water. A triple wall of fortifications protected the city on the western side, the land side. There were towers at intervals of two hundred feet, and built into the innermost wall were barracks for troops, stables for horses and elephants, and huge store-houses for food and hay.

In return for the industrial products Carthage exported, she received gold, ivory, hides, and slaves from Africa, silver and other metals from Spain, amber and ambergris from the northern lands. Sicily supplied oil and wine, Sardinia grain, copper, and silver. At first, trade was principally by barter; the Carthaginians struck coins rel-atively late. From the fourth century B.C. onward they used bronze coins, and from the third century silver.

The city council and the annually elected chief magis-trates, the two *suffetes* (*shofetim* = judges), were drawn from the leading commercial families. The tribute from African peoples, the taxes from subject cities, and the high customs and port duties imposed on every foreign merchant ship, together with the profits of her own trade, made Carthage the richest city in the Mediterranean, aside from Egyptian Alexandria. But she did not win this rank until the third century B.C.; her rise had been long and slow.

Carthage had become a Great Power. Aside from her strong position in Africa, Punic troops were garrisoned in southern Spain, in the Pityusæ, in the other Balearic islands, in Corsica, Sardinia, and Sicily. Sicily, for so long the apple of discord between the Greeks and Carthagin-ians, served the same function between the Carthaginians and the Romans. A local conflict in the Sicilian town of Messina resulted in an armed clash between the rivals, which became the proximate cause of the First Punic War (264-41). The outcome of this war robbed the

Carthaginians of their naval supremacy. Ultimately, the
Second Punic War (218–1) smashed the power of Carthage.

The Carthaginians had to surrender all their possessions outside of Africa, give up their war elephants and
almost all their warships, and pay enormous reparations.
Yet only a decade later Carthage surprised the Roman
Senate by offering to pay forty annual installments of
the war reparations all at once, and to assist Rome in
her impending Syrian war by building a fleet. Carthage
had recovered with unexpected rapidity. The Punic merchants had lost only a part of their capital and none of
their land, while their commercial adroitness had remained and their enterprise had increased. The East was
now the chief object of their trade. In the ports of the
Hellenistic world Carthaginian merchants were omni-
present. They were, after all, Orientals themselves; they
spoke every language, accepted all currencies, delivered
any kind of goods. And at home their agriculture once
more flourished. Carthage was close to regaining its former rank.

The war that Rome fought in 146 B.C. was a purely
preventive war, unjust from the humane point of view,
obvious and inevitable from the imperialistic point of
view. The Carthaginians made every effort to avoid this
war. When a Roman army stood at the gates of their
city, they surrendered 200,000 pieces of equipment, 2,000
catapults, and all their ships. But Rome insisted that they
abandon their city and settle ten miles inland, where
henceforth they would be without communication with
the sea. That demand the Carthaginians resisted with
the courage of despair. The women sacrificed their hair
to be made into strings for new catapults. Every day
140 shields, 300 swords, 500 lances, and 1,000 catapult

shots were produced. Nor was all this done on orders from the city council; the people flung themselves heart and soul into the defense effort. They responded to every action of the Roman besiegers with some counter measure. When the Romans blocked the old exit from the harbor, the Carthaginians dug a new one; and when the Roman catapults obtained command of both exits and cut off all import of food, the Carthaginians patiently endured hunger and continued to reject all demands for capitulation.

In the spring of 146 B.C., Scipio Æmilianus, the Roman general, gave the order for the final grand assault. His troops conquered the naval harbor, forced their way into the lower city, and at last reached the main square at the foot of the citadel. The houses along the main streets went up in flames, but still the Carthaginians did not surrender. From every window, from every roof, behind every corner, they fought. Soldiers, burghers, even the women battled on for six days and six nights.

On the seventh day General Hasdrubal surrendered with the last fifty-five thousand Carthaginians. He emerged from the temple of Eshmun, to which he had fled at the last. All around the city was burning, and as he stepped forward to confront Scipio, his wife and two children rushed into the flames.

The city was leveled to the ground and its soil cursed. Carthage had ceased to exist. Its fate was the same as that it had inflicted earlier upon other trade rivals; had Hannibal won the Second Punic War, he would probably have done the same to Rome.

Among the first Romans to break into the city was Tiberius Gracchus, later to win fame as tribune of the people. His brother Gaius disregarded the curse that had been laid upon the soil of the city, and planted on the spot the first Roman colony in Africa. Julius Cæsar continued the project. In 44 B.C., the year of his death, or shortly afterward, the "Colonia Julia Carthago" was established, but outside the accursed area. Octavian sent more colonists over, mainly army veterans. A new city arose, with large blocks of houses and regular streets. A great aqueduct alleviated the water shortage of Punic times and the city could have fountains and baths. A theater, circus, and amphitheater were built. Soon the Roman colony had become the intellectual and political center of the province. Poets and rhetoricians, saints, and heretics lived there; it underwent the rule of the Vandals, the Byzantines, and finally the Arabs. The ruins of this Roman city are located a few miles northeast of Tunis. But of ancient Carthage, the onetime capital of the Punic Empire, virtually nothing remains.

VIII

CITIES AND LEGIONARIES

A PIPELINE FOR WINE. THE SYBARITIC WAY OF LIFE.
ANTI-NOISE CAMPAIGN IN ANTIQUITY. COMPETITION
FOR THE OLYMPIC GAMES. MUSICAL COUNTEROF-
FENSIVE. RICH CAMPANIA AND THE QUEEN OF ROADS.
HANNIBAL AS LIBERATOR. THE SOLDIERS WHO WIN-
TERED IN CAPUA. THE RANKS OF CITIES. THE RESTIVE
MOUNTAINS. THE CITY BUILT IN A YEAR. ARAB MAR-
KET IN TIMGAD. REFUGE FOR HERMITS AND DOORLESS
MONASTERY.

SYBARIS WAS situated on the western rim of the bay
that is incised into the sole of Italy's boot. It is barely
150 miles westward from the island of Corfu. Framed
by a chain of hills, the city lay in the coastal plain between
the Sybaris and Crathis rivers like a gigantic theater open
to the sea. Back of it the mountains rose like terraces
to a height of seventy-five hundred feet. It is a lovely
portion of this earth, a richly blessed land.

The fertile soil returned the seed to the sower with
hundredfold increase. The grapes clung to the vines until
the first frost, affording a splendid late vintage; moreover,
the crop was so big that vast cellars had to be dug to
house it. Some of the wine was taken to the city by cart,

for home consumption; but the rest, according to Athenæus, was sent by earthenware pipeline directly to the coast, where huge clay vessels were filled and loaded aboard the ships. The wooded mountains supplied lumber and pitch for shipbuilding; the slopes of the hills provided ample pasture for cattle, goats, and sheep; the flowery glades favored beekeeping. Honey, wax, wool, and every imaginable kind of food was abundant throughout the whole district around Sybaris.

Greeks from Achæa and Trœzen in the Peloponnesus had settled here in the eighth century B.C. In this beneficent and hitherto sparsely inhabited region the new city-state flourished mightily.

In the "old country," the southern part of the peninsula from which the settlers had come, lay the famous military city of Sparta. Here meals were community matters, provided by the state and planned along typically austere lines. A man from Sybaris once partook of such a meal. Like his hosts, he reclined on a wooden frame instead of a couch, and ate the plain fare. His comment was significant: "In the past I used to be greatly impressed when I heard how brave were the Spartans in battle," he said. "But now that I have come to know you, I no longer see anything remarkable in it. The most arrant coward would sooner die than live the way you do." [1]

The citizenry of Sybaris, on the other hand, were truly masters of refined luxury and comfort. Thermæ were still unknown to them; it took Roman engineering to develop these great baths with their waters of different temperatures and their heated walls and floors. In the sixth century B.C. a gentleman was still content with an ordinary

---

[1] This anecdote is told twice by the grammarian Athenæus, who evidently considered it revealing (IV.138d and XII.518e). Appended to the second passage are many details about life in Sybaris. Further sources are Strabo, Herodotus, Diodorus, Justinus.

bathtub filled with hot water by slaves; to keep the temperature even, more hot water was constantly added. A slave might be too hasty, of course, and scald his master. In Sybaris a solution was found to this problem: the bath slaves had their feet tied together so that they could not run too fast with the jugs of water.

After the bath, the Sybarite went to dine. (Breakfast and lunch were of little importance; the principal meal was taken late in the afternoon.) Friends were invited; uninvited guests, too, were always welcome. Greek meals might consist of a wide variety of foods—poultry, fish, pork, veal, and kid. But a meal consisting of several courses succeeding one another in carefully planned order was first developed in the West, in Sybaris and Sicily.

For soups and sauces there were spoons; otherwise, everyone ate with his fingers. Slices of bread served as plates. People usually reclined by twos on the dining-couches; beside them stood small tables. Slaves brought in the platters, served the food, removed the tables after the meal, and poured washing-water over the guests' hands. Dessert consisted of cheese, fruit, and cake. Only then was the wine brought in and drunk mixed with water. Such caution was necessary, for the Sybarites did not want to become inebriated—at least, not too soon. The wine was so strong that the addition of water did not impair its taste or aroma. In winter, mulled wine also was drunk, spiced with honey, myrrh, aloes, saffron, or calamus. It was mixed in large vessels and ladled into the beakers. The tableware of the rich was of silver in other places besides Sybaris. But Sybaris boasted a peculiar custom of its own: every dinner guest had his own chamber pot. This could not even be considered shocking; respectable women did not take part in these banquets, and as a great many liquids were drunk, the idea was to save the diners the trouble of leaving the room frequently.

Luxury was carried so far that the Sybarites kept dwarfs and lap dogs to entertain them. To all other nations, both Greek and barbarian, this seemed a repulsive habit. Equally abhorrent were the way Sybarite boys were dressed in purple with gold braid in their hair, and the convention that required young men to dress in Milesian wool. For parades, the five thousand knights of Sybaris wore ornamental cloaks dyed with saffron over their cuirasses.

ANCIENT GREEK BASKET-CHAISE WITH TEAM OF MULES.

These knights constituted the upper class. The younger members of this equestrian class retired from the city during the summer; they went to a cooler region higher up in the mountains and spent their time in amusements. Their chief sport is suggested by the name of this summer resort: "Grotto of the Bathing Nymphs." As a matter of fact, the heat in the city was really unendurable during the summer. The sun beat down upon the mountain-ringed plain; fresh breezes could be expected only in the early morning and late evening.

The Sybarites were not fond of rising early, and they prized their sleep at night (or by day when they had celebrated all night) so much that they forbade all noisy

The citadel at Mycenæ. A ring of stone slabs surrounds the conference ground; below this are the shaft-graves of the rulers.

PLATE XXXIII

The cave of the Cumæan sibyl, discovered in the cliff at Cumæ (Kyme) in 1932.

PLATE XXXIV

A remarkable example of ancient engineering skill: the half-mile-long tunnel connecting Lake Averno with Cumæ, built by Augustus for strategic reasons.

Lake Averno, near modern Naples, was considered one of the entrances to the underworld.

PLATE XXXV

Greek temple in Marmara, a suburb of Delphi
—the seat of the famous Delphic oracle.

PLATE XXXVI

The governor's box in one of the two amphitheaters at Carnuntum, one of the most important Roman garrisons on the Danube.

Carnuntum: in the raw climate of Pannonia, Roman heating engineering proved its worth. This house in the civilian city, which served as a tavern and brothel, had an ingenious floor-heating system.

PLATE XXXVII

Bronze statuette of a Negro boy, one of
the treasures of the museum at Carnuntum.

PLATE XXXVIII

Bust of a young boy, from Carnuntum.

PLATE XXXIX

Ruins of the Roman garrison town of Thamugadi (Timgad), in Algeria.
Founded by the Emperor Trajan, A.D. 100, it was destroyed along with the
other legionary city of Lambæsis by Berber tribes in the sixth century.

PLATE XL

ng down the main
e of Thamugadi
d the arch of Trajan.

The Temple of Venus
at Thamugadi.

PLATE XLI

A relic of the Roman occupation of Africa: the triumphal
arch of Diocletian at Sbeitla (ancient Sufetula) in Tunisia.

PLATE XLII

Etruscan burial chamber with "armchair" on which urns were placed.

PLATE XLIII

Small bronze statue of an Etruscan warrior, in the Egineta
style, now in the Museo Archéologico in Florence.

PLATE XLIV

Etruscan buck goat from
Bibbona in Tuscany.

Etruscan bronze chimera—a mythical monster with the head of a goat,
a lion's body, and a serpent as a tail—found at Arezzo in Tuscany.

PLATE XLV

Terra-cotta head of an E[t]ru[s]can warrior, from about 500 [B.C.]

An Etruscan chariot, sixth century B.C., beautifully sculptured in bronze.

PLATE XLVI

Bronze statuette of an Etruscan warrior setting out for battle. From the fifth century B.C.

Mural in a tomb in the Etruscan city of Tarquinii, sixth century B.C. It depicts the favorite occupations of the dead prince: fishing and bird-hunting.

PLATE XLVII

The excavation of the Great Bath at Mohenjo-daro, one of the two chief cities of the pre-Aryan culture that flourished in the Indus Valley more than five thousand years ago.

An inscribed stamp seal fro the ruins of Mohenjo-daro still undeciphered script Indus Valley culture a above the finely worked of a humped and dewlappe

PLATE XLVIII

trades. Smiths, metalworkers, and carpenters had to locate their workshops outside the city proper. Not even roosters were permitted in the city.

All over Greater Greece tales were told of the indolence of the Sybarites. When a citizen of Sybaris left the city for the country, he went by chariot, of course. But, even so, the story was that he took three days to cover a day's journey. One Sybarite is said to have suffered a stroke from overexertion after merely watching a group of ditch-diggers. When a runner at the athletic field of the neighboring city of Croton toed the cinders on the track to loosen them for a good jump-off, a horrified visitor from Sybaris asked him whether they did not have slaves for such work. Naturally the pipeline for wine from the cellars directly to the port—an eminently sensible technical innovation—was considered proof of the laziness of the Sybarites.

While such stories may in part have been mere gossip, they possess a certain historical value, and occasionally they serve not only to describe the mode of life and the wealth of the Sybarites, but also to indicate the sources of that wealth. It was no coincidence that the young men of Sybaris wore Milesian wool. Not that Sybaris lacked wool of her own; she even had her own plants for purple-dyeing. In spite of this, no import duty was leveled on garments from Miletus. For the friendship between Miletus and Sybaris was very close; the commercial interests of the two cities complemented one another neatly. Sybaris supplied raw materials, slaves, and foodstuffs (along with the goods already mentioned, fish mayonnaise and fruit syrup were among the specialties of the city); from Miletus came the products of an already advanced industry, and all the precious goods of the Orient.

Sybaris had no proper harbor, but that was no great hardship. Cargo vessels were heavy, shallow ships with bulky hulls and without prows; they could simply be drawn up on the beach. These ships did not bring wares for Sybaris alone, great though the needs of the rich, spoiled city were. Friendship with Sybaris threw open an extensive sales territory to the exporters in Miletus and other Asia Minor cities. By crossing the mountains to the west and northwest of the city, columns of mules could reach the coast of the Tyrrhenian Sea in a two-day journey. Sybaris had bases on that coast, as we have already mentioned in connection with Pæstum. The trade route ran on unobstructed to the rich and haughty Etruscans, who welcomed and paid well for all imports.

This middleman's position contributed at least as much as the fertility of the district to making Sybaris wealthy and powerful. Its dominions extended over more than twelve hundred square miles—that is to say, over a greater area than Attica. Twenty-five cities and four native tribes were subjects of Sybaris. The silver coins of the city were gladly accepted as currency throughout the entire eastern Mediterranean area. These coins, called *staters,* were equal to four drachmæ; the face of the coin showed a bull with turned head, while its other side showed the same image in reverse.

Their wealth allegedly led the Sybarites to try to outdo the Olympic Games, which were of such importance for all of Greece; at the same time as these games, similar contests were held in Sybaris. But, though the Greeks were good businessmen, they continued to prize the victor's wreath fashioned of sprigs from the sacred olive tree more than the silver wreath that rich Sybaris offered.

There must have been doubts that so much wealth, comfort, and carefree happiness could last, and an embassy from Sybaris went to the oracle at Delphi to inquire how long their good fortune would continue. The reply was reassuring: not until they began to show more honor to a mortal man than to a god would war and internal discord descend upon them.

When the inevitable catastrophe came at last, the explanation was sought and found. A citizen of Sybaris had been lashing a slave, and had pursued him with the whip even when the unfortunate man fled into a temple. But when he ran on and sought refuge at the tomb of his master's father, the master finally desisted: the Sybarite revered his father more than the god. Thus the oracle was fulfilled and the time had come for an end to the city's good fortune. But perhaps economic rivalries are a better explanation of the disaster that befell this rich commercial city.

On the same southern Italian coast, about sixty miles southwest of Sybaris, where the gulf merges with the open sea, lay the city of Croton. It possessed the one good harbor of the region, but lacked the fruitful hinterland with which Sybaris was blessed. Croton, consequently, was almost entirely dependent upon maritime commerce. Naturally, it was painful for the people of Croton that most goods from Greece and Asia Minor were shipped to Sybaris and from there transported overland. There were other disparities besides commercial rivalry. The Crotonese had an aristocratic constitution and lived modest and moralistic lives under the guidance of Pythagoras, the philosopher.

In Sybaris there was a certain amount of friction between citizens of Achæan and of Trœzenese descent. In addition, there was the natural conflict between the poorer classes and the rich. A man named Telys became leader of the popular party and set himself up as tyrant.

He expelled the five hundred richest citizens and confiscated their property. The exiles fled to Croton and sought protection at the altars of the gods. Pythagoras came to their support, and the Crotonese went to war on their account. So, at any rate, the tradition goes, as reported by the Sicilian historian Diodorus. Some of the details he adds seem scarcely credible. Some three hundred thousand Sybarites allegedly marched to battle against one hundred thousand Crotonese. Milon, a consistent winner in the Olympic Games, is said to have led the men of Croton, wearing the Olympic wreath on his head and equipped like Heracles with lionskin and club. By sheer physical strength he is supposed to have forced the enemy to retreat. A trick is also said to have aided the Crotonese. The Sybarites had developed the art of manège to such a fine point that their horses had learned to prance in time to the music of flutes. Hearing about this from the Sybarite refugees, the people of Croton took flutists along with them when they marched to battle. These musicians played a dance just before the cavalry attack was to begin. The Sybarite horses pricked up their ears, abandoned their military gait, left the line of battle, and pranced toward the flute-players! Thus the Sybarites lost their picked cavalry troops. . . .

Local tradition among the Sybarites gave a rather more credible reason for the defeat: that the enemy obtained aid from Dorieus, a prince of Sparta who had set out as a soldier of fortune and had just arrived from Africa with a sizable body of troops. His tough, battle-scarred veterans proved more than a match for the effete knights and ill-trained foot soldiers of Sybaris.

At any rate, the war between the two cities did not last long. Within seventy days Sybaris was conquered and plundered. But because the war had been fought not only for the cause of the political exiles, but on account of serious commercial rivalries, the defeated city was not permitted to rise again. It was totally demolished, and the stream bed of the Crathis River was diverted over the ruins, so that nothing remained.

This destruction took place in the year 511 B.C.[2] The surviving Sybarites fled, as has been mentioned earlier, to Poseidonia and to their other commercial bases, Laos and Skidros. In the middle of the fifth century their descendents once more founded a settlement named Sybaris on the Crathis River, but this, too, was destroyed by the people of Croton after a space of only five years. A third city of the same name was established in 444 B.C. with the aid of Athens; silver coins of that city are extant, bearing on one side the familiar bull and on the reverse the head of Pallas Athene. After a while the city became a Panhellenic colony, and its name was changed to Thurii. Hippodamus of Miletus, the foremost authority in city-planning, laid out the city in conformity with his theory, with regular streets intersecting at right angles. This city flourished for nearly a thousand years, down to the era of the Goths. But its history cannot be considered a continuation of the history of Sybaris.

The original stock, haunted by dreams of past glory, emigrated from Thurii. Once again they founded a new city. This time it was located on the border of Croton's territory. But this New Sybaris never developed into a town of any importance, and somewhere in the middle of the fourth century B.C. it was overrun by the native peoples of the peninsula, like so many other of the Greek cities of Italy. The age of great colonization was over.

---

[2] According to Gustave Glotz and Robert Cohen: *Histoire Grecque*, Vol. I (Paris, 1938). Most other histories give the year as 510. The German historian Julius Beloch calls the story that the river was diverted over the ruins of Sybaris a "silly fable."

Of Sybaris there remained only the name and the reputation for wealth and luxurious living.

"Of all landscapes, not only of Italy but in the whole world, Campania is the most beautiful. No climate is more pleasant, no soil more fruitful. Flowers bloom there twice a year, and legend speaks of the rivalry between Bacchus and Ceres in this region. Nothing can be more hospitable than the Campanian coast. Here lie the famous ports of Caieta, Misenus, and Baiæ with its thermal springs, the lakes Lucrino and Averno, each like some tranquil backwater of the sea itself. Here are mountains clothed with vines, Mounts Gaurus, Falernus, Massicus, and, most beautiful of all, Vesuvius, whose fire equals that of Etna. Here are cities by the sea, Formiæ, Cumæ, Puteoli, Naples, Herculaneum, Pompeii, and the chief of them all, Capua, which was once counted among the three greatest cities of the world, along with Rome and Carthage." These are the words of the historian Florus, writing in the second century A.D. His praise is by no means exaggerated; the soil is fruitful to this day. According to Strabo, it yielded splendid grain, especially wheat; in some districts the millet was harvested twice and the spelt thrice a year, vegetables as often as four times. The wine was world-famous. The district was populated by sturdy Oscan peasants, but the ruling group were the Etruscans who back in 600 B.C. had settled in a city south of the Volturnus (Volturno) River and named after this stream.

Over the years the Samnite farmers from the near-by mountains found the city more to their liking than their own pasture lands. Large numbers of them filtered peaceably into the city, until they and the native Oscans dominated the life of the city. The Etruscans, exhausted by many wars, formed only a weak upper crust. In the year 424 B.C. a great festival was held. When the Etruscans, heavy with food and wine, lay sound asleep, a terrible bloodletting began. Next day the Samnites were masters of the city, which they renamed Capua.

At this time Rome was still at war with her neighbors to the south, the Volscians. Campania remained studiously aloof from this conflict. But not a hundred years later envoys from Capua came to the City of the Seven Hills to beg for help. The Samnites had prospered in the rich plain; they had mingled with the Oscans to form the new nation of Campania, had discarded their rude manners and learned from neighboring Kyme to read and write, while at the same time remaining tillers of the soil. Their aristocratic youths practiced equestrian exercises, but, on the whole, the urban Samnites were no longer the tough fellows they had once been. Now their cousins came down out of the mountains, a rude folk such as they themselves had been a century before, attracted even as they had been by the fertile soil. From Mount Tifata, east of Capua, fighting hordes descended into the plain, defeated the Capuans in a pitched battle, and besieged the city.

Perhaps the Capuans remembered that bloody night when their forefathers had wiped out the Etruscans, and could see themselves suffering a similar fate. The growing military power of Rome seemed to be their sole hope. When the Roman Senate refused to defend Capua against the mountain people, the Capuans (according to the Roman historian Livy) simply repudiated their political independence and declared themselves subjects of Rome.

To hold on to this new possession, however, Rome had to fight a number of long and bloody wars against the Samnite mountaineers. But the Capuans had done well to choose Roman rule in preference to subjugation by the mountain tribes. In the year 312 the Appian Way was built from Rome to Capua. The whole length of this "queen of roads" was paved with slabs of stone, and was wide enough for two wagons to drive side by side. Bridges carried the road over rivers, levees protected it when it ran through marshlands. The construction of the Via Appia was one of the great feats of Roman history. Although built for military reasons, it proved enormously valuable for commerce. All the goods from the Orient which arrived in the Campanian port of Puteoli had to be transshipped through Capua in order to reach Rome. All travelers from Rome to the south also passed through Capua. Thus, the wealth of the city increased constantly. Lavishness extended even to the burial of the dead. The tombs, underground vaults comparable to Etruscan graves, were embellished with magnificent frescoes and the ceilings were draped with cloth of gold. The language of the city remained Oscan, and Oscan words were engraved on the copper coins, but gold and silver coins bore Latin inscriptions.

In spite of the riches and security the rule of Rome had brought them, the Campanians were not overfond of the Romans. During the long struggle with the Samnites, Capua once proved to be unreliable. Punishment fell swiftly: Rome confiscated the precious Falernian district as far as the Volturno River and distributed the land among needy Roman citizens. Roman prefects were appointed to rule the territory of Capua and Cumæ, thus reducing the powers of the native magistrates. On the other hand, sixteen hundred Campanian knights who had remained loyal were rewarded with Roman citizenship.[3]

As was the case almost everywhere in the ancient world, there were sharp tensions in Capua between the leading citizens, who controlled the city council, and the common people. The rich were closely allied to Rome by commercial interests and family relationships; Rome had gone so far as to grant the *jus connubii,* the law recognizing the validity of marriages between the inhabitants of the two cities. Hence, Capua adhered to Rome even during the Second Punic War when Hannibal crossed the Alps and penetrated into Italy. But after the Roman defeat at Lake Trasimenus (217 B.C.) there was open talk in the common people's party of an alliance with Hannibal. After the Battle of Cannæ the city council yielded and concluded an advantageous separate peace with Hannibal. Under its terms the city was to remain independent and no Campanians would be required to serve in the Punic army. Romans who had remained in the city were cruelly put to death. Men, women, and children marched to meet Hannibal and cheered their "liberation." At the end of the year Hannibal led his army to Capua to go into winter quarters there.

For most of the soldiers of the Punic army that was the pleasantest winter of their lives. The cavalrymen from the plains of Numidia, the wild Iberians, and the

[3] Livy VIII.11. Modern scholars incline to give little credence to some stories of this Roman historian. Livy himself says frequently that his sources are doubtful. However, Amedeo Maiuri, the foremost authority on the history of Campania, vigorously defends him against charges that he lacked knowledge of the region and the facts. Maiuri's essay on the subject, *"Con Livio a traverso il Sannio e la Campania,"* was published in the August 1950 issue of *Atene e Roma.* We have bypassed the disputed issues and have, in the main, followed Livy's account. Additional sources are various other essays by Maiuri and the article "Capua," by Christian Hülsen, in Pauly-Wissowa: *Realenzikopädie.*

mercenaries from the mountains of Gaul had never known
the pleasures of urban life. Hannibal had not established
a camp, but had quartered his soldiers in the city itself.
There they slept until midday—in a real bed perhaps
for the first time in their lives. They became aware of
how good it was to have a roof sheltering them from
the winter rains, of how warm it was before a charcoal
brazier. Although they did not attend the theater, they
soon learned to appreciate the joys of warm baths; they
learned to drink the best wines, to eat and sleep, revel
and make love as they pleased. These soldiers had plenty
of money; here they could spend the pillage of the last
several years. And often they did not have to pay at all,
for the Capuans did all in their power to keep the army
in the city as long as possible. The thought was gradually
beginning to steal upon them that once the Carthaginians
departed, they would have to bear the brunt of war alone.

Hannibal never won another victory like that of
Cannæ. After the winter at Capua his soldiers had little
taste for sleeping on the bare ground. Capua had compensated them for the terrible crossing of the Alps and
for their many other hardships, but it had not strengthened them for new undertakings of the same kind. Many
came creeping back to their sweethearts; Capua became
a gathering-place for deserters.

And then the hand of war fell heavily upon Capua
itself; for the first time the rich city faced famine. The
fields could not be tilled because Roman troops were
near by; they were occupying the Samnite mountains and
seemed to be preparing for a siege. Alarmed, the Capuans
sent envoys to Hannibal, who was at Taranto with his
army, and asked for provisions. But Hannibal's supply
column was intercepted by the Romans; an inconclusive
battle was fought under the walls of the city, and then,

in 212 B.C., a regular siege was begun under the direction
of both Roman consuls.

The city was completely encircled and all imports were
cut off. By the first months of the following year the
poor and the slaves were already suffering hunger. The
Campanian cavalry launched small and successful sorties,
but whenever the fighting was on foot the Roman infantry proved superior. At last Hannibal realized that he
would have to come to the aid of the city or lose the
respect of his allies in Italy. He arrived with an army
that included thirty-three elephants. The Romans re-
pelled his attack, and the Capuans, who had supported
Hannibal with a vigorous sortie, suffered heavy casualties.

After this defeat the Punic general tried another tack:
he marched against Rome itself. But the Romans did not
abandon their siege of Capua; they sent only a part of
their army to Rome to protect the capital. The citizens
of Capua dangled between fear and hope. When at last
they saw the detached elements of the Roman army
returning, they realized that Hannibal had failed to conquer Rome and had given up the struggle. At that they
lost courage. The populace gathered in angry mobs,
forced the city council to assemble, and commanded the
nobles, on pain of violence, to attend it. The council discussed capitulation. Vibius Virrius, who five years earlier
had instigated the Capuan defection to Hannibal, drew
up a frank inventory of Capua's crimes against Rome and
the punishments that might attend them. While envoys
were departing for the Roman camp, he invited his
friends to his house. Twenty-seven of the nobles came.
They dined together once more, drank their delicious
Campanian wine one last time, and then took poison.
Next day the Porta Jovis opposite the Roman camp was
thrown open. One legion and two cavalry detachments

entered, occupied the other gates, gathered all weapons in the city, and took the Punic garrison prisoner. The city councillors were placed in chains; 2,270 pounds of gold and 30,200 pounds of silver were confiscated.

No one had expected a mild punishment; many Capuans, in fact, feared that the city would be leveled to the ground. The Romans, however, were harsh but not unreasonable. The city of Capua was dissolved as a political unit, but the houses and even the city walls were untouched.

The nobility of Capua, however, was virtually extinguished. Many citizens were settled elsewhere, or even sold as slaves, their punishment depending upon the degree of their collaboration with Hannibal. Farmers, merchants, artisans, freedmen, and many ordinary citizens remained in the city. The farmlands and public buildings were declared Roman property; city council and popular assemblies were abolished. Roman citizens were settled on land that had formerly belonged to Capua; Roman colonies were established along the coast in Puteoli, Volturno, and Literno. And gradually the fertility of Campanian soil and the happy situation of the city repaired the harm that the disloyalty and folly of her citizens had wrought.

Moreover, these Capuans were hard-working. The products of their domestic industries continued in demand throughout Italy. Perfumes and rugs, baskets and rope, pails, jugs for oil, water, and wine, and a great variety of bronze utensils were manufactured in Capua.

Rome continued her policy of settling needy citizens in Campania. But these new colonists soon grew overproud in the possession of their old citizenship and their new prosperity. The chiefs among the Roman colonists did not call themselves *duumviri* (equivalent approximately to "mayors"), as was customary in other cities, but arrogated to themselves the title of *prætor*. Like high officials in Rome, they were attended by lictors bearing the famous fasces. Those who had hungrily pursued minor offices in Rome could feel like little kings in Capua. The proverbial arrogance of the Capuans was evidently not inbred in the Campanian stock, but was an outgrowth of the fortunate economic conditions of the district. When Senatorial investigators came from Rome, they were regarded as alien intruders, and in their turn they found much to criticize in Capua.

In his oration *De lege agraria,* Cicero, who was consul in 63 B.C., declared: "The Campanians are always proud of the yield of their fields, of the size of their fruits, and of the cleanliness, efficient planning, and beauty of their city. This wealth and abundance in everything has been the prime cause of notorious Campanian arrogance." Thus, there was nothing new in the Campanian attitude. But now the Roman colonists had gone so far as to install in office one hundred councillors, ten augurs, and six *pontifices* (priests). "Their Capua has developed on a plain and is laid out in broad avenues. They will mock and despise Rome, which bobs up and down on hills and valleys, crowds story upon story in its buildings, and can claim no especially good streets, nothing but narrow alleys."

Perhaps Cicero really felt strongly about Campanian arrogance; perhaps he was exaggerating somewhat for political ends. At any rate, Rome needed more territory for her propertyless populace, and in Campania there was ample land. In 59 B.C., therefore, Julius Cæsar sent twenty thousand colonists to the region, each with at least three children. Mark Antony followed his example fifteen years later, and Octavian also. The land was state property, after all, and Rome had often promised her soldiers that they would be rewarded with farms after their period of service was over. When not enough land was available, some property-owners were simply expropriated.

To compensate the old families, Rome gave Capua valuable farmlands on the island of Crete and built her an aqueduct at home. This aqueduct swooped down from Mount Tifata to the east of the city. Built with the familiar handsome Roman arches, it was a fine addition to the landscape and, of course, enormously valuable to the city. The native Capuans had reason to be content.

Henceforth they lived peaceable lives, taking little interest in the current of world events. They had their theaters and baths, their amphitheater seating forty thousand spectators—the second largest in Italy—their forums, and a capitol with a temple of Jupiter that was dedicated by the Emperor Tiberius in person. Near the amphitheater a fine triple-gated archway spanned the Appian Way. In the city's temple of Artemis the priests displayed an age-old silver cup that looked like Nestor's drinking-cup as described by Homer; an inscription it bore in letters of gold actually declared it to have been in that ancient king's possession. The old extramural temple of a mother diety existed no longer. Soon also Christianity came to Capua. The city had its Basilica Apostolorum long before the new religion was officially sanctioned.

How in the course of centuries the rank of cities changes, how old ones decline simply because they cannot keep pace with the growth of others, and how new ones rise to greatness, we may learn from the didactic poem *Claræ Urbes* (*Famous Cities*), by Decimus Magnus Ausonius, the fourth-century poet. Naturally he names "golden Rome, the home of the gods," as the first of cities. Then follow Constantinople, the new capital of the eastern part of the Empire, and Carthage, which had long since regained its ancient rank. Almost the equal of these both in size and in the vices and restlessness of the populace are Antioch in Syria and Alexandria in Egypt, both at that time more than half a millennium old. Treveri, present-day Trier, is assigned sixth place— testimony of the remarkable development of provincial cities during the early centuries of the Roman Empire. Mediolanum (Milan) takes seventh place; there, we are told, "everything is wonderful—the quantity of goods, the innumerable well-kept houses, the lively spirit of the peo- ple and their cheerful temperament."

The poet continues: "And I do not wish to pass over Capua, great for its nearness to the sea, its way of life and food, its pleasures and wealth and former fame." Then he speaks of the by now remote days of Capua's disloyalty to Rome, and concludes: "That prosperous city, mighty in treasures, was once a second Rome and could carry her head as high as Rome. Now, however, she has lingered behind and barely takes eighth place." (After Capua there follow Emerita in Spain, which today is the small town of Merida; Athens, the city of culture and philosophy; then the Sicilian cities of Catina (Catania) and Syracusæ. The last three "famous cities" were in France: Tolosa [Toulouse], Narbo [Narbonne], and Burdigala [Bordeaux], the poet's home town.)

Even after being sacked by the Vandals under Geiseric in A.D. 456, Capua was able to recover. It survived the wars that followed the rule of the Ostrogoths in Italy. Under the Lombards, Capua resigned its position as capital of Campania to Benevento, where the Lombard dukes resided; but the city continued wealthy. This

wealth, however, proved something less than a blessing,
for it lured the Saracens, who were at this time the
scourges of the Mediterranean. Saracen pirate ships from
Africa, Crete, and Spain raided the coasts of Italy, conquered Sicily, and threatened Rome herself. In A.D. 840
they destroyed Capua, and this time the destruction was
final.

Its successor, Capua Nuova, was built about two miles
farther to the west. In the immediate vicinity there is a
village known as Santa Maria di Capua Vetere. The ruins
present a dreary appearance. Nowhere else, scarcely even
in Rome itself, has so much been plundered. Two thousand years ago Julius Cæsar's colonists opened and
robbed ancient graves of whatever struck them as valuable. Men of later centuries did likewise. Whatever antiquities had not been stolen and sold abroad—and their
number was paltry in comparison with the city's original
treasure trove—had been deposited in a museum. And
during the Second World War this museum was destroyed by bombs.

But the soil of Capua still contains surprises. In the
spring of 1955 a man bought a piece of land there with
his winnings in the soccer pool. When he had the foundation for a house dug, a splendid mosaic floor came to
light.

In Capua, as in Sybaris, beauty and the more gracious
side of life triumphed over militarism. Both cities, however, displayed only one aspect of urban life in antiquity.
The harsher aspects of life, leaving little room for myth,
were represented by the garrison cities whose sites were
chosen for strategic reasons.

At the death of Augustus in A.D. 14, Roman soldiers
were established on the coast of the North Sea and on

the Black Sea, on the border of the Sudan and at the Strait of Gibraltar. These troops defended the frontiers of Rome; under their protection, trade and agriculture bloomed and cities grew larger and more beautiful. But the camps in which the soldiers themselves lived had for many centuries been constructed on the same rectangular plan, surrounded by a trench and protected by a rampart and palisades. Where the camp was to be permanent a solid wall was built.

Early in the second century A.D. the Third Legion was shifted from the Numidian city of Theveste (present-day Tebessa in Algeria) some 105 miles farther westward. This move was designed to keep a closer watch on the dangerous bandits of the eastern Atlas Mountains, who had ever been arch-foes of peaceful farming communities. The mountain range was flanked by a network of forts, and the new camp of the Third Legion was set up about one hundred miles from the coast. It was in the region that serves as a corridor between the Sahara and the cultivated coastal plain known as The Tell—a region restive to this day.

The tiny Berber village of Lambæsis, near which the Legion and therefore the governor had now settled, became the most important place in the province of Numidia. The presence of the Legion brought material advantages. Wherever soldiers are, tavernkeepers and merchants appear. Artisans and washerwomen, stableboys and draymen are needed, and a good many soldiers will look for a girl among the village beauties.

The life of the Roman professional soldier was occasionally dangerous but for the most part infinitely monotonous. He had to serve out his twenty years; he knew no other existence but that of the camp, and could hope for nothing more than becoming a centurion someday.

But the unvarying round of service in camp or on campaign, with a little relaxation over wine and dice or a
visit to the Berber village on duty-free evenings—all this
underwent a fundamental change in April of A.D. 193
when the soldiers of the Fourteenth Legion, at the other
extreme of the Empire, proclaimed their commander,
Lucius Septimus Severus, emperor.

The distant spot where Septimus Severus had been
proclaimed emperor was at Carnuntum, one of the most
important of the camps at the Danube, situated some
twenty-five miles east of Vindobona (Vienna). The
soldiers serving there were mostly Celts from upper Italy.
They had had little difficulty striking up alliances with
the womenfolk of the Celtic-Illyrian peasantry of the
vicinity. (These Celts had been transplanted by the
Romans from their mountainous homes down into the
plain. Their new settlement soon developed into a city.
Trade—the Amber Route leading from the Baltic to the
Adriatic Sea crossed the Danube at this point—plus the
fertility of the land and the presence of the garrison
itself all combined to make conditions favorable to urban
expansion.) Now Severus ruled that the legionaries
would henceforth be permitted to contract legal marriages with their mistresses and live with them; they need
stay in camp only when on duty.

One of the reasons for this edict was Severus' wish to
enlist in the army the sons of the legionaries, who by
that time were readily available as new recruits. Since
as soldiers these young men were entitled to Roman
citizenship—whereas their citizenship status had been
unclarified before—their fathers obeyed the imperial
edict eagerly and rapidly everywhere.[4]

---

[4] In the long run the edict was unfortunate for the Empire: it im-
mobilized the army.

To return to Lambæsis: the Legion camp there, which now also became the world of the legionaries' sons, was 1,600 feet long by 1,320 feet wide, with four gates protected by strong bastions, these being the termini of the camp streets. The streets crossed about midway, thus dividing the camp into four quarters, each with its houses for officers, its barracks, stables, storerooms, cisterns, and its catapults lined up along the walls patrolled by the sentinels.

BUILDING A CAMP, AFTER A RELIEF ON THE COLUMN OF TRAJAN.

About a mile away the city of Lambæsis sprang into being. Here the soldiers lived with their families during their term of service, and here they usually remained as veterans, planting their vegetables and raising their domestic animals. When the hunters from the mountains or the nomads from the desert made a raid against the fields of the peaceable farmers, the former soldiers seized their arms with as much alacrity as those still in service. What they lacked in youthful strength they made up for in experience. In return for such services the governor, in the name of the emperor, assigned them additional land to till. As armed farmers they constituted reliable supplementary fighting forces. They were needed; though the Romans had strong *auxilia* (troops of subject and allied peoples) consisting of Spaniards, Corsicans, Sardinians, Gauls, Dalmatians, Palmyrene archers—who were particularly skilled in desert warfare—and Berbers, there was only the single legion of actual Roman troops in the land. At full strength this legion had some five to seven thousand men. The Third Legion was a famous one; in gratitude for its aid against a rival, Emperor Septimius Severus had conferred upon it the honorary title of *Pia Vindex,* the "Dutiful Avenger."

Lambæsis, then, had become a city. A boulevard nearly a mile long, the Via Septimiana, led from camp to city, passing through a triple-gated triumphal arch at the foot of the city hill. A similar arch arose in front of the capitol, chief temple of the city, while a third was later erected on the road from Lambæsis to the neighboring town of Verecunda, some two miles away. On the Via Septimiana, just outside the city, an amphitheater was built. Lambæsis had become an outpost of Roman civilization.

The Legion did not confine itself to military duties alone. The monuments that lined the boulevard between the camp and the city were its work. The soldiers built roads and bridges, improved and maintained irrigation installations and aqueducts, reclaimed bogs, planted trees and hedges.

Such works of civilization were not undertaken only in Lambæsis or only after Septimius Severus had become emperor. There was, for example, Thamugadi, twenty-five miles east of Lambæsis and situated at an elevation of thirty-three hundred feet above sea level. A century earlier Emperor Trajan had declared this small military post a settlement area for discharged legionaries, thus establishing a further center of Roman life and manners. Veterans of the Thirtieth Legion, known as *Ulpia Victrix* (Ulpia was Trajan's family name), built the city within a year, so it is said, and settled down there. The buildings they erected formed the core of the city, which was as regular as a chessboard. However, it soon outgrew the rectangle of fortification walls.

Situated as it was on a plateau, Thamugadi's pretty country houses and hedged farmsteads could be seen from far off by the Berbers who came to the city on market day. Everything they saw must have served to convince them that the Romans were here not as oppressors, but as teachers of a better way of life. Thamugadi could well stand comparison with far older cities. In fact, it was in some respects superior to these, for here there had been no need to make the city plan conform to venerable existing structures. As soon as Emperor Trajan established the colony, the forum had been laid out with classical Roman amplitude and balance. It was a square paved with bluish limestone slabs, surrounded by colonnades in the Corinthian style. On its northern side a flight of stairs descended six feet to the level at which one of the main streets began. Close to this stairway, at the northern end of the colonnade, and scattered over the square itself, stood large bronze and marble statues of gods and emperors, governors and city fathers; some of these figures were mounted on horses, while some were even standing in chariots.

Town hall, orator's platform, court buildings, and shops surrounded the forum. On the northeast corner was a handsome public comfort station with lavatories and flush toilets. Arm rests in the shape of dolphins separated the seats; there were some twenty-five of these. The plumbing functioned perfectly. There was also a market place with a two-story market building, as well as public and private baths. The thermæ in the southern part of the city had a beautiful mosaic floor and a semicircular public toilet with twenty-eight seats.

Thamugadi was especially distinguished by its library. Books were not cheap, of course. Only the rich could afford a sizable number of scrolls. But here in this North African soldier's town, scrolls filled niches and shelves in a public reading-room. Here a retired officer could look up handbooks of strategy and study the history of former wars. A budding advocate would find all the lawbooks he needed. He could have one of the library slaves bring him Cicero's orations and see how that great man had won seemingly hopeless cases. The citizen of Thamugadi with scientific interests could study the works of Aristotle, if he read Greek; if not, he could find in Pliny more information than his head could retain. The young lover could revel in Catullus or borrow verses from Ovid for his own love poems, unless he chose rather to sweeten renunciation by a passage from some Stoic philosopher. The magistrate planning a theatrical performance could select something suitable from the comedies of Plautus or Terence. The public library was the greatest treasure of Greco-Roman culture in Thamugadi.

Second in importance came the theater, a semicircle cut in the Greek fashion into the slope of a small hill. There was room here for some four thousand spectators. Two vaulted passages led to the orchestra, the handsomely paved semicircular area in front of the stage. Behind the rows of seats reserved for the dignitaries of the city rose the seats for the ordinary citizens, three tiers with steps between, crowned by a colonnade.

Performances took place in the early morning. The audience settled on the steps, spreading a coat or blanket under them if the stones were still cool from the previous night. Their feet rested on the next lower step, behind the backs of their fellow citizens. But there was still room in between for the barefoot Berber boys who clambered about loudly proclaiming in barbarous Latin the attractions of the fruit, cakes, and wine they offered for sale. Those who had come without breakfasting could have a bite before the curtain dropped, disappearing into a broad channel in front of the stage. The sight of this stage with its small steps and its niches at the front was impressive indeed to anyone who saw it for the first time—to the Berber, say, who was being taken to the theater by his Roman brother-in-law. And how exciting was the per-

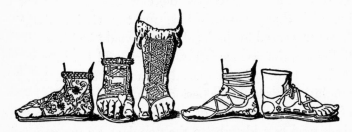

ROMAN FOOT-COVERINGS.

formance itself, whether it was a drama, a farcical mime, a ballet, or a clever pantomime in which the entire action was represented without words, merely by movements, facial expression, and the musical accompaniment.

Those who preferred the cruder sort of entertainment would have to go to Lambæsis or some other neighboring town where there was an amphitheater in which gladiators put on their bloody contests and wild beasts fought men or other animals. (Here in Africa there was no lack of wild animals; in fact, the amphitheaters of Italy were supplied with lions, bears, panthers, and buffalo from this province.) Different sectors of the amphitheater were assigned to different districts of the city, so that there would be no quarrels over seats.

In distant Carnuntum on the Danube a similar principle was followed; sections of the amphitheater were reserved for the rural populace of various districts. This city had no theater at all; evidently the taste of the inhabitants was on a lower level than that of the North Africans. But it did have two amphitheaters. One of these, seating thirteen thousand persons, was reserved primarily for civilians. The other held about eight thousand persons. It had been erected by the "mayor" Domitius Zmaragdus, a Syrian by birth, at his own expense. This second amphitheater primarily served the soldiers of the garrison, though of course there was a place of honor, opposite the governor's box, for the civil authorities. Beasts captured in the local forests would be turned loose to fight in the arenas: bears, wolves, wild boars, aurochs, and, as an occasional special attraction, a lynx. But the amphitheaters had uses besides this. They were the scenes of all great assemblies, of parades, sometimes of political trials, and of addresses to the populace by the governor.

The legion stationed in Carnuntum was the Fourteenth, nicknamed Apollinaris. Under Vespasian and Titus it had helped to conquer Jerusalem (A.D. 71). From its service in the East it had brought the cult of Mithras, the Persian god of light, to Pannonia, as the Roman province along the Danube was called. As in so many of the cities of Italy, Africa, and Gaul, a great variety of gods was worshipped in Carnuntum: Roman gods, numerous Oriental divinities, and indigenous Celtic-Illyrian deities, some of whom had been given Latin names. Aside from their political dislike of Christianity, the Romans were tolerant. But at the beginning of the fourth century there was even a small Christian congregation in Carnuntum. Sixty miles farther south, in the Pannonian city of Savaria (now Szombathely), Quirinus died a martyr's death in A.D. 308.

In North Africa the new religion had appeared even earlier. Shortly after the death of Severus (A.D. 211) a scandalous event involving a Christian legionary occurred in Lambæsis: true to the spirit of Christian love, this man cast away his sword—and at a public festival, at that!

By the middle of the century there were large Christian communities throughout North Africa. The province bred saints, fathers of the church, martyrs—and heretics. In Thamugadi, where several churches and two baptisteries had been built, the heretical sect of the Donatists under Bishop Optatus had a cathedral of their own.

Similar in origin, the garrison cities of the Roman Empire also resembled one another in the process of their decline. In Africa, the granary of the Empire, the economic depression of the fourth century A.D. did not cause as much distress as in Pannonia in the north. But in both provinces the barbarian threat was equally dangerous, and the defenses were inadequate.

Carnuntum was situated directly on the border of the region inhabited by Germanic tribes. Even after economic crisis and the constant horrors of war had reduced the civilian city to a filthy, half-deserted village, the Legion camp continued to play its part in the strategy of the Empire. But not for long. In the later part of the fourth century Germanic tribes began to migrate across the Danube; some the Romans admitted voluntarily, some they could not keep out. These tribes settled for a while, then wandered on. Fields were devastated, farms destroyed. The Roman civilian populace retreated to Italy; the native farmers joined the Germans. And then came the Huns.

The Germanic Vandals, who had passed through Pannonia in A.D. 401, landed in North Africa in May of 429. But the Vandals themselves did not bring about the downfall of the Roman cities in Africa. They pillaged, killed, and defaced, expropriated land, and let roads and irrigation works fall to ruin. Nevertheless, they were as eager to be supplied by the native farmers as the Roman overlords had been, and forbore to scorch the earth. But the Vandals had overthrown Roman order without being able to substitute an adequate order of their own. First the masses of native farmers rose up and destroyed the manor houses of their former masters. Then the Berbers descended from the mountains. There was no longer a Roman army to stop them. Thirsting for loot, they fell upon the flourishing cities of the lowlands. Like so many others, Lambæsis and Thamugadi went up in flames.[5]

The ruins of both cities continued to play some small part in the struggle of the Byzantines, who were trying to restore the Roman Empire, against the Vandals and Berbers. From the remains of buildings that had once been the pride of the citizenry of those cities, fortifications were built. These fortresses protected the rural populace, but the cities themselves had already fallen. Thamugadi alone continued to lead a pitiful existence as a beleaguered center of the Catholic Church until the seventh century. Then the Arabs came and completed the work of annihilation.

Strangely enough, these same Arabs have kept coming

[5] Our statements on Lambæsis and Thamugadi are drawn from Julien: *Histoire de l'Afrique du Nord* (Paris, 1951), and St. Gsell: *Les Monuments antiques de l'Algérie* (Paris, 1901). On Carnuntum we follow lectures by Rudolf Egger of Vienna and *Carnuntum*, by Erich Swoboda (Vienna, 1953).

ever since to the site of Thamugadi, now called Timgad, to hold a weekly market. They continue to do so to this day, though they must ride a considerable distance. Its very distance from other populated centers was the factor that saved Thamugadi from the fate of so many ancient cities. It was not robbed of its stones because these would have had to be transported too far. When the French began excavations there in 1881, they soon laid bare so astoundingly complete a picture of the city that they were tempted to speak of an Algerian Pompeii. Rarely mentioned by classical writers, Thamugadi is famous today. In the excavated Roman theater Parisian troupes give festival performances for which special trains travel from Paris through Marseille and Algiers to Timgad— though Thamugadi is a dead city, a single luxury hotel is all that stands on the site of Timgad.

Although the many other Roman garrison cities were built in as short a time as Thamugadi, Carnuntum, or Lambæsis, many endured for two thousand years. Numerous cities in Spain, France, Germany, Austria, and other countries were founded on Roman camps.

One of these is the Roman citadel on Mount Sinai which Emperor Justinian built in A.D. 530 for the protection of the hermits and desert saints living in the vicinity. As a fortress its site was extremely ill-considered, for it can easily be commanded from the surrounding hills; in fact, the Emperor had the architect responsible for it beheaded. But as a monastery it survived the centuries, sheltering an enclave of Greek monks in the midst of Arab territory. Although visitors no longer have to be drawn up with a winch, as was once the case (because originally the monastery had no gate), the high wall that still surrounds it is the very one built by Justinian's luckless architect.

IX

DIM SCRIPTS AND DARK ORACLES

WHITE STONE AGE MEN IN THE FIFTEENTH CEN-
TURY. CAVE CITIES AND DUAL KINGSHIP. STRANGE
JUSTICE. THE ETRUSCANS IN THE ALPS. ROME'S FIRST
KINGS. THE SCIENCE OF THE LIVER. STAGNATION ON
THE INDUS. THE PRIEST CITY WITH THE SACRED
BATHS. THE ARYAN INVADERS. THE CHARIOT CON-
QUERS CULTURE. THE GREAT CITY OF SHANG. COSMO-
POLITAN KARAKORUM. THE RESIDENCE OF THE TAR-
TAR KHANS. THE REVOLT OF THE BEARDLESS. 5000
ASTROLOGERS. THE PROVINCE OF BEAUTIFUL GIRLS.

IN THE year 1417—seventy-five years before the discovery of America—a flotilla of stately warships sailed
from a Spanish port to conquer a few islands in the Atlantic Ocean. Jean de Béthencourt, a Norman knight in
the service of Queen Catharine of Castile, was in command of the fleet.

The goal of his expedition was the group of islands
known today as the Canary Islands. Their existence had
been known in antiquity; in fact, they were supposed to
be the Isles of the Blessed, the Insulæ Fortunatæ, where
certain privileged human beings lived on in eternal bliss
after their earthly course was run. That entertaining col-

lection of wondrous tales which was once actually ascribed to Aristotle, *De mirabilibus auditis,* tells of a lonely island in the sea, beyond the Pillars of Heracles, wooded, well watered, and fertile, which had been found by the Carthaginians. They had been so struck with it that the Carthaginian authorities had to forbid on pain of death any voyage or settlement there, for fear of losing all their citizens.

But the island was not uninhabited, and it was probably the hostility of the natives, rather than fear of any law, that prevented the famous Carthaginian seafarer Hanno from establishing a colony there.

In the following centuries pirates and slave-hunters visited the islands frequently. The Canaries lie only about sixty miles off the northwest coast of Africa; it was therefore no great feat to rediscover them. The story has been told elsewhere of the islanders' brave resistance, of the violence and duplicity of the Spaniards, of the fruitless intervention of the Portuguese, and of the many times the would-be conquerors were fended off before the islands were at last subjugated in 1473. But what concerns us here are two ancient cities on Gran Canaria, the most important of the islands, and the people who dwelt in them.

At the time the Spaniards landed, the natives of the island were still living in the Stone Age. With implements made of stone and the bones of goats they tilled the soil, sewed clothing, and cut their hair. With stone saws they worked palm trees into timber for the doors of their houses. They fought their battles with javelins tipped with goat horn, with wooden clubs, and with stones. And yet they were not, properly speaking, "savages." The people on Gran Canaria (not the inhabitants of the neighboring islands) believed in a single god named Acoran, lived in monogamous marriages, spared women, children, and sanctuaries in wartime, engaged in single combat and in such sports as running, stone-throwing, and mountain-climbing. They had their own script. Most astonishing of all, these natives were whites. They were of the same race that scratched famous pictures on the walls of caves in southern France and Spain during the last Ice Age—descendants of Cro-Magnon man, one of the ancestors of the present-day European. Cut off from the advancing civilization in Europe and Africa, these white islanders had clung to a Stone Age culture until, in the fifteenth century A.D., they found themselves confronted by their more highly civilized cousins from the mainland.

The natives were "primitive" to the extent that they believed in the honor and good faith of their enemies, and trusted an oath sworn upon the Host, before a priest, by the Spanish governor, Pedro de Vera. Their whole mode of life suggested intellectual capacities of a high order. However, none of the several scripts found on the island can thus far be deciphered.

Tomas Arias Marin y Cubas, a Canarian historian of the seventeenth century, possessed and edited a Spanish manuscript of the period of the conquest. In it two ancient cities of the natives are mentioned. They were located near the Canarian royal city of Telde, which was later favored by Spanish noblemen as a resort and which has retained its old name down to the present time. Of the two older cities, however, no trace remained. According to the old manuscript, the Canarians lived "in Cendro, a large settlement of earthen-roofed houses, like baking ovens; also in caves . . . and in Tara, a village of farmhouses and of caves cut in white stone. These settlements are on small hills separated by ravines."

We have one additional report on these cities. It is to

be found in the most important source for the Canary Islands, an Italian manuscript by the architect Leonardo Torriani of Cremona, who visited the islands toward the end of the sixteenth century. He says of Telde: "This is a very small town with 300 hearths, situated on a river, in the vicinity of two large ancient settlements which in the Canarian language are called Tara and Cendro. Old inhabitants maintain (and the remains bear them out) that these cities were of great extent, and that the number of houses came to as many as 14,000. Part were above ground; the houses were small and round, with narrow streets between; these were the homes of the poor. Another part lay underground, dug out with great industry; these houses were the homes of the nobles and the rich."

These cities, since effaced, were situated on the plain about nine miles from the southeast coast of the almost circular island of Gran Canaria, and just slightly farther from the mountains in the west and south. These mountains, as Torriani said, "are a joy to see under the clear and bright horizon, and send fresh breezes so that the eternal peacefulness of the elements and the bliss so much praised by poets seem to dwell here."

A city of fourteen thousand houses seems scarcely credible, but we have no way of checking this account. On the other hand, Torriani does give a description that permits us to reconstruct the appearance of the houses. The round dwellings of the poorer class consisted of stones laid dry, without mortar; they were low huts, but well built. The roof was made of palm trunks with a layer of sod on top.

The Canarian men wore short skirts of palm leaves and rushes laboriously woven on a kind of loom. These were worn belted around the waist; goatskins covered

the upper part of the body. Goats were the most important of their domestic animals. As we have mentioned,
the horns and bones provided weapons and tools; the
skins, carefully tanned and sewed, were made into caps
as well as jackets. The women dressed entirely in goatskins. In winter the people wore cloaks of fleece. Of the
other domestic animals, the Canarians had sheep, swine,
chickens, sheepdogs, and greyhounds, but no cattle or
horses. (In fact it was the horses of the Spanish conquerors and not their firearms which gave them their superiority over the natives—as was later true in America
also.) Bread was unknown; wheat and barley were eaten
in meal form. They also had legumes, dates, figs, and
olives.

The common people had shaven heads. The most de-
spised trade was that of the butcher. Men worked as
carpenters, builders, rope-makers, and tanners, but most
other crafts were in the hands of the women, who also
painted the houses, using vegetable dyes. However,
women were not held in subjection; a number of them
even functioned as priestesses. For fishing, leather lines
and hooks of goat bones were used, also nets woven of
grasses and strips of palm wood. The fishing ships were
dugout canoes equipped with rudders and palm-leaf
sails; in these the coasts of neighboring islands were visited, and occasional raids carried out.

The high priest, called Faicagh or Faycan, was at once
a magistrate, teacher, and doctor. Nobility was not he-
reditary; the Faicagh conferred nobility upon those who
from their youth had been generous, merciful, open-
handed, and brave, had never robbed cattle or entered a
slaughterhouse. As a sign of their distinction such men
wore their hair long, below their ears. The underground
dwellings in which the kings and the nobles lived were

pleasantly cool in summer and warm in winter. They were not pits, however; the rooms were cut into the slopes of hills, so that there was space for window openings above the door.

With its pleasant climate and simple, honest folk of peasants and shepherds, the island might well have seemed one of the Isles of the Blessed. It had a dark side, however: its system of justice. A murderer was not prosecuted if he entered openly through the door of a house to commit his deed. Only assassins were punished by death, and their relatives were considered dishonored. For the murder of a highly placed person there was a curious punishment. As the Canarians thought that death

FIGURE OF A SHIP CARVED ON ROCK, FROM THE CANARY ISLANDS.

was not the worst fate, they let the evildoer live and instead killed the person he loved most—wife, son, friend, sweetheart, or father—reasoning that sorrow was a worse punishment than the death penalty for the murderer himself.

The same type of justice prevailed on the neighboring island of Fuerteventura, which was divided into two kingdoms, each under the common rule of a king and a priestess who at the same time was supreme judge. Gran Canaria likewise had two kingdoms, but there religious authority—the supervision of sacrifices—was in the hands of a Faicagh. The Canarian custom is reminiscent of the pre-Greek and early Greek dual kingship in Mycenæ and Tiryns, of the selection of two consuls in Rome, and of two suffetes in Carthage.

This is not the sole ethnological relationship between the Canary Islands and the Mediterranean area. In architecture, in the construction of tombs, in script, ceramics, and seals there are astonishing parallels to early Mediterranean civilizations, as Dominik Wölfel the Austrian scholar, has demonstrated. Wölfel is also the discoverer of the Torriani manuscript; but for his decades of research, we would know virtually nothing about the ancient native cities of Tara and Cendro. And yet we know not much more of this people than what the sixteenth-century traveler has told of them, since their own script remains a riddle. A few years ago a faint hope was awakened that the Canarian script might eventually be solved; this was at the time the first news of the decipherment of Cretan "Linear Script B"—which was just possibly related to Canarian—spread through the world of scholarship. But the hope proved illusory; only the Greek words in the Cretan script could be read, not the Cretan language itself. For even when the phonetic value of individual signs is known, the road to a full knowledge of a language remains long and uncertain. This holds true for the Canary Islands, as well as for that other ancient Mediterranean people who must occupy a considerable space in any consideration of ancient civilizations: the Etruscans.

The Etruscan script is fully readable, for the Etruscans employed an archaic form of the Greek letters. A few words of the language are explained in ancient lexicons; a few other words philologists have deduced. Nevertheless, the language as a whole remains unknown, and there seems little prospect that it ever will be known. All that we can be sure of is that Etruscan was not a member of the Indo-European family of languages.

. . .

The great tribal migrations that caused upheavals in the eastern Mediterranean world during the twelfth century B.C. also affected a rather unimportant seafaring people who lived on the western coast of Asia Minor. They recovered very slowly from the tempests that had passed over them. Some, however, went westward in search of new homes, and these became powerful and famous. They were the Tyrsenians, who may have been the same people who were known wherever Latin was spoken as the Etruscans.[1]   In the course of their sea voyages the Etruscans had come upon the thinly populated but ore-rich western coast of Italy, opposite the island of Corsica. The land attracted them, and soon after 1000 B.C. the first wave of immigrants came across the sea, followed about two centuries later by another. The new settlement flourished.

Strictly speaking, these settlements were not entirely new. In most cases the immigrants established themselves in places where the earlier inhabitants had already found favorable living conditions. These natives were Umbrians of Italic (which is to say Indo-European) stock; the name lives on as one of the regions of modern Italy. Some of them retreated before the invaders; some remained to live under foreign domination as the herdsmen and farmers they had been before.

---

[1] In ancient times opinions differed on the origin of the Etruscans, and the question has not yet been settled. In addition to our much-cited ancient authors, Herodotus, Strabo, Livy, and Athenæus, whose comments on the Etruscans must always be taken up with considerable discretion, we have based our account mainly on: *Etruscologia*, by Massimo Pallottino (Milan, 1947); *Etruskische Frühgeschichte*, by Fritz Schachermeyr (Berlin, 1929); the chapter entitled *"Die Etruscer"* in *Italien und Rom*, by Franz Altheim (Amsterdam, no date); *Itinerari dei musei e monumenti d'Italia*, Vol. 70 (*Cerveteri*, by Massimo Pallottino) and Vol. 75 (*Tarquinia*, by Pietro Romanelli). Finally, we are obliged to Dr. Marchese, head of the museum at Tarquinia, for his friendly and informative explanations.

Populonia, on a steep promontory opposite the island of Elba, was one such settlement where the oval huts of the Umbrians yielded to the rectangular homes of the Etruscans. These were laid out in regular order and built upon firm stone foundations.

About one hundred miles farther to the southeast was the city of Agylla, situated on a rock cliff that dropped off steeply on three sides and was accessible only from the northeast. A long wall with eight gates protected the city. Under its Etruscan name of Cære it became a famous sea power, though for its own safety it was not situated directly by the sea. Centuries later Strabo extolled its inhabitants for not having practiced piracy (obviously an exceptional case) and for sending votive offerings to the temple of Apollo at Delphi.

Like Cære, Tarquinii was also situated a few miles from the coast. It, too, rose up on a rocky hill, with the citadel capping the peak in the eastern part of the city. According to tradition, the name went back to Tarkon, who was either the brother or son of Tyrsenus, the mythical prince who led the emigrants from Asia Minor, or a grandson of Heracles. In actual fact the name Tarkon is related to that of a divinity of Asia Minor—Tarku. In Lydia a Zeus Targuenus was worshipped at one time.

Tarkon is said to have founded all twelve of Etruria's great cities. The truth was, it required the labor of several generations before even the coastal region came under the control of the Etruscans. Nevertheless, the new arrivals from the East were superior to the Italic tribes in the art of warfare. They fought in ordered line of battle, employing lances, short swords, and battle axes; their bodies were protected by round shields, helmets, breastplates, and cuisses, all of metal. Native subjects served in the ranks of the infantry. Once established, the Etruscans still followed their ancient tradition of fighting in chariots, armed with javelins, long swords, or double-bladed axes; they were slow to lay aside their old-fashioned weapons and fight as cavalry. Even so, horses and chariots frequently served only to transport them to the battlefield; there they leaped to the ground and fought on foot.

The city of Tarquinii had extended its dominion into the interior as far as Lake Bolsena (twenty miles north of the city) early in its career, even before the second wave of immigration. Within this territory are the ruins of six towns with fortifications and necropolises of their own. Not even their names are now known. Gradually the Etruscans' influence penetrated still farther. On the one hand, they were reinforced by kinsfolk who continued to come from Asia Minor, where in the meanwhile their civilization had reached higher stages. On the other hand, Greek colonization in Italy barred them from expanding farther along the coasts and forced them inland. During the period after 800 B.C. they built, on the sites of older Umbrian settlements, those other cities which Tarkon had supposedly founded. Then the Etruscans turned north and on the plain of the Po established another twelve cities. They spread until they reached the Adriatic Sea. They also ascended into the Alps beyond the Po. Traces of their civilization can be found as far as Tyrol.

Their rule extended across Latium and southward to Campania; we have already spoken of the Etruscan cities in that region. Once again there were twelve. This number was not a chance one; it was a sacred number in the Ægean region whence they had come, and also farther east, in lands that had once exercised a profound cultural influence upon them.

"Etruria was so powerful that it filled not only the land but the sea as well with the fame of its name, throughout the whole length of Italy from the Alps to the Sicilian Sea," commented Livy five hundred years afterward (Book I, Chapter 2). Yet, for all their power, the Etruscans did not possess a unified state. All their accomplishments in culture and politics, all their conquests and wars were actions by individual cities, kings, and princely houses.[2]

One of the most important of the Etruscan families were the Tarchna, who, like the city of Tarquinii, derived their name from the god Tarku. They were responsible for an event of world-historic importance.

As early as the seventh century B.C. the Etruscans had invaded Latium, culturally as well as militarily. Præneste (present-day Palestrina, a town of seven thousand inhabitants)—founded, according to legend, by Telegonus, the son of Odysseus and Circe—was the center of their power. It possessed a citadel and princely mausoleums. From this citadel the Ruma family ruled over the Latin villages on the Palatine and Esquiline hills above the Tiber. Perhaps one of the village chiefs was named Numa, Ancus, or Tullus—names attributed by tradition to the early kings of Rome.

When the settlement had expanded to include the third hill, the Quirinal, a common center became necessary. The marshy low ground between the hills, where formerly the dead had been buried, was drained; this became the site of the forum. Under the rule of nobles from Tarquinii the villages grew into a city; its name was derived from the Etruscan clan of the Ruma (in Etruscan

---

[2] For example, in the naval battle of Alalia only the ships of the city of Cære fought on the Carthaginian side against the Greeks. The conquest of Rome and the war against the Latins and the Greeks of Kyme was undertaken by King Porsena of Clusium alone.

u and *o* were written with the same letter, *y*). On the next hill, the Capitoline, the king's castle was erected; also a temple for the three Etruscan gods who were named Tin, Uni, and Menerva (the later Capitoline triad Jupiter, Juno, and Minerva). At the foot of this hill a splendid royal tomb with high-vaulted dome was built. Later, under the name of Tullianum, it served as Rome's jailhouse.

Thus, Etruscan kings were rulers of Rome. They headed the Latin League, but had no say at all in the Assembly of the Etruscan League. The latter was restricted to the twelve foremost cities—including Tarquinii, Cære, Populonia, Clusium, and Veii—whose representatives met in this Assembly and elected one of their number as the supreme king. Every city provided a lictor, who carried the bundle of fasces with ax inside; originally this had been a double-bladed ax, the ancient Mediterranean symbol (well known from Crete) of the power of a sacred king. The king, whose title was *lauchme* (Latin *lucumo*), was not only chief magistrate, holding a public audience every week; he was also supreme warlord and the foremost religious authority.

The insignia of his office—golden crown, scepter, purple toga, throne, and fasces—remained even after the Etruscans had taken part in the general political development of the Mediterranean world, the change from kingship to aristocratic republic. In this evolution the Greeks had preceded them quite early, and the Phœnicians between the eighth and fifth centuries B.C. In all Etruscan cities except Veii the kings were overthrown. Sometimes these upheavals were followed by short periods of anarchy, as was the case in Clusium, for example, and by military dictatorships like the one of Servius Tullius in Rome, which interrupted the succession of Tarquinian kings. The last of the Tarquinians was expelled from Rome by an aristocratic palace revolution, not by an uprising of the native populace against the Etruscan masters.[3] Livy's account of these events is based almost entirely upon family chronicles, but it has historical validity. He narrates, for example, that the Tarquinians fled to Cære, and their family grave has been found there.

The Etruscan historians cannot speak to us. We know that there were some, but we do not even know their names. "I have it on good authority," writes Livy,[4] "that in those days young Romans generally learned Etruscan letters as they now do the Greek." After the expulsion of the Tarquins, Etruscan artisans, architects, and artists continued to live in Rome, whereas Italic youths lived with friends of their families in Etruscan cities, absorbing the learning their more rural homes could not give them. In so doing they were entering a world which must have seemed familiar to them in many external features, but which in essential matters was completely foreign.

The first sight of an Etruscan city could not help impressing a Roman or Italic youth. Here were thick city walls, strongly fortified gates, regular streets. The houses were spacious, with rooms opening on an interior courtyard that admitted light and air. Some buildings were veritable palaces, entered by imposing portals, with upper stories and long balconies supported on columns. As was the rule in antiquity, there was little furniture. But what there was had been made with artistry. There were beds with carved legs, embroidered blankets and many-colored

---

[3] According to Roman tradition, as recorded by Livy (I.59), the leaders of the conspiracy were Brutus, King Tarquin's nephew and commander of his bodyguard; Lucretius, the king's commandant of the city; and Tarquinius Collatinus, another kinsman of the ruler.

[4] Livy IX.36.3: *"Habeo auctores vulgo tum Romanos pueros, sicut nunc Græcis, ita Etruscis litteris erudiri solitos."* The word *litteris* can also be taken to mean letters in general, not only language and script.

bolsters; there were armchairs and chests. At night the rooms were illuminated by oil lamps, sometimes made of bronze, that hung from the ceilings.

A young man who was present at a feast in such a dwelling could tell garish tales of the Etruscans' life when he returned to his home. Abundance of food and wine was nothing special, of course. But among the Etruscans the womenfolk participated in the meal, sharing the wine and drinking toasts. Wrestlers and gladiators appeared for the entertainment of the guests, and their contests were accompanied by music. Zithers and flutes (the flute was the national instrument of the Etruscans) also played joyous dances. Women and men whirled about, not only their legs but their arms, their heads, their whole bodies swinging in time to the rapid beat. After a while the musicians themselves began to dance.

Such customs might seem strange to the Italic visitors but certainly not unpleasant. But they must have wondered at the Etruscan habit of using matronymics as well as, or instead of, the patronymic customary among the Greeks and almost all other peoples. We may see in this adoption of the mother's name a relic of the ancient Mediterranean matriarchal society; but the Italic youths perhaps surmised that these Etruscans were not sure who their fathers were. And in fact the Etruscans occasionally held such wild revels that the matter might well be in doubt. It was said that Etruscan servant maids wore nothing at all when they served their masters at meals.

Even more peculiar was their religion. This, in fact, was alarmingly alien. There was none of the comfortable relationship of the worshippers to the rural divinities, the "I give so that you will give" spirit of the Romans and other Italic tribes, none of the simplehearted sacrifices for rich harvests and fertility of the cattle, or of thank-offerings after the harvest was in. Nor was there any realistic observation of nature. The Etruscans believed in the permanent presence of higher powers, gods, demons, and innumerable spirits whose will must be discovered at every moment and be obeyed according to rules fixed with painful exactitude. The Roman philosopher Seneca formulated the matter very well, for the gulf still persisted in his time, the first century A.D. "This is what distinguishes us from the Etruscans: we believe that lightning arises because the clouds clash; they believe that the clouds clash in order for there to be lightning." [5]

The Etruscans had special books for interpreting lightning as an expression of divine will, books for explaining other omens, books on the hereafter, on rituals, and on haruspicy (divination from entrails). Of all the branches of the "science" of augury, this last—and especially divination from the liver of a sacrificed animal—was the most important method for determining the future and the will of the higher powers. The practice derived from the Orient. In Mesopotamia, too, there were demonstration models for apprentice augurs like the one found in Piacenza: a bronze representation of a liver divided up into numerous areas with appropriate inscriptions on each, so that the fledgling priest could learn how to interpret the condition of the liver.

The Italic peoples took over much from the Etruscans—the concept of *lares* and *penates* as household gods, the concept of the *manes* or spirits of the dead—yet the interpretation of lightning and similar omens remained a highly specialized matter. Consequently, until late in the imperial era they had to resort to Etruscan priests (*harus-*

[5] Seneca: *Quæstiones naturales* II.32.2.

pices) when an augury was needed, just as they resorted to Chaldeans for the interpretation of dreams. Once when the Romans were again fighting the city of Veii and had no Etruscan haruspex to augur for them, they were greatly distressed by a disturbing omen: the water of Lake Alban had risen considerably for no apparent reason. At last there seemed nothing for it but to kidnap a haruspex from the city they were besieging. Being cautious people, however, they also sent a delegation to the oracle at Delphi to check on the Etruscan's predictions.

A deity of the earth or of the underworld named Veltha, Valtune, or Voltumna, who was represented sometimes as a monster, sometimes as bisexual, sometimes as a bearded, armed man, evolved into the supreme god of Etruria. His temple was probably situated at Volsinii, the city that gave its name to the Lake of Bolsena. In olden days the supreme Etruscan king had been elected there, and long after the rule of kings had come to an end the high priest continued to be chosen at Volsinii. Pan-Etruscan festivals and games were held there annually, and played the same part for the Etruscans as the Olympic Games did for a Greece similarly divided into numerous city-states.

Circus games were highly favored by the Etruscans, both as pure sport and as entertainment for the masses. In the great arena, chariots and horses raced, wrestlers and boxers fought, strong men and slender youths ran races, naked or in heavy armor, and displayed their skill at broad jumping and pole vaulting. There were acrobats, equestrian artists, referees. Women as well as men thronged the stands to watch.

The Etruscans built canals in the Po plain and aqueducts throughout their dominions; they practiced mining, had specialized industrial regions, and exported

their wares as far as Athens. But all these achievements
do not make them seem so "modern" as the equality
they permitted women in ordinary life. To the Greeks,
whose women lived within doors in almost Oriental se-
clusion, such manners must have seemed sheer immoral-
ity. All the tales the Greeks told one another about the
life of the Etruscans, and about the freedom of their
women at feasts, in sports (at which, of course, the
women wore no clothes), and in love, bordered on the

MURAL IN CLUSIUM: WRESTLING MATCH.

(from Massimo Pallottino: Etruscologia; *Milan, 1947)*

obscene. On the other hand, the Etruscan ladies were
praised as exceedingly beautiful; they had at their command all the grace, all the arts of body-culture, and all
the capacity for sensual pleasure of a wealthy, high-bred
aristocracy.

The story goes that Etruscan power in upper Italy
came to an end on account of a beautiful woman. She
was the wife of a nobleman named Arruns. The king of
Clusium fell in love with her, and ravished her. By way
of reprisal, Arruns invited the Gauls of what is now
southern France to invade Italy. Eager for the wines of

Italy, for the luxury and lovely women of Etruria, the wild Gallic hordes fell upon the Etruscan cities. Pillaging and burning, they marched through Italy. The fate of Rome, which had already become a dangerous rival of the Etruscans, became linked one more time with the destiny of her former masters and teachers. When the Gauls destroyed Rome, the Etruscan city of Cære sheltered within its walls Rome's vestal virgins and her images of the gods. And with their own city a smoking ruin, many Romans emigrated to Etruscan Veii.

But Rome soon recovered and renewed her hostility to the Etruscans. Malaria in the coastal cities, combined with the two-front war against the Gauls and Rome, ultimately broke the power of Etruria. But even with the Romans in control, the outward changes were small; the soil remained fertile, the mines lucrative, and the people industrious and artistically gifted.

During the struggle with Hannibal the Etruscan cities were still strong enough to provide welcome and valuable support to the Roman navy. The list of their contributions throws light on the economic conditions in these cities in an age when piracy and commercial monopolies had already run their course. Cære supplied grain and other provisions for the ships' crews, Populonia provided iron, Tarquinii canvas for the sails, Clusium grain and lumber. In both the inland and the overseas trade many other Etruscan wares were much sought after.

A Roman *prætor* meted out justice instead of the Etruscan *zilath;* many of the old Etruscan families had lost their wealth; and Etruria was crowded with colonists from Rome and Latium. But, despite these facts, the cities changed little outwardly. The merchant wrote out in the Latin language lists of the same goods his grandfather had recorded in Etruscan. Shoemakers and leatherwork-

ers, weavers and potters went about their tasks in the
open air. Goldsmiths and masons filled the streets with
the noise of their work. The peasant toiled in his fields;
the overseer drove the mine slaves into the bowels of the
earth; the ferryman and the river boatman continued to
transport iron, gold, and silver. The Etruscan cities remained prosperous, though political upheavals and malaria had reduced their population and though, within
the Roman Empire, they no longer were so important as
they had been as independent city-states.

A good many of these cities have survived to this day,
among them Arezzo, anciently Arretium, with its manu-
factures of arms and beautiful vases; Populonia, now a
fishing village; and Chiusi, ancient Clusium. Other cities
of Etruria like Pisa, Perugia, and Florence did not really
begin to flourish until Roman times. Some fell to ruin in
the course of centuries. The foremost of these was Veii,
Rome's old enemy. In 396 B.C., Veii was conquered after
a ten-year siege. The inhabitants were sold into slavery,
and the later city, Municipium Augustum Veiens, never
developed into a place of any importance.

A curious fate was reserved for the Etruscan city of
Cosa, so the story goes. It was situated at a strategic point
on the coast, and was therefore strongly fortified. There
were stout towers, an almost square city wall made of
huge polygonal blocks of stone, and an acropolis. Neither
earthquake nor human enemy destroyed this city; it was
visited by such a terrible plague of mice that the citizens
had to leave. At the beginning of the fifth century A.D.
the abandoned walls still stood.

Cære was deserted by its inhabitants after having stood
for more than two thousand years. They fled from the
menace of the Saracens and from malaria, and founded
a town named Ceri near by. In Old Cære (Cerveteri, as

it is called in Italian) only a very small part of the former area of the city is inhabited. What made the place famous is the cemetery. It truly deserves the name *necropolis,* city of the dead. Regular streets lead between the funeral mounds. The vaults are furnished like regular homes for the dead.

Tarquinii, the most important of the Etruscan cities (it once had more than one hundred thousand inhabitants), was destroyed by its neighbors. Back in the eighth century the Saracens stayed just long enough to plunder the city and then moved on. But no new life sprang into being on the ruins, for the ruins were not permitted to lie where they were. They were used as building material for the houses of the neighboring town of Corneto, two miles farther to the south. Corneto was built on ground where an outlying fort of Tarquinii had once stood. It rested on old fortification walls, underground vaults, and the remains of an ancient aqueduct. In the thirteenth century A.D., Corneto was a flourishing city of thirty-five thousand inhabitants; today it has no more than eight thousand. The medieval city walls still stand, and a splendid Renaissance palazzo houses the rich Etruscan museum. During the twenties of the present century Corneto was renamed Tarquinia. A river valley separates the town from the hill that is still called La Cività (The City). On this hill, scattered among fields of grain, are to be found a few ruins of ancient Tarquinii.

Here, too, the tombs of the nobility have been excavated. The Roman art-dealer Augusto Jandolo has recently published an account of their discovery. As a boy he had been present at the opening of an Etruscan sarcophagus. "It was no easy undertaking," he writes, "to move the lid. At last it rose, stood on end for a moment, and then fell heavily down on its other side. And then

I saw something I shall remember to my dying day. Inside the sarcophagus I saw resting the body of a young warrior in full accouterments, with helmet, spear, shield, and cuisses. Let me stress that it was not a skeleton I saw; I saw a body, with all its limbs in place, stiffly outstretched as though the dead man had just been laid in the grave. It was the appearance of but a moment. Then, by the light of the torches, everything seemed to dissolve. The helmet rolled to the right, the round shield fell into the collapsed breastplate of the armor, the cuisses flattened out at the bottom of the sarcophagus, one on the right, the other on the left. At the first contact with air the body which had lain inviolate for centuries suddenly dissolved into dust. . . . In the air, however, and around the torches, a golden powder seemed to be hovering."

The admission of fresh air also affects the decaying stone of the vaults; the ornamentation begins to crumble and the paintings to peel off. Consequently, it has been decided to remove such art works and preserve them in museums. What a profound impression the still-preserved graves make! Their murals provide a splendid insight into the Etruscan character. In the vaults of the dead the Etruscans represented everything that had mattered to them while they lived: hunting and fishing, sports, feasts, dancing. There is in these early Etruscan murals a naïve joy in the beauty of life. On the other hand, we can also see what transformations their attitude toward life underwent when they became conscious of the decline of their power. The paintings in vaults dating from after the decisive defeat by the Greeks and after the heavy Etruscan casualties in battles against the Romans and Gauls are full of reminders of the terrors of the underworld; there are many snake-haired demons and

messengers of death. Among these grim pictures, however, we may see the smiling face of a charming girl of
the noble Velcha family.

The Etruscan nation has assimilated with the Italian
people. Their civilization has made vital contributions to
the civilization of Europe. And the austere beauty of their
landscape and their women has remained to this day.

To no country in the world is the sentence from Herder
quoted at the beginning of this book more applicable than

GREEK FUNERAL.

to India, the "Italy of the Orient." There, in truth, man
treads upon the roof of his own house. And in the valley
of the Indus, especially, innumerable deluges have laid
layer upon layer of mud over the cultures that sprang
up along the shores of the great river.

Thus, the Indian historian Banerji, seeking an ancient
Buddhist monastery perhaps fifteen hundred years old,
came upon an age-old city underneath the walls of the
monastery—a city from which the Buddhists had taken
the bricks for their building. Other excavations upriver
along the valley of the Indus as far as the Punjab gradually brought to light some fifty towns and cities of varying sizes, two of which had plainly been the metropolises
of an extensive and well-organized civilization. These are

Harappa, situated about sixty miles southwest of Lahore on a tributary of the Indus, and Mohenjo-daro, on the lower reaches of the Indus. These cities were the focuses of a tremendous ellipse that enclosed a cultural area larger than the approximately contemporaneous river civilizations in Mesopotamia and lower Egypt. The carefully planned layout of the cities and of the surrounding arable lands suggested that a strong, highly centralized government had ruled this region for at least a thousand years (from 2500 to 1500 B.C.) until Aryan tribes on an incomparably lower level of civilization poured into the valley of the Indus and destroyed the cities of the Harappa culture.

Discovery of the Harappa culture enabled archæologists to assign a "beginning" to Indian history. Those most familiar with the age-old spiritual tradition of India had all along thought it impossible for Indian civilization to have taken its origin from the Aryan invaders. Now excavations in numerous places proved conclusively that the Aryans had in fact shattered a highly developed existing civilization from which numerous strands of later Indian life have derived.

The Indus culture had a hieroglyphic script that has not as yet been deciphered. This inability to read the literary remains constitutes a grave handicap for archæology. On the other hand, it has been possible to form a reliable picture of this ancient Indian civilization because of its extraordinary uniformity over a long period of time and over an extensive area. The handicraft products of the culture, especially the ceramics, were amazingly standardized throughout the whole region. Even more surprising is the fact that each of the nine strata of ruins at Mohenjo-daro, resulting from repeated prehistoric floods of the Indus, show that the earlier city plan and architectural principles were retained. Can we imagine a central European city like Zurich, Munich, or Milan being repeatedly destroyed by earthquakes and floods and consistently rebuilt in the same fashion, so that it would look today as it did at the time of Charlemagne? Such incredible conservatism is characteristic of India, however, and is reflected today in the faithfulness to tradition of contemporary Hindus. As a result, the Indus civilization was curiously without a history. No early forms have been found. We know only the culture of the period of maturity, which lasted unchanged for at least a thousand years and would probably have gone on still longer if barbarian peoples had not invaded the valley.

It is a culture that, so we now consider, appeared suddenly. Before it, nothing comparable existed in India; in this respect it resembled the culture of the Sumerians, who said of their predecessors in a hymn: "They knew neither bread for nourishment nor clothing for covering their bodies. They walked on the bare ground, ate grass with their mouths like sheep, and drank water out of ditches."

The size of the cities presupposes an organized agriculture capable of providing sufficient surplus beyond the needs of the farmers to supply the urban population. Huge pit silos, such as were utilized in ancient Rome two thousand years later, have been found. Intensive tillage seems to have been practiced at the cost of personal liberty and the peasant's standard of living, for not even the most rudimentary agricultural machines were used. (A similar contradiction between primitive agriculture and impressive architecture is found in pre-Columbian cultures of Central America. There were no mills; grain was pounded. Barley, wheat, sesame, field peas, and cotton were raised. (Fragments of red cotton cloth were found adhering to a silver vase found in Mohenjo-daro.) Cotton textile formed the Indus culture's chief article of export to Mesopotamia and East Africa.

Agriculture, brick-manufacturing, weaving, pottery, and probably other occupations were, as we would say today, "nationalized." Today the region where this ancient civilization flourished is a wasteland of broad belts of sand alternating with islands of jungle; it is hard to imagine that such land could have supported a lively agriculture. The excavated cities themselves supply the explanation. They were not built of sun-dried brick, but of extremely uniform baked bricks that would be impervious to constant rains and floods. Seals made of hard stone, soft steatite, ivory, and clay bear the image of the water buffalo, so that the fauna as well as the architecture point to the climate's having once been moist. Nowadays this part of the Indus valley receives a bare minimum of water from irrigation canals, but in those days it must have lain on the fringes of the monsoon rains. Much later, in fact, the scholars who accompanied Alexander the Great on his invasion reported a land of rich vegetation. Moreover, the drainage systems of the two great cities—with covered sewers such as are rare in the Orient even today—suggest that rainfall was heavy and regular.

Besides the two metropolises, many other cities have been found. There was a strongly fortified commercial city in the vicinity of Sutkagan-dor; a city near Chanhu-daro in Sind; another farther up the Indus, situated on a plateau forty-two hundred feet above sea level, a still nameless city that was destroyed before Harappa. The excavations begun there in 1954, mainly by French archæologists, have made no great strides due to persistent bad weather.

On the other hand, our knowledge of the two principal cities of the Indus culture is complete enough to provide us with a more comprehensive picture of prehistoric urban life than any we possess from other cultural areas.

The great navigable river was the principal artery linking Harappa and Mohenjo-daro, but it was also a terrible destroyer, repeatedly visiting tremendous floods upon the two cities. Given the location of the cities, defense against these floods always had to be the prime concern. Perhaps it was the necessity to build good levees that made such capable architects of the men of Harappa. No matter how often the river devastated the city, it was always rebuilt again at the same spot, as though water were its indispensable element. River water was, in fact, everywhere available, for there were great public baths and innumerable bathrooms. Perhaps there were religious reasons for remaining close to the river, destructive as it was.

The cities were laid out on a regular plan, usually with rectangular streets, some of a generous width. The wind from the mountains could sweep through these streets, bringing fresh air, though the houses themselves had only narrow window slits just below the ceilings of the rooms, and the façades were almost solid. Although most of the houses had two or more stories (houses more than thirty-five feet high have already been excavated), the citadels both in Harappa and in Mohenjo-daro towered commandingly over all the other buildings. They were built on huge pedestals that probably served to raise them above the flood level. The citadels were a rectangular complex of buildings measuring about four hundred yards in length by two hundred yards in width. Terraces seem to have been intended for religious processions or public festivals.

The buildings within the citadel were of an almost exclusively public character. One of these, the largest, was a bath of imposing dimensions. A large pool lined with smooth brick formed the central feature; it was surrounded by numerous disrobing-rooms and chambers for warm baths, massage, and rest. A second huge building, notable for its aggregate of small rooms, was a kind of school, either a seminary for priests or a college for officials (possibly priests and officials were one and the same). A large hall with a roof supported on pillars may have served for assemblies.

From the available evidence it appears that the citadel was the center of both religion and government. The great granaries were also included in the citadel, and a tremendous temple topped the whole complex of buildings. This temple would no doubt have been the crowning glory of the excavations at Mohenjo-daro, but it has not proved possible to dig for it because the mound under which it lies—like so many other ancient sanctuaries—now supports another temple, a Buddhist stupa of the third or fourth century A.D. which the excavators have been reluctant to remove.

What sort of religion was practiced by the inhabitants of the ancient Indus culture is as yet unknown. A number of small female figurines made of various materials have been found, suggesting that some sort of mother goddess was worshipped. This hypothesis is supported by a seal representing a woman from whose womb a plant emerges. That is, the maternal principle was equated with the earth and with growth; goddesses of this sort, *gramadevatas*, are common in rustic Hinduism. A male god is represented several times in characteristic yogi posture and surrounded by animals, like the god Shiva in later Hinduism. Since the Harappans also practiced a fertility cult, there were small symbols of male and female sexual organs. However, nothing really conclusive can be said about the religion until the script has been deciphered. It is striking that the existence of a temple underneath the stupa at Mohenjo-daro has been assumed, and that in Harappa the brick-robbers apparently removed an entire temple, while in none of the other cities has there been found any building that can be definitively recognized as a temple.

The script has so far resisted all attempts at decipherment largely because no text of more than twenty-odd symbols has been found. Most of the inscriptions are limited to three or four symbols found on seals. Altogether there were some four hundred signs, of which two hundred and fifty appear to have been basic and the rest variants. Some had numerical value, others appear frequently at the ends of words, but their meaning remains obscure.

The difficulty of interpretation makes all the more intriguing the mysterious life of the people themselves— a life that, to all appearances, was even in the days of the Harappa culture itself a life of concealment. The reason probably lay in the rigid authority of the central power. As this power seems to have survived unimpaired for a thousand years, it was in all likelihood a priest-kingship. For the laws of a religion are more binding and more apt to survive the passage of time than the vicissitudes of a court and of dynastic succession. In the Harappa civilization the individual had his assigned role, even though he might be a freeman and not one of the innumerable slaves whose uniform dwellings have been excavated. Music, dancing, and public life were organized on a religious basis. Even sociability was supervised.

Rooms in Harappa and Mohenjo-daro were illuminated

by oil lamps, provided with wooden furniture and mats
of reeds; hides and cloth were probably also used. In the
warm, damp climate not much clothing was worn, but
perhaps this was compensated for by the large number of
ornaments of copper, silver, gold, and precious stones.
The women went naked except for a short cotton skirt.

SEAL FROM MOHENJO-DARO, CIRCA 2000 B.C.

(from Gisbert Combaz: L'Inde et l'Orient Classique; *Paris, 1937)*

However, necklaces, armlets, and fancy girdles were not
enough to satisfy their vanity; they affected a kind of
tall, fan-shaped headgear, while the men wound great
lengths of cloth around their bodies. In a cache that, to
all appearances, contains the loot of a burglary, numerous
pieces of gold and silver jewelry have been found; the
Harappans were skilled at working metals as well as at
smelting them.

Considerable artistic skill is indicated by the bronze statuette of a lithe-limbed dancer, a naked girl wearing the same sort of jewelry and coiffure that can be seen on vase paintings. There is an inimitable grace in the pose—so much so that at first the great age of the statuette was seriously doubted. The circumstances of the find, however, are unquestionable evidence that this statuette

STATUETTE OF A DANCING GIRL, FROM MOHENJO-DARO.

(from Gisbert Combaz: L'Inde et l'Orient Classique; Paris, 1937)

was in fact a product of the Harappa culture. In addition to the workshops of artists there must have been a considerable industry for the production of drinking-cups, for in the vicinity of wells tremendous quantities of cup fragments of the simplest manufacture have been found. These had obviously been thrown away deliberately. Apparently the Harappa people had a taboo against drinking twice from the same vessel—as do contemporary Hindus—so that the cups were smashed after use.

It is always a venturesome business to draw conclusions from pictures or sculptures about the lineaments of a race or the appearance of its people. Interpretation of skeletal finds is a safer procedure. Apparently two races lived in the cities on the Indus. One of them was medium-sized, with dark-brown to olive-brown skin color, dark hair, and large dark eyes, long heads and faces, and narrow, rather prominent noses. This same type is still found in northwestern India. The second, more primitive element in the population must have been the aboriginal inhabitants of the country. They display a distinct kinship with the Australian peoples and with the Veddas of Ceylon, and apparently belonged to the race that emigrated to Australia from India, via Ceylon and Melanesia. They are small, black-haired, with wide faces, broad noses, and protruding lips. This type is still to be found in central and southern India. They must have formed the working class of the Harappa culture. They were the ones who dug the canals, molded the bricks, hauled the stones, and pounded the grain, while the other group ran the farms, planned the cities, engineered the buildings, and formed the official class.

For a thousand years and more the people of Mohenjo-daro and Harappa had scarcely any enemy but the waters of the great river. Only four of over forty excavated settlements show signs of fortifications. But in the last century of the Harappa culture human foes appeared. The fortifications of the big cities were reinforced, especially at the west gates. The rigid empire of priest-kings, in which the common people unprotestingly accepted the yoke and could amuse themselves only in secret, was forced on the defensive. A few at a time at first, but later in ever larger groups, wild tribes from the mountains descended upon the Indus valley. Five, ten times, perhaps oftener, the walls fended them off. But at last came a mighty wave that smashed everything before it.

Whole groups of skeletons in unnatural postures have been found, people killed in the streets, others with their heads cut off—testimony to the butchery committed by the Aryan invaders in the metropolises of this ancient civilization. The time of this invasion was approximately 1500 B.C.

The barbarians must have been amazed, for they found countless objects whose use was a mystery to them: hundreds of types of children's toys; scented oils, charcoal pencils, and red ocher for cosmetic use; metal mirrors, combs of ivory, and jewelry, enormous quantities of jewelry. When the last of those strange people who had created all this lay bleeding in the broad avenues, the Aryan invaders settled down and made themselves at home. They chose, however, not to live in the great brick buildings with bathrooms, kitchens, and drains; rather, they kept to the round huts and tents to which they were accustomed, furnishing these with mats taken from the empty houses.[6]

The cities vanished; the city-dwellers died at the hands of the conquerors. But in the villages and in the countryside smaller groups of natives were permitted to live. They were important to the barbarians because they possessed all sorts of skills, because they could weave cloth and make pottery. Thus, many of the traditions of the Indus culture, perhaps the very ones that had penetrated

---

[6] For a long time the Aryans were supposed to have brought civilization into India. In recent years this theory has been definitely disproved by scholars. Stuart Piggott states emphatically in his *Prehistoric India* (Penguin Books, 1950): "The Aryan advent in India was, in fact, the arrival of barbarians into a region already highly organized into an empire based on a long-established tradition of urban culture."

most deeply among the people, survived over the centuries in spite of the Aryan invasion, and have deeply
affected Hindu culture right up to the present.

The barbarians who poured into the valley of the Indus
had only one great advantage over the Harappa people:
an invention more likely to be conceived by a pillaging,

MINIATURE FROM HARAPPA.

(from Gisbert Combaz: L'Inde et l'Orient Classique; *Paris, 1937)*

migrating people than by crowded urbanites. This was the
war chariot.

This deadly vehicle appeared for the first time around
the middle of the second millennium B.C. Beside the
driver stood a noble warrior in heavy armor, with perhaps a squire behind him. No battle line of infantry
could resist the attack of a squadron of chariots. And so
the savage warriors triumphed wherever they appeared,
and the turmoil they brought with them was propagated

like a wave. From the Hoangho to the Vistula, from the Nile to the Indus, city folk found hiding-places for their jewelry and valuables, while homes and palaces went up in flames. The broad steppes between the Black and the Caspian seas may have been the homeland of these pillaging cattle-breeders; but their victories affected ancient, highly developed civilizations thousands of miles away. During this time of trouble Crete lost her hegemony in the Mediterranean, Egypt bowed under the rule of the shepherd-kings, Babylon was plundered. New empires came to the fore, like that of the Hittites in Asia Minor. In some places the bloody nightmare passed swiftly, leaving behind nothing but a horrible memory—and knowledge of the chariot, which henceforth was used for hunting as well as for war. Sometimes invaders destroyed whole cultures, as they did in the valley of the Indus; sometimes they created new cultures, as in China. There the Shang Dynasty, its power based upon the chariot, brought the first Chinese urban civilization to its peak in the Hoangho region. While the Etruscan cities and the Harappa cities vanished without leaving behind a single readable message, China's civilization has been continuous. A virtually unbroken line leads from the legendary "Great City of Shang" down to historical times.

The world under the earth, the realm of demons and graves, occupies a peculiarly important place in the psychology of the Chinese. For thousands of years—in fact, up to a few decades ago—the Chinese had no community cemeteries. Each family established its graves anywhere, the place being determined by all sorts of magical calculations and cosmic considerations. Consequently, the soil of this most ancient civilized people has become, in the course of its long history, virtually sacred. It is an-

cestral soil in the most literal sense, and as such invio-
lable. That fact has caused difficulties wherever a railroad
or a streetcar line had to be laid, and it has made extensive excavations, such as archæologists have carried out in
Egypt, Mesopotamia, or Italy, almost impossible. Thus the
oldest cultural heritage of mankind, the only one that extends in a long chain of dynasties from the remote past
to the present, is also the least well known. What we do
know is not sufficient for us to form even so much as a
vague conception of the extent and the importance of the
potential archæological riches the land must hold.

For centuries the peasants of the district of Anyang,
north of the Hwang Ho River, had been plowing splinters
of bone and fragments of tortoise shell out of the earth
and selling these to pharmacists as dragons' bones—a
favorite cure for all sorts of diseases. Eventually archæologists were given the chance to undertake excavations,
though at times these had to be carried out under military protection. The scientists persisted, in spite of the
wrath of the populace, and so discovered the "Great City
of Shang." The city hitherto had been known only from
the legend of Pan Keng, who was supposed to have
founded this first capital of China around 1400 B.C. Under
the wind-deposited thick layer of loess, which had preserved the city of Shang through the millennia, were
found a great many beautiful sacred vessels of bronze,
etched with animal motifs and partly coated with a mala-
chite-green patina. In addition, some thousand headless
skeletons were found; the skulls had been preserved in a
separate place. These were evidently prisoners of war,
who had been sacrificed by the hundreds.

The king's wives and numerous members of his court
were also killed in order that they might accompany the

dead sovereign to the hereafter—a custom that was practiced among many other ancient peoples in Asia, Africa,
and America.

As yet, study of the Great City of Shang is still in its
initial stages. We do not even know the manner of its
destruction. Indeed, such riddles are the rule. The vast
Chinese Empire seems to have swallowed up the past
utterly; history vanishes without a trace under the sands
of its great deserts or the mud of its giant rivers. Only
by chance, it would seem, is it restored to the world
when, say, an earthquake opens a crevice in which archaic
pottery, grave-offerings, and tools of vanished epochs are
discovered.

Twenty-five hundred years after the founding of the
Great City of Shang, another Chinese capital was will-
fully deserted, the population expelled from it, and a sea
of houses abandoned to decay. And this was done on
the word of an astrologer. The man who obeyed the
star-gazer's oracular pronouncement was one of the greatest conquerors in history, a man noted for his firm grasp
on reality: the great Kublai Khan.

"Khambalu is situated on a great river in Cathay and
in ancient times was an extraordinarily splendid and
royal city. The name itself means: the City of the Sovereign. But His Majesty being told by astrologers that this
city would rise in rebellion against its master, he decided
to build another capital on the other side of the river . . .
so that the new and the old city would be separated only
by the stream flowing between them. The newly built
city was given the name Tai-du, and all Cathayans had
to leave the old city and make their homes in the new.
Some of the inhabitants, however, whose loyalty was

under no suspicion, received permission to remain, especially since the new city could not shelter the tremendous population of the old one."

Evidently, to judge by this account of Marco Polo's, Kublai Khan trusted his astrologers but did not think it necessary to disrupt things unnecessarily. He believed

KUBLAI KHAN (1216–1294), FOUNDER OF MONGOL DYNASTY, FROM A CHINESE ENGRAVING.

and did not believe; had he been fully convinced of the danger, he might very well have abandoned his plan to establish his capital in China and have returned to Karakorum, where the other Tartar khans had resided.

Kublai's decision resulted in the abandonment to decay and eventual annihilation of two cities: Karakorum, the old capital, and Khambalu, the capital threatened by rebellion.

The ruins of Karakorum lie north of the Gobi Desert, in so deserted a region that modern scholars give its position by latitude and longitude. We must admire the courage and pertinacity of the travelers who reached the city under the primitive conditions of the Late Middle Ages, on orders from the pope, as ambassadors of Saint Louis, or as simple merchants. For there were several, perhaps many. Giovanni de Piano Carpini arrived at Karakorum in 1246. He was followed six years later by the Minorite friar Rubruquis (Ruysbroek). Their accounts afford a vivid picture of the bustling life of Karakorum, which at that time was the heart of the greatest empire in the world. Peoples from all parts of the globe lived in the city, each nation having its own quarters and streets. There were Germans, who were prized as artisans, Frenchmen, Englishmen, Hungarians, Arabs, and of course Chinese. Around the palace of the Great Khan stood twelve houses of worship of different nations—evidence of the tolerance of the Mongolian ruler. In other respects, too, his city was orderly and rational. "The city wall had four gates; outside the East Gate was the grain market; outside the West Gate the market for sheep and goats; at the Southern Gate the market for oxen and drays; and on the north the market for horse traders."

Of this great capital of the Middle Ages no more can be seen today than an occasional low wall of rammed earth.

The fate of Khambalu was not much kinder. At the time the Chin emperor Utubu fled from it, leaving the city to Kublai Khan, Khambalu already had a history of at least two thousand years. It is mentioned as the capital of earlier empires. From the tenth century A.D. on, it won fresh importance as the residence of the Tartar *khitan,* and later of the Manchurian Chin Dynasty. But this long history weighed less with Kublai Khan than the predictions of his astrologers. He expelled all the natives ex-

cept for his own officials and some people he considered
not dangerous. Among these were the prostitutes, who
were allowed to keep their old homes in Khambalu. Since
their numbers had swelled to twenty-five thousand because of the numerous foreign diplomats and dignitaries
visiting the court of Kublai Khan, Khambalu can scarcely
have been left empty. But it acquired a rather odd
reputation as a result of their presence.

Moreover, as long as Kublai Khan lived, the city remained the residence of the officials he had brought with
him. For all their collaboration, he did not trust the
natives; evidently the Chinese officials who served Kublai
were not among the best elements in the Chinese bu-
reaucracy. Nevertheless, they could scarcely have been
more corrupt than the Arab minister named Ahmed, in
whose hands Kublai Khan had placed the most important affairs of state, leaving the other eleven members of
the Supreme Council to play a very minor part during
Ahmed's twenty years in office. This Ahmed, whom
Marco Polo calls Achmak, sold government posts for
money or for the favors of beautiful women, arbitrarily
condemned men who criticized him or who refused him
their daughters, and in general behaved so badly that at
last his administration became too much even for the
long-suffering Chinese. At last one year, when Kublai
Khan had retired to his summer castle, two Chinese
named Chen-ku and Van-ku broke into Ahmed's palace,
which was still at Khambalu, and assassinated him. The
subsequent investigation revealed so many crimes committed by Ahmed with the assistance of his sons that
Kublai confiscated the minister's property and had seven
of the sons executed.

The prophecy had thus been fulfilled, though the revolt had been directed not against Kublai Khan himself

but against his prime minister. Since Ahmed the Arab had worn a short beard and the Chinese conspirators were smooth-faced, the rebellion against Ahmed was called the Revolt of the Beardless.

The Mongolian invasion had broken the prosperity of still another city, Hangchow, which Marco Polo calls Kinsay. From what he tells us of King Fakfur of Kinsay, it is not surprising that the King was unable to put up an effective resistance to the warlike Mongolian hordes. The Venetian writes:

"Occasionally accompanied by his Queen, at other times by some of his women, the King visited the lake to seek amusement in the silk-covered barks that sailed upon it, and to visit the temple of idols which stood on the shore of this lake. The two other divisions of his seraglio had the most beautiful groves, pools, gardens full of fruit trees, and also enclosures for all kinds of game such as antelope, deer, hare, and rabbit. Here, too, the King amused himself in the company of his ladies, of whom some drove in carriages and others rode on horses. Aside from the King, no man was permitted to be present at these parties. The women, however, were accustomed to hunt with dogs. If they wearied, they returned to the pleasure groves by the shores of the lake, laid their raiment aside, and leaped into the water; they swam gaily about, some here, some there. The King watched this spectacle. Thereafter, they returned to the palace. Occasionally he had the midday meal served in one of these groves, where the branches and foliage of the tall trees provided dense shade, and these same ladies surrounded him and served him."

Uncharitably, the Venetian concludes: "Thus he whiled away his time amid the debilitating charms of his women and in utter ignorance of the trade of war, and the consequence was that his softness and his cowardice permitted the Great Khan to deprive him of his glittering sovereignty and to drive him shamefully from his throne."

Fakfur's splendid palace was already decaying in the time of Marco Polo; the walls around parks and the game enclosures had collapsed, the trees had been felled, and the animals had run off or been stolen.

On the other hand, Khambalu and the new city of Tai-du across the river, which was still under construction, were in his time centers of vigorous trade and churning life. The new city of Tai-du contained only the palace of the Great Khan and some government buildings. In spite of the move across the river, Khambalu was far more densely populated for a while than the new city, hemmed in as it was within walls. As Kublai Khan also wished to keep his palace city free of everything dishonoring or unpleasant, executions took place in Khambalu, the dead were buried there, and all the less savory trades were practiced there. Moreover, caravans from foreign parts had to put up in the decaying houses of old Khambalu.

Most such caravans brought Indian wares: gems, spices, pearls, aromatics. The importation of raw silk at times attained the volume of one thousand wagonloads a day—hardly less than two hundred tons! This mountain of raw material was woven in Khambalu into cloth that ranged from the heaviest brocade to the most diaphanous gauze. What was not used at the court was exported.

The consumption of the court itself must, however, have been tremendous. Although we must always approach with caution any figures given by medieval writers (it seems scarcely likely that each of Kublai Khan's four principal wives actually had "ten thousand other women" in her retinue), all reports of foreign ambassadors agree in describing a court of unparalleled luxury. The basis of such magnificence was the income the Great Khan derived from his vast empire, which he apparently administered with the greatest adroitness. It is well known that Kublai Khan, following an already established Chinese practice, issued paper currency.[7]

We possess only scattered reports that do not make too clear his ingenious system of tribute, tolls, and, above all, indirect taxes. Of the latter, the salt tax alone brought in from the province of Kinsay eighty tomans of gold annually (between fifteen and seventeen million dollars). On wine, on fermented beverages made from rice, and on spices, a tax of three and one-third per cent was imposed, and the import duty usually amounted to ten per cent.

Kublai Khan's philanthropy, which Marco Polo praises so highly, seems to have been limited largely to the capital itself, where twenty thousand bowls of rice were issued to the poor each day. The state treasury bore only part of the cost of armaments. It provided the raw materials. The weaving of uniforms for the army, for example, was done free by the weavers, who were required to give one day's work a week to the Great Khan. But if his armed forces were cheap, his astrologers were expensive. Kublai Khan employed no less than five thousand astrologers, drawn from all the nations of the world which had produced adepts in this science. Christians, Mohammedans, and Chinese divided the favor of the Great Khan and provided him with precise calendars for the year and for the next month. Although they were

---

[7] Kublai Khan was not the first; Oktai Khan had issued paper money in 1236, and the rulers of the Chinese Chin Dynasty are said also to have established a paper currency. The first issue of paper money in China probably took place in the ninth century A.D.

paid salaries by Kublai, they were also permitted a certain amount of private practice and sold their horoscopes and special prophesies to the merchants and diplomats who visited or lived at Khambalu.

Their most eager customers must have been the innumerable women of the harem. Unlike his grandfather Jenghis Khan, who had his officers bring him the most beautiful girls from all the provinces he conquered, Kublai Khan preferred a particular type: the girls of the Mongolian people who had settled in the vicinity of the Great Wall, the Kungurat (whom Marco Polo called "Ungut").

"Kublai is of medium height," writes Marco Polo. "His limbs are well formed and his whole body very well proportioned. He has a light complexion, suffused with a slight redness like the lovely flush of the rose, which lends a great deal of charm to his appearance. His eyes are dark and beautiful, his nose well-shaped and prominent.

"When His Majesty wishes the companionship of one of his empresses, he either sends for her or betakes himself to her palace. In addition the Great Khan has a number of concubines who are brought for his use from a province in Tartary named Ungut. In this province there is a city of the same name whose inhabitants are famous for the beauty of their features and the light coloring of their hair. Thither he sends his officials every year, or even more frequently. These select four to five hundred of the choicest young maidens according to their beauty.

"The number the Great Khan desires are then selected out of these chosen girls, and brought to his court. As soon as they are presented, he has another examination made by a special commission of overseers, and a new

selection is made, of which twenty or thirty are kept for
his bed. These girls are first placed in charge of ladies of
certain nobles of his court, whose duty it is to observe
them attentively at night in order to make sure that they
sleep quietly, do not snore, have a pure breath, and are
free of unpleasant odors in all parts of their bodies. After
they have passed this strict test, they are divided into
groups of five, each of which groups must attend three
days and three nights in His Majesty's inner chamber,
performing all services that are required of them. When
this is done, they are relieved by another group, until
the whole number of them have performed their service;
then the first five begin again from the beginning. But
while one group serves in the inner chamber, another is
posted in the adjoining room outside, so that if His
Majesty should wish anything, such as food or drink,
the first group passes his orders on to the other, who
immediately bring whatever has been requested. Thus
the task of waiting upon His Majesty is performed solely
by these young girls.

"The others among them, upon whom a lower value
has been placed, are assigned to various gentlemen of
the court, whom they serve in cooking, in the making of
clothing, and in other useful things. And if any gentleman
belonging to the court should express the desire to take
a wife, the Great Khan gives him one of these ladies, with
a handsome dowry. In this manner he takes care of all.
One might ask whether the people of the province do
not feel offended to have their daughters snatched vio-
lently from them by the emperor. Not at all; on the
contrary, they regard it as an honor and a sign of favor
shown to them. Those who are the fathers of pretty girls
feel extraordinarily flattered that His Majesty should
condescend to choose one of their daughters."

In view of such an influx of pretty women into the capital city, it is easy to imagine that the looms and embroidery chambers of Khambalu were kept busy. In those days there was not much else to spend money on besides clothing (food was comparatively cheap), and fine garments were a favorite gift, a part of the annual salary, and often amounted to a decoration or order of merit when conferred by the Emperor. On his birthday Kublai Khan wore an especially fine robe of cloth of gold and presented many of his princes, nobles, army officers, and high officials with garments of silk shot through with gold, or with girdles of yellow leather embroidered with gold and silver.

As the Chinese city of Tai-du filled with houses and people, the old city of Khambalu diminished in importance. The rich families moved across the river to be close to the Great Khan. It was no longer considered respectable to dwell in the old capital, which was now swarming with prostitutes and foreigners.

Kublai Khan had certainly been one of the greatest rulers in world history. He was succeeded, however, by weaker Mongol emperors who were ruined by the same faults that Marco Polo attributed to the Chinese emperors before Kublai.

Khambalu declined, and the new city, which was ultimately named "the northern capital"—Peking—spread out along that bank of the river to which the astrologers' warning did not apply. Diagonally across from the walled Tartar city arose the populous Chinese quarter, absorbing more and more of the common people who at first had remained in Khambalu. The houses of Khambalu which still stood collapsed during the great earthquakes of 1662 and 1730. On October 12, 1860, Peking was occupied by combined English and French troops, and every time the Chinese did not keep some agreement, one or another of the historically important buildings in the vicinity of Peking was plundered and burned down. In the course of this protracted succession of struggles and retaliations, all that might have been considered the ruins of Khambalu was destroyed. The existence of the "new" city (by the nineteenth century more than six hundred years old), its size, and the incomparable charm of the older parts of it, still surrounded by walls, have made the memory of ancient Khambalu pale. The old city not only vanished, but has been forgotten. For thousands of years it was the residence of great rulers, but the greatest of them distrusted it, and the action he took cut its history off short. Kublai Khan abandoned the city of Khambalu to decay, and British and French cannon wiped out the last traces of its existence.

EPILOGUE

T HERE ARE only a few tranquil islands of the past in this modern world, islands like that Île Saint-Louis in the Seine, in the heart of Paris, where almost every house bears a memorial tablet reminding visitors and occupants of its colorful history. We, the human race, determine the fate of ancient buildings. From human beings they acquire life, but they also radiate life back into our world. It is possible to build anew after great disasters, but it is not possible to take up all the old threads. A new house, a different street, another city make a break in our lives. Continuity is difficult to establish within new walls. Roots are lacking, and the sum of all the lives that have warmed the old stone in the succession of generations is lost.

What a sense of familiarity, of native's return, we feel when our foot, idly probing the tidal ooze along the Frisian coast, encounters the stone rim of a well where maids gathered and gossiped seven hundred years ago, before the flood came. As in a dream we wander among the age-old dwellings along the coast at Baiæ, now inhabited by the poorest of the poor, who smilingly invite us to enter and assure us that here, on this very spot, Agrippina once lived.

We dive down into the past as into a sea whose bottom is littered with everything imaginable: skeletons in the embrace of death, traces of crimes and of repulsive greed, but also the mysterious smile of some unknown hetæra or vestal virgin, or the silent beauty of marble gods. There is some risk in taking the plunge; these depths draw us, hold us fast with the glitter of vanished glories. Many a searcher has never found his way back because he chose not to, preferring to live with Homer, Herodotus, Dante, and Marco Polo rather than with daily newspapers and television.

Nevertheless, we would not wish our probing of the past to be construed as a flight from the present. We have looked about with an affection prompted by the fear that tomorrow or the day after it may be too late to see anything at all. It is true that lost cities are being uncovered every day, ancient homes and palaces being excavated. But when this is done, the protective covering of lava, clay, or rubble is inevitably removed. The old cities become once more a part of our world, and rain and wind complete the work begun thousands of years ago by volcanoes or the weapons of men.

Yet there was also an element of confidence in our backward look. The man of Harappa who created the tiny bronze statuette of a dancing girl is closer to us than the destroyer Pizarro, who lived three thousand years later. And against the mercenary soldier who threw the first torch into the library at Alexandria there stand all the scholars and scientists who have sought to restore the treasures of the mind and spirit which long ago went up in flames at Alexandria.

CHRONOLOGICAL TABLE

B.C.

3000 Maritime communication between Mesopotamia and the cities of the Harappa culture on the Indus.
Origin of the city of Babylon, which, however, did not acquire importance until *c.* 2000 B.C.
Culture of the oldest layer of excavation at Troy.

2500 Presumed peak of the Harappa culture.
Founding of the second city on the hill of Troy.

2400 First Egyptian sea voyages to the Rhodesian gold mines.
Inscriptions at Mohenjo-daro.

1700 (to about 1600) Invasion of the Hyksos in Egypt.

1550 (to about 1050) Shang culture on the Hwang Ho in China.
Indo-Iranian nomads from Afghanistan invade the Harappa culture.

c. 1500 A tremendous volcanic eruption destroys the island of Santorin (Thera) in the Ægean. Sodom possibly destroyed at this same time.

1501 (to 1480) Hatshepsut, wife of Thutmosis III, equips an expedition to the coast of Somali.

1365 The sixth city of Troy destroyed by an earthquake.
Destruction of the city of Ugarit (now Ras Shamra).

1300 Italic peoples migrate into Italy from the northeast.
The Great City of Shang becomes capital of the Shang Empire, which is later called Yin (to 1050).

1250   New foreign population using iron at Troy.
Beginning of the great migrations in the eastern Mediterranean area. Moses leads the Israelites from Egypt to Palestine (around 1230). Phœnicians settle coastal regions in Spain, especially in Andalusia.

1200   Paris, prince of Troy, mentioned in Hittite sources.

1100   The Jews have by now conquered and settled Canaan. Phœnician settlements on the western coast of Morocco (to 950) and trading voyages to far places.

1000   Copper-smelting furnaces in Ezion-Geber.
First wave of Etruscan emigration reaches Corsica.

960   (to about 925) King Solomon's trade with East Africa and southern Arabia.

950   Documentary mention of the city of Khambalu in China.

880   (and later) Flourishing of the maritime cities of Tyre and Tartessus; legendary founding of Carthage by Dido.

800   Second wave of Etruscan emigration. Etruscan towns in central Italy flourish.
Supposed lifetime of Homer.

750   Greek colonies in Spain and southern France (Marseille).

735   Greeks found Messina and Syracuse.
Supposed lifetime of Hesiod.

600   Height of Babylon's power and building of the Tower of Babel (temple of the god Marduk).
Carthage founds colonies in West Africa, southern France, Sardinia, Sicily, and Spain.

594   On orders from Pharaoh Necos, Phœnicians sail from the Red Sea and in a three-year voyage circumnavigate Africa.

587   (to 539) Babylonian Captivity of the Jews.

575   Nebuchadnezzar II lays out the Hanging Gardens.

550   Writing down of the major parts of the Old Testament.

540   (or 535) Naval victory of the Carthaginians and Etruscans over the Greeks at Alalia (Corsica).

539   King Cyrus of Persia conquers Babylon.

529   The Greeks found Dicæarchia in lower Italy (on the site of modern Pozzuoli).

511   Destruction of the city of Sybaris.

510   End of Etruscan kingship in Rome.

495   (or 484) Birth of Herodotus.

474   Greek naval victory over the Etruscans at Kyme.

427   Birth of Plato.

424   Death of Herodotus.

396   Rome conquers and destroys Etruscan Veii.

347   Death of Plato.

343   Capua becomes dependency of Rome.

330   Alexander the Great attempts to rebuild the Tower of Babel.

323   Death of Alexander the Great, who in the thirty-three years of his life founded more than seventy cities.

309   The Romans conquer Etruscan Perusia (Perugia).

273   Poseidonia is renamed Pæstum.

212   The Romans conquer Syracuse; death of Archimedes.

200   Empire of the Huns in Mongolia and Turkestan.

146   Carthage destroyed by the Romans.

63   Birth of the Greek traveler and geographer Strabo.

A.D.

37 Birth of the Jewish historian Flavius Josephus.

79 Pompeii and Herculaneum destroyed by eruption of Vesuvius.

100 Thamugadi (Roman military camp) founded.

128 Completion of military camp at Lambæsis.

170 Geography and world map of Ptolemy.

200 New period of prosperity for the city of Carthage. Earliest possible date for the foundation of the Manamatapa kingdom south of the Zambezi River.

272 Emperor Aurelian conquers Palmyra.

300 White-skinned men found the kingdom of Ghana in West Africa.

372 The Huns cross the Volga from east to west; their pressure upon the East Goths precipitates the *Völkerwanderung*.

395 Probable destruction of the Breton city of Ys by high storm tide. (Another possible date is 441.)

400 Tiahuanaco art in the Andes.

410 Plundering of Rome by the West Goths.

439 The Vandals under Geiseric conquer Carthage.

452 Fleeing from Attila, mainland Venetians found the lagoon city of Venice.

530 Emperor Justinian founds the military camp on Mount Sinai.

600 Epidaurum, commercial city in southern Dalmatia, is destroyed in the course of the Slavic invasion.

751 Victory of the Arabs over the Chinese at Samarkand. The most populous cities in the world at this time are Shang'an (China) and Byzantium.

827 The Saracens conquer Sicily.

840 The Saracens destroy Capua.

850 Greatest expansion of the Tiahuanaco culture.
Building of the acropolis of Zimbabwe (Rhodesia).

869 Height of the Khmer culture in Indochina. Death of King Djayavarman II.

1000 Growth of power of the Incas in Peru; downfall of the Tiahuanaco culture. According to Heyerdahl: beginning of emigration to Polynesia of Kon-Tiki worshippers.

1050 Height of Viking city of Haithabu in Schleswig.

1098 Danes destroy the fortress of Jomsburg (probably identical with Vineta). King Djayavarman VII ruling in Angkor (to 1218).
Building of the Bayon temple.

1207 Destruction of the pirates' haven at Cumæ.

1254 Lifetime of Marco Polo (to 1324).

1259 Kublai Khan comes to power and founds Peking (1279).

1362 Supposed destruction of Rungholt in great North Sea flood.

1480 Chinese fleet visits East Africa.

1492 Columbus discovers Cuba and Haiti.

1503 Portuguese settlements at the mouth of the Zambezi and barter trade with the Manamatapa kingdom.

1538 The Spaniards discover the ruins of Tiahuanaco.

I N D E X

Abyssinia, 58, 210, 211; *see also* Ethiopia
Academica (Cicero), 174
Achæans, 240, 242, 262, 267
Acoran, 293
Acropolis, of Zimbabwe, 191-2, 221, 223, 344
Adam of Bremen, 23
Adria, 79
Adriatic Sea, 75-7, 79, 150, 188-9, 282, 301
Ægean Sea, 182, 231, 233, 240, 340
Ægina, vii
Æmilianus, Scipio, 259
Æneas, 83, 161, 169, 228, 248, 250, 253
Afghanistan, 340
Africa, 9, 29-30, 34, 182, 190-223, 253-60, 268, 280-94, 327, 341, 344
Agamemnon, 240, 242
Agisymba, 194
Aglibol, 137
Agrippa, 246
Agrippina, 178, 338
Aguntum, 151
Agylla, 300
Ahaziah, King, 202
Ahès, 13
Ahhiyawa, 236
Ahmed, Arab minister to Kublai Khan, 330-1
Aksum, 210
Alalia, 188, 302n, 342
Alamans, 247
Alaska, 118
Alba, Duke of, 170
Alban, Lake, 307
Alcacova, Diego de, 212
Alexander Severus, Emperor, 177
Alexander the Great, 130-3, 316, 342
Alexandria, 6, 23, 160, 164, 167, 257, 279, 339
Algeria, 281
Algiers, 291
All Saints' Day Flood, 18, 23-4
Almeida, Don Francesco d', 211
Almeida, Laurenço d', 212

Alps, 74, 87, 150, 157, 228, 244, 274, 301-2
Altheim, Franz, 299n
Amalfi, 86-7, 170
Amatha, 7
Amazon River, 30
Amazons, 29
Amber Route, 71-2, 282
Ambidravians, 151
Ambisontians, 151
Amenophis II, Pharaoh, 198
America, 29-31, 39, 49, 54-5, 57, 59, 64, 66, 202, 256, 292, 296, 315, 327
Amina, Queen, 206
Ancus, 302
Andalusia, 181, 189
Andes, ix, 57-8, 66, 208, 343
Angkor, 39-41, 44-8, 55, 344
Angkor-Vat, temple of, 47
Angola, 212
Annals (Tacitus), 98
Antioch, 134, 229
Antiquities of the Jews (Josephus), 6
Antony, Mark, 135, 172, 277
Anyang, 326
Apennines, 74
Apollo, 99, 300
Apollodorus, *quoted*, 88
Appian Way, 272, 278
Aquileia, 150-1, 158
Arabia, 128, 133, 141, 175, 186n, 191, 198, 201, 209-11, 341
Arabs, 23, 124, 138, 146-8, 165, 180, 192, 194, 203-4, 206-7, 211, 213, 215, 260, 290-1, 329-31, 343
Aramaic language, 126, 255
Arcadius, 146
Archimedes, 228, 342
Arezzo, 310
Arganthonius, King, 184, 188
Argissa, 235
Argos, 76, 234-5
Ariovistus, 154
Aristodemos, 244-5
Aristophanes, 78, 189
Aristotle, 37, 84, 286, 293; *quoted*, 77-8
Aristoxenos of Taranto, *quoted*, 84

Armenia, 33, 124, 128, 134, 144
Arretium (Arezzo), 310
Arruns, 308
Artemis, 278
Aryan tribes, 314, 323, 323n
Asclepius, 256
Asia, 9, 30, 34, 38, 49, 55–6, 191, 202, 313–37; *see also* Asia Minor
Asia Minor, vii, 17, 81, 102, 117, 125–6, 128, 141–2, 144, 150, 162, 183–4, 189, 230–1, 233, 236, 241, 266–7, 299–301, 325
Assuan, 190
Assyria, 122, 202, 236, 254
Atella, 91
"Atellan plays," 91
Athalaric, 177
Athenæus, 176, 262, 262n, 299n
Athens, 74, 78, 142, 269, 279, 308
Athos, Mount, 132
Atlantic Ocean, 13, 18, 26, 30, 34, 180, 292
Atlantis, viii, 29–38, 187n, 202
Atlantis-Helgoland, Motherland of Aryan-Germanic Racial Thoroughbreeding and Colonization, 29
Atlas Mountains, 30, 89, 281
Atreus, 236, 240
Atria, 76–9
Attalus, King, 162
Attarissiyas, 236
Attica, 266
Attila, 343
Augustine, Saint, 168
Augustus, Emperor, 137, 157, 167, 245–6, 280; *see also* Octavian
Aurea, Saint, 170
Aurelian, Emperor, 143–6; *quoted,* 145–6, 343
Aurignacian period, 58
Ausonius, Decimus Magnus, 278–9; *quoted,* 279
Australia, 197, 322
Austria, 151, 154, 159, 291
Avaris, 9
Averno, Lake, 173–4, 176–7, 246, 250, 270
Aversa, 91
Aymaras, 60, 64
Azores, 29–30
Aztecs, 59

Baal, 121, 130
Baalshamin, 136
Babel, Tower of, 134, 138, 341, 342

Babylon, ix, 119, 121, 123–34, 236, 325, 340, 341, 342
Babylonian Captivity, 126, 341
Babylonian language, 122, 126
Babylonians, 120, 123, 131–2, 138
Bacchus, 270
Bætis, *see* Quadalquivir River
Baiæ, 104, 170–9, 189–90, 245–6, 270, 338
Balearic Islands, 257
Balkans, 242
Baltic Sea, 21–3, 25, 72, 182, 282
Banerji, 313
Bantus, 204, 208, 220
Barotse, 208
Barros, João de, 192; *quoted,* 194
Basilicata Mountains, 81, 87
Basques, 31
Bassikunu, 207
Bassus, Cerronius, 145
Bassus, Lucilius, 79
Bastetanic people, 185
Battuta, Ibn, 207
Baumann, Hermann, 219n
Bayon Temple, 44–5, 47, 344
Beck, Horace, 214–15
Bekr, Abu, 146
Bekri, El, 206–7
Bel, 137
Belian gate, 121
Beloch, Julius, 269
Bellamy, H. S., 58
Belloso, Diego, 40
Benamatapa, 192
Benevento, 279
Benjamin of Tudela, 147
Bennett, Wendell C., 66n
Bérard, Jean, 238n
Berbers, 165, 207, 253, 281–5, 287, 290
Béthencourt, Jean de, 292
Bible, 5–8, 10, 181, 196–7, 201; *quoted,* 5–6, 135, 197, 200, 201, 202; *see also* Genesis, Book of
Bible societies, 196
Black Sea, 80, 231, 281, 325
Blankenhorn, Max, *quoted,* 7
Blegen, Carl William, 242
Bodhisatva Avalokitesvara, 47
Bolivia, 63
Bolsena, Laice, 301, 307
Bombay, 212
Bonepe, *see* Ponape
Bordeaux, 279
Borneo, 39, 215
Borsippa, 128
Braghine, 31

Brazil, 66
Brest, bay of, 15
British Isles, 28, 256; *see also* England
Brittany, 13–17, 20, 180*n*, 181, 343
Brutus (Etruscan), 304*n*
Bucco, 91
Buddhism, 47–8, 56, 313, 318
Burdigala (Bordeaux), 279
Burma, 38–40, 46
Busch, Andreas, 24, 27; *quoted*, 24
Byzantines, 23, 247–9, 260
Byzantium, 23, 168, 211, 343; *see also* Constantinople

Cádiz, *see* Gadir
Cælius, Marcus, 173
Cære, 300, 302*n*, 303–4, 309–10
Cæsar, Julius, 154, 171, 177, 178, 186*n*, 248, 260, 277, 280
Caieta, 270
Calabria, 81
Calamis, 179
Calancha, Antonio de la, 60
Calasasaya, 63
California, 118
Caligula, Emperor, 140, 164
Callao, *see* Lake Titicaca
Cambodia, 39–40, 45
Cameroon, 256
Campania, 79, 88–9, 92–3, 97, 102, 105, 114, 160, 166, 242–7, 270–4, 277, 279, 301; *see also* Cumæ
Canaan, 9, 11, 12, 341
Canary Islands, 29, 33, 292–8
Cancale, 15
Cannæ, Battle of, 84, 273–4
Canton, 210
Cape Guardafui, 196
Cape Miseno, 93
Cape Skagan, 25
Capitoline Hill, 303
Capri, 87
Capua, 149, 160, 243, 270–9, 342, 344
Capua Nuova, 280
Caracalla, Emperor, 167
Carales (Cagliaria), 167
Carinthia, 151, 154–5
Carlos III, King, 87
Carnac, bay of, 15
Carnuntum, 288–9, 290*n*, 291
Caroline Islands, 49, 50, 53
Carthage, 133, 160, 228, 253–9, 270, 279, 297, 302*n*, 341, 342, 343

Carthaginians, 32, 161, 182–4, 188–9, 293
Caspian Sea, 131, 325
Cassiodorus, 93; *quoted*, 177–8
Cassites, 122
Castile, 292
Castor, 79
Catania, 279
Catherine, Queen of Castile, 292
Catholic Church, 290; *see also* Christianity
Catiline, 95
Catina (Catania), 279
Caton-Thompson, Gertrude, 214–17, 221, 223*n*; *quoted*, 223
Catullus, 286
Caucasus, 29
Celtic language, 158
Celts, 14, 17–18, 74, 150, 153–4, 157–9, 182, 186*n*, 187, 282
Cendro, ix, 294–5, 298
Central America, 29, 49, 55, 315
Ceram, C. W., 231*n*
Ceres, 86, 165, 270
Ceri, 310
Cerveteri, 307–8
Ceylon, 29, 40, 322
Chad, Lake, 206, 209
Chalcis, 187
Chaldean gate, 121
Chaldeans, 307
Chamisso, Adelbert von, 50
Chanhudaro, 316
Charlemagne, 15, 206, 231, 315
Charles XII, King, 147
Chartres, Cathedral of, 47
Chausey Islands, 15
Chen-ku, 330
Chichén Itzá, 55
Chile, 55
Chin dynasty, 329, 333*n*
China, 38, 40, 46, 211, 325–37, 341, 343, 344
Chinese, 44, 46, 48, 191, 211, 213, 215, 325–37
Chisium, 309
Chiusi, 310
Christ, Jesus, *see* Jesus Christ
Christian Topography, 37
Christianity, 14, 15, 21, 23, 41, 52, 56, 62, 134, 168, 211, 246, 252, 278, 288–90, 294, 329, 333
Chronica Slavorum (Helmold), 21
Cicero, vii, 95, 172, 173, 177, 286; *quoted*, 93, 277
Cilento, 83
Cimbrians, 160*n*

Circe, 302
Cissian gate, 121
Civita Castellana, 69n
Claræ Urbes (Ausonius), 278–9
Claudius, Emperor, 159, 164
Cleopatra, 135
Clusium, 302n, 303, 308, 310
Cocceius, 245–6, 249–50
Cohen, Robert, 231n, 269n
Collatinus, Tarquinius, 304
Colombia, 57, 315
"Colonia Julia Carthago," 260
Columbaria, 166
Columbus, Christopher, 197
Comacchio, Lake, 74, 76
Commedia dell'arte, 91
Commentarios Reales (Vega), 56
Concarneau, bay of, 15
Condate, 17
Condevincum, 16
Confessions (Augustine), 168
Constantine the Great, 168
Constantinople, 168, 247, 279; see also Byzantium
Contenau, Georges, 125n, 129
Corfu, 261
Corinth, vii, 142, 182
Cornelius, Publius, 162
Corneto (Tarquinia), 311
Corsica, 184, 188, 257, 284, 299, 341, 342
Cosa, 310
Crassus, Licinius, 171
Crathis River, 261, 269
Cremona, 85, 295
Crete, ix, 29, 77, 89, 233, 236–7, 240, 251–2, 278, 280, 298, 303, 325
Critias (Plato), 34–8
Crœsus, 74
Cro-Magnon man, 294
Croton, 265, 267–9
Cuba, 344
Cubas, Tomas Arias Marin y, quoted, 294
Cumæ, 89–90, 176, 245–51, 270–2, 344
Cuzco, 64
Cybele, 102, 162
Cyclops, 32–3, 234
Cyprus, 127, 235
Cyrus, King, 119n, 126, 128, 184, 342

Dædalus, 77, 252
Dahut, Princess, 13, 14
Dalmatia, 284, 343

Damascus, 137, 147
Danauna, 33
Danes, 21, 23, 344
Dante, 339
Danube River, 71, 155, 282, 288–9
Dar For, 205
Dardanelles, 233
Darius, King, 128, 130
Darius III, King, 130–1
Dark Ages, 79
Darwin, Mount, 208
David, King, 196
De lege agraria (Cicero), 277
De mirabilibus auditis, 293
De mirabilibus auscultis, 77
Dead Sea, 6–8, 10, 12
Delphi, 74–5, 162, 267, 300, 307
Deluge, 5
Denmark, 21
Der-el Bahri, temple of, 195
Descriptio insularis Aquilonis (Adam of Bremen), 23
Dicæarchia, 69, 342
Dido, 228, 253, 256, 341
Dinocrates, 132
Diodorus, 185n, 186n, 262n, 268
Diomedes, King, 76–7
Dionysius of Halicarnassus, quoted, 75, 89
Dioscuri, temple of, 168
Disselhoff, Hans Dietrich, 32, 66n; quoted, 32, 64–5
Diu, 212
Djayavarman II, King, 46–7, 344
Djayavarnum VII, King, 47, 48, 344
Dodona, 75
Donatists, 289
Donnelly, Ignatius, 31
Dorians, 242
Dorieus, 268
Dossennus, 91
Doumer, Paul, 41
Dounarnenez, bay of, 16
Duomo, 86

East Africa, 211, 219n, 223n, 316, 341, 344
East Goths, 343
Easter Island, 55
Edrisi, Abu Abdallah Mohammed ash Sherif al, 23
Egger, Rudolf, 290n
Egypt, ix, 8–9, 11, 29, 34, 89, 125, 128, 130, 133, 139, 142–4, 164, 167, 197, 201, 208, 215, 233, 236, 279, 314, 325–6, 340, 341

Egyptians, 33, 70, 138, 165, 191, 195, 197, 198
Ehrenreich, Paul, 57
Eichem, 10
Eider River, 25
Elba, 300
Elephantine Island, 190
Elliptical Temple, 191-2, 221
Eloth, 197
Emerita, 279
Emesa, 142
Encyclopedia (Pliny the younger), 135-6
England, 181, 329, 336-7
English Channel, 28
Epidaurum, 343
Epirus, 161
Eridanos River, *see* Po River
Eritrea, 209-10, 215, 251
Erythraa (Frobenius), 209
Eshmun, 256, 259
Esquiline Hill, 302
Ethiopia, 133; *see also* Abyssinia
Etna, 69, 270
Etruria, 74, 82, 133, 300, 302, 307, 309
Etruscan language, 298, 302-3
Etruscan League, 303
Etruscans, 32, 72, 74-5, 77, 82, 88-90, 161, 183-4, 244-5, 248, 266, 270-1, 298-313, 325, 341, 342
Euphemos, 184
Euphrates River, 6, 124-5, 135, 144
Europe, 30-1, 33-4, 40, 202, 213, 233, 294, 313
Eusebius, 242-3
Ezion-Geber (Tell-el Kheleifeh), ix, 197, 199, 201-2, 341

Fakfur, King, 331-2
Falerii, 69n
Falernian district, 272
Falernus, Mount, 270
Fallmerayer, Jakob Philipp, *quoted*, 12
Fatu Hiva, 53-4, 62
Fausta, 169
Felix, Julia, 101
Felix, Minucius, 168
Felix, Spurius Julius, 101
Ferrara, 76
Février, F., 141n
Fidenæ, 161
Finsler, Georg, 231n
Fiumicino, 165
Flanders, 25-7

Florence, 310
Florus, *quoted*, 270
Formiæ, 270
Fourteenth Legion, 282, 288
France, 89, 279, 291, 294, 308, 329, 336-7, 341
Franciscans, 40
Franks, 247
Frazer, Sir James, 209-10
Frisian Islands, 25, 26, 28, 338
Frobenius, Leo, 203, 219n; *quoted* 205-6, 209, 222
Fuerteventura, 297

Gadir (Cádiz), 181, 189
Gæta, 170
Galen, 93
Gallic War (Cæsar), 154
Gamboa, Pedro Sarmiento de, 60
Gardoine, 15
Gargoris, King, 183, 186
Gaugamela, 131
Gaul, 17, 29, 154, 165, 256, 274, 284, 288, 308-9
Gaurus, Mount, 176, 270
Geiseric, 279, 343
Genesis, Book of, 5-6, 9n; *quoted*, 5-6, 8, 111
Gerar, 199
German Archæological Institute, 235
Germania, 154
Germans, 19-21, 155, 165, 290, 329
Germany, 33, 291
Geron, King, 181, 183
Ghana, 206-7, 343
Ghent, 25
Giants, 29, 58-61
Gibraltar, Strait of, 180-1, 188-90, 281; *see also* Pillars of Heracles
Glotz, Gustave, 231n, 269n
Glueck, Nelson, 198-9
Glycera, 132
Gobi Desert, 328
Goes, de, *quoted*, 192
Gomorrah, 7, 12, 111-12
Gonzalez, Blas Ruiz de Hernan, 40
Gothic War (Procopius), 14
Goths, 29, 141-2, 169, 246-7, 269, 343
Gracarca, Mount, 151-2
Gracchus, Gaius, 259-60
Gracchus, Tiberius, 259
Gradlon, King, 13
Gran Canaria, 293-5
Grand Lama of Lhasa, 47
Great City of Shang, 325-7, 340

Great Lake, 39, 48
Great Revolution, in Canton, 210
Greece, 71, 74, 80, 87, 142, 183, 233, 235-6, 242-4, 248, 265, 267
Greek language, 138, 158, 255-6 298
Greeks, 23, 69, 72, 74-5, 77, 80, 88, 90, 94, 138, 149, 165, 182-3, 185-8, 190, 230-1, 240, 254-6, 297, 302n, 307-8, 312, 341, 342; see also Achæans, Hellenes
Gregoriopolis, 170
Gregory IV, Pope, 170
Grousset, René, 44
Guadalquivir River, 180
Guatemala, 31
Gyges, 74

Habis, King, 183
Hadramaut, 139
Hadrian, Emperor, 136, 177
Hadrianopolis, 136
Haggard, H. Rider, 196
Hairanes, 140
Haithabu, 25, 344
Haiti, 344
Halauruans, 151
Halieutica (Oppianus), 17
Haman, 7
Hambruch, Paul, 49-51, 53
Hamburg, 25
Hammurabi, King, 122; quoted, 129-30
Han Emperors, 38
Hangchow, 331
Hanging Gardens, 122, 132, 342
Hannibal, 69, 84-5, 91, 161, 259, 273-6, 309
Hanno, 256, 293
Hansa, 21
Harappa, 314-25, 339, 340
Harpalus, 132
Hasdrubal, 259
Hatshepsut, Queen, 195-6, 340
Hauptmann, Gerhart, 20n
Hebrews, see Israelites
Hecuba, 238
Heine-Geldern, Robert, 49
Helgoland, 28-9, 33
Helius, 71
Helmold, 21
Hennig, Richard, 20, 25
Hephaistion, 132
Hera, 79, 81, 83, 86, 109
Heracles, 79, 88-9, 183, 268
Herakleion, 89, 90; see also Herculaneum

Herculanean Gate, 92
Herculaneum, 7, 93-4, 97, 99, 102-3, 109-10, 113, 114n, 166, 170, 187, 270, 343
Herder, Johann Gottfried von, 313
Herodotus, 119n, 190; quoted, 123, 187-8, 256n, 262n, 299n, 339, 342
Hesiod, 341
Heyerdahl, Thor, 53, 61-2, 67; quoted, 53-4, 344
Hiero, 245
Hieron, 161
Himilco, 255-6
Hindus, 131, 321, 324
Hippodamus, 269
Hiram, King of Tyre, 185, 196-8, 200
Hispania, see Spain
History of the Inca Kingdom (Gamboa), 60
Hittite Empire, ix, 122, 231n, 236, 242, 325, 341
Hoangho River, 325
Homer, 32, 143, 228-30, 237-8, 278, 339, 341
Horace, 170, 177-8; quoted, 170
Hörbiger, Hans, 57-8
Hortensius, Quintus, 95, 172
Hülsen, Christian, 273n
Humboldt, Alexander von, quoted, 62-3
Hungarians, 329
Huns, 290, 342
Hwang Ho River, 326, 340
Hyksos, 9, 340
Hymyarites, 210
Hyrcanians, 131

Iberia, 183, 188, 190
Iberians, 182, 186n, 187, 273
Icarus, 77
Ice Age, 294
Ile Saint-Louis, 338
Iliad (Homer), 228-9
Ilion (Troy), 242
Illyrian tribes, 150, 282
Incas, 55-7, 64, 67, 69, 208, 344
India, 33, 45, 46, 49, 124-5, 132-3, 139, 146, 198, 201, 211-13, 313-25, 332
Indian Ocean, 178, 191, 196, 205, 209, 211-12, 214
Indians, American, 56, 60, 62; see also Aztecs, Incas
Indicopleustus, Cosmos, 211
Indochina, 39-41, 46, 344

Indo-European linguistic family, 33, 77, 87, 187n, 298, 299
Indus River, 117, 313-14, 316-17, 340
Indus hieroglyphic script, 314, 319
Ionia, 188
Ionian Sea, 81
Ireland, 33, 181
Iron Age, 242
Ischia, 252
Ishtar, 123
Ishtar gate, 130
Isis, 99-100, 114, 209n
Isles of the Blessed, 14, 184, 292, 297
Israel, 8, 201; see also Palestine
Israelites, 8, 12, 341; see also Jews
Issos, 130
Istrians, 150
Istros River, see Danube River
Italy, 34, 68-114, 149-50, 160, 162, 242-53, 261-80, 282, 287-8, 290, 299-313, 326, 340, 341, 342
Ithaca, 240

Jade Bay, 28
Jakub, Ibrahim Ibn, quoted, 22
Jandolo, Augusto, 311
Jansonius, quoted, 20
Japan, 33, 50
Jarhibol, 137
Jason, 79, 80, 88
Java, 59
Jehoshaphat, King, 202
Jenghis Khan, 334
Jericho, 232n
Jerusalem, 65, 111, 126, 185, 200-1, 288
Jesuits, 41
Jesus Christ, 67, 74, 89, 138
Jews, 8-10, 12, 111-12, 126, 138, 165, 183, 195-8, 200-2, 204, 211, 341
Jomsburg, 344
Jomsviking Saga, quoted, 21
Jordan River, 6
Josephus, Flavius, 6, 198, 343
Judah, 202
Julien, Ch. André, 256n, 290n
Julius II, Pope, 170
Jumneta, 19, 22; see also Vineta
Juno, 165, 303
Jupiter, 99, 165, 278, 303
Justinian, Emperor, 291, 343
Justinus, 77, 186n, 262n
Juvenal, 185n

Kaffa, 209
Kao-Mon, 45
Karakorum, ix, 328-9
Kenner, Hedwig, 160n
Kenyon, K. M., 223n
Khambalu, ix, 327-37, 341
Khmer, 39-48, 51, 63, 344
Khorsabad, 129
Kiel, 21
Kien, Jang, 38
King Solomon's Mines (Haggard), 196
Kinsay (Hangchow), 331, 333
Klagenfurt, 154, 159
Kleito, 35
Klopeiner, Lake, 154
Königswald, G. H. R. von, 59
K'oniraya, 57
K'oni-tikki, viii, 57, 60-2, 64, 67, 344
Kon-Tiki, see K'oni-tikki
Koulen, Mount, 47
Krickeberg, Walter, 57
Kuala Sensing, 214
Kubary, W. S., 49, 50
Kublai Khan, 56, 327-37, 344
Kültepe, 126
Kungurat, 334
Kyme, 89, 242-5, 271, 302n

La Città, 311
Lago Fusaro, 252
Lahore, 314
Lambæsis, 281-4, 287-91, 343
Land of the Two Rivers, 9; see also Mesopotamia
Laos, 40, 81, 269
La Paz, 63
Las Casas, Bartolomé de, 212
Latin language, 138, 158, 255, 287, 299
Latin League, 303
Latium, 83, 301-2, 309
Latobius, 155-6, 159-60
Lebanon, 127-8
Lembas, 204
Leo IV, Pope, 170
Letters (Pliny), 105-8
Lex Claudia, 149
Libya, 34, 190, 254
Ligurians, 187
Limpopo River, 202, 204
Lisbon, 204, 212
Literno, 276
Livy, 77, 85, 163, 271, 273n, 299n, 304n; quoted, 302, 304
Locmariaquer, 17

Lombards, 248, 279
Longinus, Cassius, 141-2
Lot, 8, 12
Louis, Saint, 329
Lübeck, 21
Lucania, 81, 83
Lucarno, Lake, 176, 246, 270
Lucretius (Etruscan), 304n
Lusitanians, 186
Lydia, 183, 300

Maccus, 91
Macedonians, 131
Magadoxa, 211
Magdalensberg, 159
Mainake, 184, 188
Maiuri, Amedeo, 80n, 114n, 178-9, 179n, 273n
Malaga, 184
Malaparte, Curzio, *quoted*, 83
Malays, 191, 213
Malraux, André, 39, 41-4; *quoted*, 39, 42-4
Mamæa, 177
Manamatapa, 186n, 205-18, 222, 343, 344
Manchurian Chin dynasty, 329
Mandalay, 38-9
Mandara, Mount, 39
Mansa Musa, 206
Marcellus flood, 19
Marchese, Dr., 299n
Marcius, Ancus, 161
Marcomanni, 155
Marduk, 131, 341
Maria Saal, 159
Marib, 210
Marismas, Las, 180
Marius, Marcus, 93, 172
Marseille, 256, 291, 341; *see also* Massilia
Martial, 85, 176-7, 185n
Massicus, Mount, 270
Massilia (Marseille), 160, 184, 256; *see also* Marseille
Maternus, Julius, 194n
Matolenim, 50, 52
Mauch, Karl, 195-6, 202, 204
Maxentius, Emperor, 168
Maximus, Saint, 246
Mayan civilization, ix
Mazaios, 131
Mecca, 65
Medes, 130-1, 188
Medieval Rhodesia (Randall-Mac-Iver), 203
Mediolanum (Milan), 279

Mediterranean area, 33, 77, 87-9, 134, 140, 142, 150-1, 181-2, 185-6, 188-91, 197, 203, 205, 223, 242, 244, 254, 256-7, 266, 280, 298-9, 303, 305, 325, 341
Megalithic culture, 186-7
Meganthropus, 59
Megara, vii
Megiddo, 10
Melanesia, 322
Melkarth, 254
Menerva, 303
Merida, 279
Meru, 39
Mesopotamia, 124, 128, 134, 139, 141, 191, 214, 306, 314, 316, 326, 340
Messenia, 236
Messina, 257, 341
Messina, Strait of, 243
Mexico, 58, 64
Micronesia, 49
Middle Ages, 86, 329
Milan, 279, 315
Miletus, 81, 189, 264-6, 269
Milon, 268
Minerva, 105, 303
Minerva Victoria, 166
Minos, 77
Minos, King, 77
Miseno, 105, 170, 174, 178, 243, 245-6, 252
Misenus, 270
Misty Sea, 184
Mithras, 165, 288
Mkes, 7
Mohammedans, 207, 211, 333
Mohenjo-daro, 314-25, 340
Mongol dynasty, 328, 336
Mongolia, 342
Monica, Saint, 168
Mons Lactarius, 104, 109, 247
Monsol, King, 205
Mont Saint-Michel, 15
Monte Grillo, 250
Monte Lattaro, 93
Monte Santo, 49, 66
Moors, 29
Morocco, 341
Moses, 183, 341
Mossul, 129
Mozambique, 212
Munich, 315
Municipium Augustum Veiens, 310
Murashu and Sons, 126, 128

Mycenæ, 213, 234–7, 240, 242, 251, 297
Mysteries, 12

Namatianus, Claudius Rutilus, *quoted*, 169
Nanking, Mr., *quoted*, 56
Nantes, 16, 17
Naples, 69, 87, 89, 91–3, 99, 102, 104, 110, 170, 176, 243, 245–8, 270
Narbo (Narbonne), 167, 279
Narses, 247
Near East, 128, 141; *see also* Asia Minor
Nebuchadnezzar, 126–8, 254, 342
Necos, Pharaoh, 190, 255, 256n, 341
Negroes, 165, 194, 203–5, 208, 212, 215–17
Nema, 207
Nero, 79, 100, 105, 174, 178
Nestor, 236–7, 240, 278
Nevermann, Hans, 45; *quoted*, 51–2
New Guinea, 58
Nibelung Saga, 247
Nicæa, Council of, 146
Nigeria, 206–7, 222
Nile River, 9, 71, 117, 190, 198, 325
Nineveh gate, 121
Nippur, 126
Nordstrand, 19, 24
Noreia, 155, 160n
Noricum, 151, 153–9, 160n
North Africa, 253, 281–91
North America, 29
North Sea, 19, 28, 33, 186, 280, 344
Notre Dame, Cathedral of, 47
Nubia (Kaffa), 209
Nuceria, 98
Numa, 302
Numidia, 273, 281
Nupe, 206
Nuzi, 126

Oceanic peoples, 209
Oceanus, 71
Octavian (Augustus), 245–6, 250, 260, 277; *see also* Augustus
Octavius (Felix), 168
Odenathus, 140–1
Oder River, 18, 23
Odoric of Portenoe, Franciscan father, 40

Odysseus, 228, 240, 302
Odyssey (Homer), 237
Oklai Khan, 33n
Old Cære, 307–8
Old Testament, *see* Bible
Olympic games, 266, 268, 307
On Animals (Aristotle), 77–8
Ophir, 196–203, 212, 215
Oppianus, 17
Optatus, Bishop, 289
Orient, 87, 231, 236, 248, 265, 272, 306, 316
Orpheus myth, 14
Oscans, 88, 90, 94, 245, 270–2
Osiris, 209
Ostia, 161–70
Ostia, Battle of, 170
Ostia Antica, 170
Ostrogoths, 246, 279
Ovid, 85, 163, 286
Ovilava, 151

Pachaiachachic, 60
Pacific Ocean, 52, 53, 67
Pæstum, 83–8, 266, 342
Paistom, 84
Palatine Hill, 95, 302
Palestine, 8–10, 29, 33, 197–9, 201, 341; *see also* Israel
Palestrina, 302
Pali, 46
Pallas Athene, 83, 269
Pallottino, Massimo, 299n
Palmyra, 135–48, 284
Pamir, 131
Pan, 31
Pan Keng, 326
Panama, Isthmus of, 57
Pan-Katara, 51
Pankatra, 51
Pannonia, 288–90
Panuco, 31
Pappus, 91
Paris, 31, 291, 338
Paris, prince of Troy, 240, 242, 341
Parmenides, 82
Parthians, 131, 136, 138
Paulme, Denise, 223n
Pauly, August, 256n, 273n
Pausanias, 184n
Pax Romana, 17, 246
Peene River, 19, 24
Pegu, 46
Peking, 336–7, 344
Pelasgians, 75, 89
Peloponnesus, 234, 236, 262
Pelops, 234, 236

Pergamon, 160, 162
Persian Empire, 121, 124, 126,
    130-1, 142, 144, 146, 342
Persian Gulf, 125
Persians, 119-22, 130-1, 138, 141,
    189, 191-2, 211
Peru, viii, 31, 40, 55-7, 61, 64-5,
    67, 197, 208, 344
Perugia, 310, 342
Perusia (Perugia), 342
Pessinus, 162
Petrie, Flinders, 199
Phæthon, 70-1, 77
Pharos of Alexandria, 164
Philippines, 40, 191, 215
Philo of Alexandria, 6, 19
Phlegræan Plain, 190, 228
Phocæa, 187-8
Phœnician language, 255-6
Phœnicians, 32, 138-9, 149, 181-3,
    185, 187-8, 190-1, 195, 201,
    204-5, 233, 253-6, 303, 341
Phythian-Adams, W. J., 241
Piacenza, 85
Piano Carpini, Giovanni de, 329
Picts, 209
Piggot, Stuart, 323n
Pillars of Heracles, 34, 184, 255,
    293; see also Gibraltar, Strait of
Piræus, vii
Pisa, 310
Pityusæ ("Pine Islands"), 254, 257
Pizarro, Gonzalo, 31, 40, 69, 194,
    213, 339
Plato, 33-8, 143, 173, 342; quoted,
    33-4
Plautus, 286
Pliny the elder, 105, 286
Pliny the younger, quoted, 105-8,
    135-6
Pnompenh, 48
Po River, 70-2, 74-6, 301, 307
Pointe de Raz, 13
Poles, 22
Polo, Maffeo, 40
Polo, Marco, 40, 327-34, 339, 344;
    quoted, 327-8
Polo, Niccolò, 40
Polycleitus, 95
Polydeuces, 79
Polynesia, 49-67, 209, 344
Polyphemus, 32
Pompe, 89-90; see also Pompeii
Pompeii, ix, 7, 89, 90, 92, 94-114,
    114n, 166, 170, 270, 291, 343
Pompey, 172, 245
Pomponianus, 107-8

Pomponius Mela, 18, 19
Pona Yat, King, 48
Ponape, 49-50, 52-3, 55
Populonia, 300, 303, 309-10
Porcius, 96
Porsena, King, 302n
Porta Jovis, 275
Portuguese, 40-1, 49, 192, 194,
    203-4, 208, 211-13, 217, 219-20,
    293, 344
Portus Augusti, 164
Poseidon, 34-6, 179, 241
Poseidonia, 81-2, 87, 269, 342
Posilippo, 171
Pozzuoli, 69, 342
Præneste (Palestrina), 302
Priam, 238, 240-1, 247
Probus, 144
Procopius, 14
Propertius, 85, 179; quoted, 172-3
Ptolemy, Claudius, 6, 194, 343
Puinipet, see Ponape
Punic Empire, see Carthage
Punic Wars, 84-5, 257-60, 273, 309
Punjab, 313
Pursta, 33
Pushukin, 126
Puteoli, 69-70, 85, 161, 163-4, 171,
    179, 245-6, 270, 272, 276
Pygmalion, 253
Pylos, 236, 240, 242
Pyrenees, 117
Pyrrhus, 161
Pythagorus, 82, 267-8
Pythionice, 132

Quadi, 155
Quarternary period, 15
Quechua tribe, 60
Quinta, Claudia, 162-3
Quirinal Hill, 302
Quiros, Pedro Fernandez de, 49

Radriani, 79
Ramses III, Pharaoh, 33, 35
Randall-MacIver, David, 203, 215
Raphael, 170
Ras Shamra, 340
Ravenna, 79
Red Sea, 134, 141, 197-201, 210,
    255, 341
Regulus, Livineius, 98
Renders, Adam, 194-5
Rennes, 17
Revolt of the Beardless, 331
Rhodes, 240

Rhodesia, 191, 205, 215–16, 340, 344; *see also* Zimbabwe
Rhodesian Beads (Beck), 215
Ribat (slave), 128
Riem, Johannes, 6
Rimini, 85
Rio Grande River, 30
Rock, Fritz, *quoted*, 56–7
Roger II, King, 23
Roman Antiquities (Dionysius of Halicarnassus), 75
Roman Empire, 79, 135, 138–42, 155–8, 163–4, 167, 247, 279, 281–91, 310
Romanelli, Pietro, 299n
Romans, 12, 16, 89–90, 92–5, 123, 133, 135, 138, 149–50, 156, 165, 183, 194n, 198, 210, 244–7, 257–60, 262, 271–7, 281–6, 305–7, 312
Romanzov, Nikolai, 50
Rome, 23, 68, 91–2, 102, 104, 139–40, 149, 156, 160–5, 168, 170–2, 184, 228, 244–5, 248, 252, 270–81, 297, 302–4, 309, 342, 343
Romulus, 184
Royal Palace of Angkor, 45
Royal Way, The (Malraux), 39, 41–4
Rubruquis (Ruysbroek), Father, 329
Rudbeck, Olaf, 29
Ruden, 18
Rufus, Curtius, 132
Rufus, Vibennius, 79
Rügen, 18, 20, 23
Ruma family, 302
Rungholt, 24–7, 344
Ruysbroek, Father, 329

Sabrata, 167
Saggi di varia antichità, 80n
Sahara Desert, 281
Saif, 206
Saint-Anne, bay of, 15
St. Gsell, 290n
St. Helena, 29
St. Veit an der Gean, 154
Salerno, 80, 83, 86–7
Salso River, 85
Samarkand, 343
Samnites, 83, 89–90, 245, 270–7
Samos, 69
San Matteo, Cathedral of, 86
Sangiran, 59
Sanskrit, 46
Santa Maria di Capua Vetere, 280
Santorin (Thera), 340

Saracens, 20, 86, 144, 170, 248, 280, 310–11, 344
Sardinia, 163, 183, 188–9, 248, 257, 284, 341
Sargasso Sea, 256
Saria, 206
Sarmatians, 165
Sarnos River, 89–90
Satadru River, 117
Sataspes, 190
Saturnia, 75, 89
Saurat, Denis, 57–9, 61–2, 67
Savaria (Szombathely), 289
Sbarco di Enea, Lo, 170
Scamander River, 231
Scandinavians, 23, 33
Schackermeyr, Fritz, 299n
Schebesta, Father Paul, 204, 209, 216, 221, 223n
Schlei River, 25
Schleswig, 25, 344
Schliemann, Heinrich, 241
Schliemann, Paul, 29
Schuchhardt, Carl, 231n
Schulten, Adolf, 186n, 189
Scipio family, 162
Scythians, 29, 131, 133
Seine River, 338
Sele River, 79–81, 109
Seleucia, 133–4
Seleucid Empire, 133–4
Seleucus, 133
Seljuks, 146
Semiramis, 120, 122
Seneca, 177; *quoted*, 306
Senegal, 206–7
Serapis, 70
Severus, Lucius Septimus, Emperor, 167, 282, 284, 289
Seville, 180
Shang dynasty, 325
Shang Empire, 340
Shang'an, 343
Shapur I, King, 144
Shardana, 33
Shautelur the Last, King, 52
She (Haggard), 196
Sheba, Queen of, 195–7, 200
Sheshonk, Pharaoh, 201
Shiva, 318
Siam, 39, 47–8, 57
Siaros River, 86
Sibylline books, 162
Sicily, 23, 77, 235, 245, 253, 257, 263, 280, 341, 344
Sierra Morena, 181
Silaros River, *see* Sele River

Silenus, 103
Simbaoe, *see* Zimbabwe
Simois River, 231
Sinai, Mount, 291, 343
Sind, 316
Siris, 81
Siva, 46
Skidros, 81, 269
Skin, The (Malaparte), 83
Slavs, 19, 21-2, 343
Social War, 92-3
Sodom, 6-12, 14, 26, 111-12, 340
Sofala, 191, 196
Solomon, King, 135, 185, 195-202, 215, 341
Solomon Islands, 197-8, 209
Solon, 34
Sorrento, 87, 91
Sosandra Aphrodite, 179
Sotha I, King, 40
Souryavarman II, King, 47
South Africa, 212
South America, 30, 39, 54-5, 57, 59, 64, 66
Southeast Africa, 207-8
Southeast Asia, 49
Spain, 17, 33, 49-50, 56, 63, 88-9, 133, 161, 180-1, 183, 188, 198, 253, 256-7, 279-80, 284, 291-4, 341
Spanuth, Pastor Jürgen, 29, 33-4
Sparta, 142, 262, 268
Spartacus, 97
Spina, ix, 72, 74-8
Spitzbergen, 29
Stabiæ, ix, 92-4, 99-100, 103-4, 107, 109, 114n
Starky, J., 141n
Steinheim skull, 58-9
Stone Age, 89, 150, 293-4
Strabo, 6, 10, 19, 74-5, 78-9, 80n, 102, 185-6, 245, 256, 262n, 270, 299n, 300, 342; *quoted*, 6, 74, 79, 85, 89, 230
Stromboli, 69
Sudan, 281
Südfall, 27
Sulla, Cornelius, 92-4
Sulla, Publius, 95
Sumatra, 40
Sumerians, 30, 121-3, 315
Sun Gate, of Tiahuanaco, viii, 55, 58, 63-4
Sundra Islands, 191
Susa, 134
Sutkgan-dor, 316
Swahili, 205

Swanscombe, 58-9
Sweden, 29
Swoboda, Erich, 290n
Sybaris, 74, 80-2, 189, 243, 261-70
Sybaris River, 261
Syracuse, 160-1, 243, 245, 279, 341, 342
Syria, 125, 128, 134, 136, 141, 143, 165, 175, 182, 197, 199, 258, 279
Szombathely, 289

Tacitus, *quoted*, 98
Tadmor, 134-5
Tahiti, 51
Tai-du, 327, 332, 336
Tara, ix, 294-5, 298
Taranto, 81, 161, 274
Tarchna family, 302
Tarkon, 300-1
Tarku, 300
Tarquinia, 299n, 311
Tarquinii, 300-3, 309, 311
Tarshish, *see* Tartessus
Tarshish ships, 185
Tartarus, 186
Tartary, 334-5
Tartessus, 181-90, 198, 202, 256, 341
Taurisks, 151
Tebessa, 281
Teheptilla family, 126
Teia, King, 247
Tei Tetua, 54
Telde, 294-5
Telegonus, 302
Tell, The, 281
Tell Beit Mirsim, 10-11
Tell Hemmeh, 199
Tell-el Kheleifeh, 199
Telys, 267-8
Temple, in Jerusalem, 111
Terence, 286
Teurnia, 151, 154-5
Teutons, 29, 160n
Thai tribes, 47-8
Thamugadi, viii, ix, 284-91, 343
Thasos, 117
Theoderic, 177
Thera, 340
Theseus, 79
Theveste (Tebessa), 281
Third Legion, 281, 284
Thirtieth Legion, 285
Thrace, 241
Thurii, 269
Thurnwald, Richard, 219n
Thutmosis III, Pharaoh, 340

Tiahuanaco, 55–67, 194, 202, 343, 344
Tiber River, 83, 160–1, 163–5, 169, 302
Tiberias, 7
Tiberius, Emperor, 278
Tibet, 39, 47, 58
Ticino River, 247
Tifata, Mount, 271, 278
Tigris River, 6, 124, 133
Tiki, 53–5
Timæus (Plato), 33–4, 37
Timbuktu, 205
Timgad, 291
Tin (Etruscan god), 303
Tin Islands, 190
Tiryns, 234, 242, 246–7, 297
Titicaca, Lake, 55, 57, 61–2, 67
Titus, Emperor, 105, 111, 288
Toledo, Don Pedro di, 178
Tolosa (Toulouse), 279
Torriani, Leonardo, 295, 298; *quoted*, 295
Totila, King, 247
Toulouse, 279
Town Museum of Husum, 24
Tracimenus, Lake, 273
Trajan, Emperor, 134, 164, 283, 285
Transjordania, 199
Treveri (Trier), 279
Trier, 279
Tripoli, 167
Trœzen, 262, 267
Trojan War, 76, 240–1, 253
Troy, 29, 161, 228, 230–3, 237–42, 248, 340, 341
Tu, of Tahiti, 51
Tullianum, 303
Tullius, Servius, 303
Tullus, 302
Turkestan, 342
Turkmenistan, 131
Tyre, 185, 187–8, 196–8, 200, 253–4, 341
Tyrrhenia, 34, 89, 188
Tyrrhenian Sea, 81–2, 86, 244, 248, 266
Tyrrhenians, *see* Etruscans
Tyrsenians, 182–3, 187, 299; *see also* Etruscans
Tyrsenus, 300

Ualata, 207
Uganda, 209, 217–18, 221
Ugarit (Ras Shamra), 9n, 340
Ugrait, 235

Uiracocha, 61
Umbria, 74, 299, 300–1
Ungut (Kungurat), 334
Uni, 303
Unyoro, 209, 217
Ur, ix, 8
Usedom, 19, 20
Utubu, Chin emperor, 329

Valgus, 96
Valley Ruins, 192
Vandals, 260, 279, 290, 343
Van-ku, 330
Varro, Marcus Terentius, *quoted*, 172
Veddas, 322
Vega, Garcilaso de la, 56
Veii, 303, 307, 309–10, 342
Velcha family, 313
Veltha, 307
Venice, 71–2, 77, 343
Venus, 165, 248
Venus (planet), 6
Vera, Pedro de, 294
Verecunda, 284
Vespasian, Emperor, 79, 288
Vesuvian Gate, 92
Vesuvius, 69, 99, 102, 105, 107, 109–12, 114, 270
Via Septimiana, 284
Vienna, 282
Vienna University, viii
Vikings, 21
Vindobna (Vienna), 282
Vineta, 19–26, 344
Virgil, 83, 85, 248–51, 253; *quoted*, 251
Virrius, Vibius, 275
Virunum, 159, 160n
Vishnu, 47
Vistula River, 325
Viteliu, 89
Vitellius, 79
Viterbo, 69n
Voccio, 154
Volga River, 343
Völkerwanderung, 246, 343
Volscians, 271
Volsinii, 307
Volturnus (Volturno) River, 270, 272, 276
Vulcan, 165

Waballath, 143
Wadi Zerka Ma'in valley, 7
Washasha, 33
Watzinger, C., 141n

Wells, H. G., 32
Wends, 21
West Africa, 341, 343
Wiesner, Joseph, 231n
Wilusa, 242
Wisby, 21
Wissowa, Georg, 256n, 273n
Wölfel, Dominik, 298
Worod, 140

Xerxes, King, 119–21, 128, 130, 190

Yacovarman I, King, 47
Yemen, 196, 210
Yin Empire, 340
Yoktans, 196
Yomsburg, *see* Vineta
Ys, 14–20, 53, 343

Yucatán, 55
Yumne, *see* Vineta

Zakkara, 33
Zambezi River, 202, 204–5, 208,
    212, 343, 344
Zanzibar, 212
Zenobia, 142–6
Zeus, 37, 252
Zeus Targuenus, 300
Zimbabwe, 191, 194–6, 203–5, 208–
    23, 344
Zmaragdus, 288
Zopyrus, 120–1
Zuider Zee, 28
Zulus, 208
Zurich, 315

□Hermann Schreiber, born in 1920, earned his doctor's degree in philosophy and literature at the University of Vienna. He has worked as an editor and lecturer, and since 1952 has devoted his full time to free-lance writing. Besides the two books written in collaboration with his brother, he has published a number of highly successful novels. His books have been translated into several European languages.

□Georg Schreiber was born in 1922, the son of a Viennese bookseller. He studied classics and archæology at the University of Vienna, receiving his doctorate in 1949. A teacher of Greek and Latin at a *Gymnasium* since 1954, he has written many articles on history and science for popular magazines, and has collaborated with his brother to write two books of popular history.

A NOTE ON THE TYPE AND PRODUCTION

The text of this book is set in Caledonia, a Linotype face designed by W. A. Dwiggins (1880–1956), who was responsible for so much that is good in contemporary book design. Though much of his early work was in advertising and he was the author of the standard volume Layout in Advertising. Mr. Dwiggins later devoted his prolific talents to book typography and type design, and worked with great distinction in both fields. In addition to his designs for Caledonia, he created the Metro, Electra, and Eldorado series of type faces, as well as a number of experimental cuttings that have never been issued commercially.

Caledonia belongs to the family of printing types called "modern face" by printers—a term used to mark the change in style of type-letters that occurred at the end of the eighteenth century. It is best evidenced in the letter shapes designed by Baskerville, Martin, Bodoni, and the Didots.

This book was composed, printed, and bound by Kingsport Press, Inc., Kingsport, Tenn. The paper was made by P. H. Glatfelter Company, Spring Grove, Penn.